WALKING
HOME

The Blue Bear:
A True Story of Friendship, Tragedy, and
survival in the Alaskan Wilderness

The Last Shot

WALKING HOME

A JOURNEY IN THE ALASKAN WILDERNESS

LYNN SCHOOLER

BLOOMSBURY

LONDON · BERLIN · NEW YORK

First published in Great Britain 2010

Bloomsbury Publishing Plc
36 Soho Square
London W1D 3QY

www.bloomsbury.com

Bloomsbury Publishing, London, New York and Berlin
A CIP catalogue record for this book is available from the British Library

ISBN 978 1 4088 1028 6

10 9 8 7 6 5 4 3 2 1

Printed in Great Britain by Clays Limited, St Ives plc

Mixed Sources
Product group from well-managed
forests and other controlled sources
www.fsc.org Cert no. SGS-COC-2061
© 1996 Forest Stewardship Council
FSC

Dedicated to the memory of Luisa Stoughton

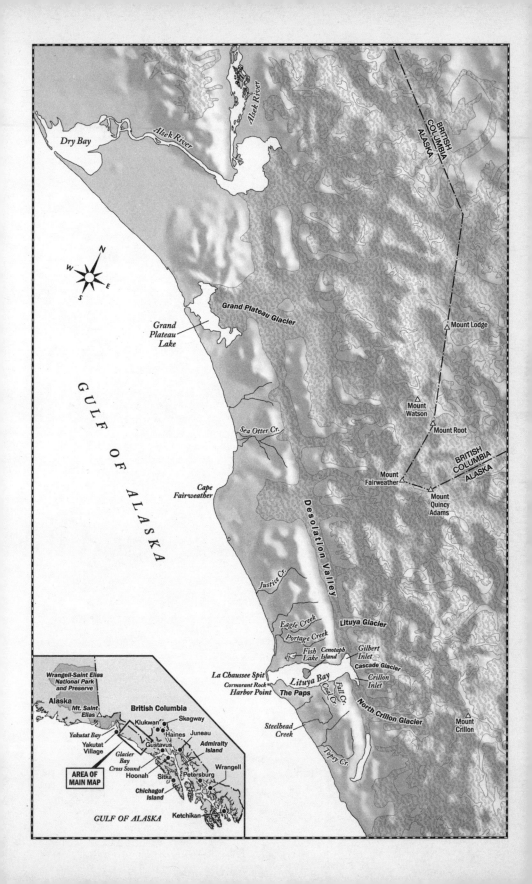

GULF OF ALASKA

Dry Bay

Alsek River

Alsek River

N
W · E
S

Grand Plateau Glacier

Grand
Plateau
Lake

BRITISH
COLUMBIA
ALASKA

Mount Lodge

Mount
Watson

Sea Otter Cr.

Mount Root

Cape
Fairweather

BRITISH
COLUMBIA
ALASKA

Mount
Fairweather

Mount
Quincy
Adams

Desolation Valley

Justice Cr.

Eagle Creek
Portage Creek

Lituya Glacier

Fish
Lake

Cenotaph
Island

Gilbert
Inlet

Cascade Glacier

La Chaussee Spit
Cormorant Rock *
Harbor Point

Lituya Bay

Crillon
Inlet

The Paps

Coal Cr.

Fall Cr.

North Crillon Glacier

Steelhead
Creek

Mount
Crillon

Topsy Cr.

Wrangell-Saint Elias
National Park
and Preserve

Alaska

Mt. Saint
Elias

British Columbia

Klukwan

Skagway

Yakutat Bay

Haines

Juneau

Yakutat
Village

Gustavus

Admiralty
Island

Glacier
Bay

Cross Sound

AREA OF
MAIN MAP

Hoonah

Sitka

Petersburg

Wrangell

Chichagof
Island

GULF OF ALASKA

Ketchikan

PROLOGUE

IN MAY OF 2007, I stood on a remote Alaskan beach, on the bank of a flooding river, desperate to find a way across. The stream of muddy, hissing water cut through a rock-studded beach and hurled itself headlong into a line of breaking waves. Every few seconds another swell rolled in from the Gulf of Alaska, rose into a steeple against the outflow of current, then collapsed in an avalanche of foam. The gulf is seldom still, and a stiff wind bullied the gray water into tumbling heaps.

To my left the river rushed straight out of a wall of thick brush. As I watched, a clump of roots torn loose by the flood swept by, washed into the surf, and was thrown back again. The clatter of cobblestones rolling downstream under the surface sounded ominously like the rattling of old bones.

I was afraid and I had been for two days. Twenty-four hours earlier I had been stalked by a grizzly in a terrifying cat-and-mouse game of such prolonged and unrelenting intensity that my insides were still shaking. The hunt had gone on for hours, and everywhere I looked I could still see the fixed stare of the bear's small, dark eyes and the rubbery black lip that hung beneath its lower jaw, swinging grotesquely out of rhythm with the animal's stride as it came for me time after time.

It was only by the slimmest chance that I had escaped, and given that I was alone in the middle of more than 2,000 square miles of wilderness, with the tenacious bear still somewhere behind me and a flooding river in front of me, my survival did not seem guaranteed. There was no way the small inflatable kayak I was carrying to ford creeks and tidal sloughs during my trek along the coast was adequate to cross the frothing river. If I didn't get swept into the surf and

1

drown, being overturned would still be disastrous; I was several days'
walk from the nearest help or shelter, and to risk losing my pack, with
the sleeping bag and extra clothing inside, was unthinkable.

I was tired, my back and feet hurt from running over boulders
and through wet sand with a heavy pack on my back, and the spent
adrenaline had been replaced by a growing dread. I had no choice but
to go upstream into the thick forest to try to find a way across the
swollen river, and I didn't want to go into the forest. To leave the open
beach where I could see in all directions and push into that tangle of
alder and devil's club where the visibility would at times be limited to
a few yards or less was too frightening. The canopy of an Alaskan
rainforest can be so thick that 80 percent of the light never reaches the
ground and the world underneath it is a silent, mossy place of deep
shadows. I couldn't help imagining the moment when one of those
shadows would begin to move and become the bear. I kept playing
and replaying a scenario in which there was a crackle in the underbrush, a glimpse of dark fur, and a sudden rush . . .

I couldn't let myself think about the rest. Since the ancestors of
the Tlingit* Indians wandered across the Bering Land Bridge and
spread into Southeast Alaska by hopscotching across ice fields and
climbing down glaciers into ice-free pockets along the gulf, the region I was in has been lightly trod. A handful of European explorers
blew through in the late 1700s, followed by a brief but furious swarm
of fur hunters in the 1800s, bent on extirpating the gulf's sea otters; a
trickle of prospectors nibbled at the sand with picks and shovels during the first half of the twentieth century. But after the Tlingit were
nearly exterminated by new diseases and the area's sole permanent
white settler died in 1939, human presence grew as thin as at any time
since the beginning of the Ice Age. Now the five-hundred-mile arc of

---

* It's commonly pronounced "KLEEN-kit" by English speakers, but the first syllable is
more properly pronounced with a breathy *l* sound that does not exist in English.

wilderness that sweeps northwest from near the present-day settlement of Gustavus to Prince William Sound is traversed primarily by
the 298 species of birds common to Alaska, which include the ducks,
sandpipers, cranes, plovers, and songbirds that migrate north along
the corridor every spring by the millions, along with occasional individuals of another 150 or so species that ornithologists refer to as
"accidentals," meaning that although they have been seen and noted
by qualified observers, they do not belong here. Rather, they have become lost or struck out on their own for unfathomable reasons, such
as the lone Steller's sea eagle (a species indigenous to the northern islands of Japan) that appeared in Southeast Alaska a few years ago and
surprised everyone by settling down with an American bald eagle for
a companion.

A new home, discovery, glory, gold, and the opportunity for un-
bridled plunder—humans have pushed into this country for a variety
of reasons throughout history, but my own was something else. I was
in flight. Two weeks earlier I had left my home in Juneau hoping to
find some relief from the exhaustion and stress that came with laboring seven days a week for months on end to build a home meant to
house a marriage that now seemed in danger of crumbling. After a
lifelong love affair with Alaska's wild places and natural history, I had
thought I might find some ease in the wilderness, a respite from the
heartache and confusion plaguing my marriage, and perhaps might
learn something that would help me form a bulwark against the short-
falls of middle age and a looming sense of mortality.

It hadn't worked out. The confrontation with the bear had left me
feeling as shaken as I had ever felt in my life, alone and off balance, as
out of place as one of the avian accidentals. I wanted out, but I was a
long way from nowhere, with a pulsing river before me and a shower
of hard rain pelting down.

I don't know how long I stood there listening to the angry growl
of the surf and sorting hopelessly through options that didn't exist,

but it was long enough for the wind to eventually work its cold hands up under my coat and push me to get moving. It was early spring, there were still patches of snow on the ground, and I knew I could either stand there until I became hypothermic, try to cross the river and risk drowning, or swallow my trepidation and plunge into the waiting forest.

What I didn't know was that the sum of the whole experience would turn out to be one of the best things that had ever happened to me. What follows is the story of how that came to be.

CHAPTER 1

I COULD BEGIN with a death, that of one James Sullivan, age forty-seven, who climbed, muttering and despondent, onto the rail of the bridge that spans the churning waters between downtown Juneau and Douglas Island. From his perch seventy-five feet in the air—closer to ninety, really, since it was low tide at the time and the tides of Southeast Alaska average fourteen feet from high to low—Sullivan could have looked south down Gastineau Channel to a breathtaking view of the blue and green mountains of the Coast Range, or to his left across the rooftops of a cluster of homes and small businesses nestled along the foot of a closer range of forested mountains.

Of course, a crowd gathered. Juneau is a small town and people care. They vote regularly, school board meetings are well attended, and every spring a large part of the population turns out to make a celebration of harvesting the litter that sprouts from beneath the receding winter snow, volunteering their time to clean the limited grid of roads that stitch Juneau to the surrounding landscape. This effort, community spirited and admirable as it is, is really no more than window dressing, an effort to impose a sense of order on what is otherwise a notably disorderly corner of the world. A small, isolated place, Juneau is composed of fewer than thirty thousand souls perched precariously amid a jumble of glaciers, ice fields, and mountains that sprawl endlessly in every direction. To seaward, a narrow archipelago of equally wild islands separates the city from the Gulf of Alaska, where files of towering gray waves throw themselves ceaselessly against the shore. The clean streets and neatly painted houses provide no more than a diaphanous, even illusory, membrane of safety between the clinging

5

pocket of humanity and the enveloping wilderness, one penetrated at will by nature's whim. During spring and summer the police column in the daily newspaper is as likely to report bears ruckusing through the streets breaking into trailer houses and kicking over bird feeders as it is episodes of drunken driving or domestic violence. More significantly, a large portion of the town sits directly in the path of one of the most dangerous avalanche chutes in the world. Every winter a broad alpine funnel pointed directly at Juneau's heart waits for an accumulation of heavy, wet snow to build on top of a layer of older snow that has been scoured to an icy crust by relentless arctic winds—a combination that will someday send several thousand megatons of snow exploding at speeds of up to 180 miles an hour through the back doors of the houses below. In 1972 one avalanche blew down the mountain and screeched to a stop at the very verge of the imaginary membrane, mere yards from a densely populated neighborhood. The powder blast generated by the slide obliterated the town from view, startling the city's residents into a breathless recognition of the true nature of their town's setting. Nonetheless, they dutifully swept away the ice crystals that settled like glittering ash across the sidewalks and within a disturbingly short time began referring to the communal brush with destruction in joking tones.

Across the board, experts agree it is only a matter of when, not if, the Big One will occur, and when it does, it will be no joking matter. But no one, to my knowledge, even considered leaving town after the '72 slide, because Juneau is, after all, a genuinely great place to live. The surrounding wilderness, for all its ability to snatch through the curtain and leave nothing in our place but a vacuum, is also a treasure chest of riches. The mountains give forth deer, wolves, and mountain goats in great numbers. Tumbling streams lined with giant spruce and hemlock trees teem with trout and salmon. The channels and passages fingering in from the gulf boil with shoals of herring, which in turn provide food for whales and sea lions that swim above a seabed alive with shrimp and crabs. At the moment Sullivan was climbing onto the rail of the bridge, I was only a short distance away, on an outing with my nephews on my boat, trying to catch some of those crabs. Our first pot came up empty, but the second held two crabs. A lone crab had wandered into the third pot, but the fourth, only a few yards away and a fathom or so deeper, broke the surface bulging with a snapping, squirming dozen. After spilling the pot's contents onto the deck, we did a quick check with a tape measure and confirmed that all of them were legal, large enough across the carapace to satisfy even a hungry man. About then was when Sullivan jumped.

"It wasn't like the movies," said a friend who grabbed Sullivan's arm as he stepped into space. Though fit and athletic, Tom admitted, "There was no way I could hold on."

My nephews and I recovered the body. As we were urged on by the yells of the crowd on the bridge, it took only a quick calculation of the current's set and drift and a search pattern of expanding squares to motor up on what from a distance looked like a scrap of rag, then, as we drew closer, became a T-shirt ballooning with captured air. Two boot heels stuck up from the water. In the roiling current, it took me two or three tries with the boat hook to snag Sullivan's belt. Then there was a burst of frantic activity as would-be rescuers in the form of two strikingly young Coast Guard personnel roared alongside and jerked the corpse from our grip onto their bright orange, overpowered emergency response craft and began a fumbling, wide-eyed CPR before zooming away to a waiting ambulance. They were trying their damnedest, but the light was already gone from Sullivan's eyes.

After we returned to the dock and cleaned our catch, I loaded the butchered crabs into a plastic cooler. My oldest nephew helped me carry the heavy cooler up the dock. Then I dropped my nephews off at home and headed out the road. For several years I had been living in a one-room cabin twenty-five miles north of Juneau, on a small, quiet cove more than halfway out the only highway that runs any distance from the mountain-corralled town. Go fifteen miles farther and the road dead-ends at a point of nowhere that serves best to remind Juneau's residents that though we may be physically attached to North America and its five hundred million or so other human inhabitants by the bedrock of the continent, we are in essence an island community, accessible only by airplane or ship.

On the day of Sullivan's suicide the twenty-five miles to the cabin was far enough for me to have time to think over the day's events. As I drove, I realized I found them neither particularly disturbing nor traumatic, probably because during my forty years in Alaska I have known death to reach up from the water, out of the trees, down from the peaks, and out of the noise and violence of avalanches, car wrecks, and bear attacks with what some might consider unsettling frequency. I am neither callous nor inured, but in trade for the vast, beautiful heartache of its landscape and other treasures, Alaska often exacts a shocking tithe. Hikers get lost and die within sight of downtown Juneau. Climbers slip and fall. Simple fishing jaunts turn tragic when a boat overturns.

Still, I mulled over what might push a man to leap off a bridge instead of simply waiting for time to throw its dark shadow over him and relieve him of his burdens. A vision of Sullivan floating with his feet slightly spread, arms at his sides, and face gray with lack of life drifted across the windshield of my truck. I saw new leather work boots with no sign of wear; unstained denim pants and a nice belt; a decent shirt; and a full head of hair only slightly in need of cutting. Not a poor man or a street person addled with drugs. So why? A savage divorce? A bankruptcy? The loss of a child?

I could not know. So I let it go and started wondering if I had any beer at the cabin to go with the crab.

The next morning I had to go back to town, a quick run to pick up building supplies for a house I had been laboring on for more than a year. After nearly three decades of living on boats and in rustic cabins, even in tents, I had finally decided to "swallow the anchor," as old-time sailors said, and settle down. The previous summer there had been a brief, explosive courtship with a woman of great charm and breathtaking beauty, and when an opportunity had arisen to build our own home near the cabin, I had decided to do as much as I could with my own hands. Half Filipino, half Chinese, slender, athletic, and exotic, she had come to me with a glitter in her eyes and open arms. "A fifty-year-old bachelor," laughed a friend familiar with my reclusive ways. "You never had a chance."

Our wedding took place amid bales of lumber and rolls of tar paper. The wedding feast was laid out on planks and sawhorses. Ed, the eighty-two-year-old owner of the cabin I was living in, gave the bride away. Ed had come to Alaska when it was still a territory, in 1946,* after training to fly torpedo bombers during World War II. Ten years later, after graduating from college in Fairbanks on the GI Bill and joining one of the earliest expeditions to put a man on top of 20,300-foot Mount Denali, he had acquired the land I was building on through a government program that gave veterans preference. He and his wife, Marjory, built their own home a few miles closer to town, rowing in every morning from a nearby island that had been homesteaded by a family named Weshenfelder in the early 1920s. The two worked from first light to last, digging a basement by hand, mixing concrete with a shovel, and moving twenty-four-foot timbers into their roadless homesite with a wheelbarrow. Marjory sprouted a seedling from a maple tree grown on the island by the Weshenfelders and planted it next to their new house. She and Ed watched it grow for forty years, while making plans to someday build a second, smaller home near the cabin. When Marjory passed away unexpectedly, Ed decided to sell the land to me, and he came around on a daily basis after I started building to keep an

---

* Alaska did not become a state until 1959.

eye on my progress. One day he arrived with a clutch of thumb-sized seedlings sprouted from Marjory's maple.

I pickaxed four holes into the stony ground on the hill below the half-framed house and watched contentedly as my new bride knelt to gently pack a mixture of potting soil, sand, and compost around the tender shoots while admonishing them in a singsong voice to grow strong. When they grew tall enough to drop seeds of their own, I thought, we would sprout some and pass them on to her two grown daughters from a previous marriage, who would in turn pass seeds to their own children someday.

Shortly after the walls were up and the roof was on, however, the marriage started to slide. Immediately after the wedding my wife had begun a new career in a field for which she had great talent, and as word of her abilities spread, she landed first one position, then another and another; by the time the windows were installed, she had not been to the building site for months. Three of the seedlings had died, and after putting out a few nickel-sized leaves, the fourth had been nipped by a porcupine. I had been glad to see a tiny new bud starting out of the gnawed stump that morning and had meant to mention it to her, thinking the news might provide a positive point to help offset a note of friction that had been building between us lately, but she had left in a rush while I was making out a list of supplies. Now, an electrician was coming by in the afternoon to help me lay out the wiring, and I had to put my worries over the troubled marriage aside.

On the way into town I swung onto a side road that curved toward the beach and bumped past an empty campground before parking under a towering spruce tree and clattering down a steep flight of stairs to a friend's home on the waterfront. Luisa had spent the last fourteen years battling breast cancer and was in slow recovery from her third round of chemical and radiological insults to her body. She was also one of those rare, naturally gracious spirits who will inevitably brush aside their own hammering misfortune to quiz a visitor on his or her own well-being.

"Was this you?" she asked, knowing the answer even as she held out the morning paper, where a photo of my boat, the *Wilderness Swift*, and the Coast Guard response boat covered half the front page. "That must have been horrible for you."

"It wasn't," I replied. What I was feeling, I realized, was something like anger. How dare Sullivan give up so easily, while someone like Luisa—breast-lopped, bald, chemical-burned, and shaky, her voice weak with tribulation—was struggling to keep the flame alive?

"It pisses me off," I said, dropping the paper on the table. "There's people like you, trying so hard, and he . . ." I did not *want* to feel any empathy. I didn't *want* to understand why someone would waste his own life. Luisa sighed, exhausted, and curved her spine into the enveloping softness of the couch before glancing out the window at a flock of goldeneyes paddling close to shore. "It's just so hard for some people . . ."

"How's your appetite?" I asked, rising to leave.

Luisa lifted her chin and smiled. There was something beatific in her eyes. "I eat like a horse," she laughed, then stifled a choking cough. I bent down to brush my cheek against hers—her skin was as soft as a baby's—then looked around the living room at the mementos she and her husband had gathered while traveling around the world making natural history films. An antique engraving of polar bears purchased in England after a trip to the Norwegian Arctic adorned the fireplace mantle. There was a photo of a much younger Luisa with a colorfully dressed African tribesman, and the massive horns of an argali sheep from the mountains of Mongolia, where two years of intense effort and genuine deprivation had made them the first people ever to film a snow leopard in the wild. For two decades Joel and Luisa had been what I think of as "burning building" friends, because I suspected that either one of them would rush into a burning building if I needed them. This may have been hyperbole, but I knew without question that they would come if I called in the middle of the night and would stand up for me if a time ever came when I could not stand up for myself. We didn't touch each other often or say certain things out loud, but they were family without the benefit of blood or genes.

"I'll check back in a couple of days," I said, retrieving my hat from the table. "See how you're doing."

"How's the house coming?" she asked, keeping her voice low to avoid another coughing fit.

I blew out a sigh, not wanting to set loose the litany of careless sub-contractors and soaring costs that seemed to boil on my lips these days. It seemed petty to even consider such things in front of someone whose every thought must be of the looming possibility of losing her own life.

She read me like a book. She and Joel had been through the same frustrations a few years earlier during the construction of their own home. "Don't worry. In another year this will all be over," she said.

"When I get the porch built, we'll sit on it and have a beer," I promised. On the way out I prayed she would still be around when the time had passed.

Two-by-fours, a box of screws, a case of silicone window caulking in tubes—one by one I checked things off my scrawled list until the truck was full and then spun out of the building yard, hurrying to get back out the road. At the last second I cranked the wheel right instead of left, deciding to head for a supermarket a half mile away. Sullivan's suicide was nagging at me, and I could grab a newspaper there, maybe learn something that would explain his jump and help lay him to rest. It seemed like a variety of death's swords and scythes had been punching holes in the backdrop of my life for months, and all morning it had been hard to stop thinking about them. Only a few weeks earlier I had found one of my neighbors, an older woman who had lived alone on a beautifully manicured piece of ground she and her long-passed husband had carved from the rocky coast back in the 1950s, dead in her bedroom, after a concerned friend had called and told me she was not answering her phone. When I found her, a medical encyclopedia lay open on a dresser by her bed, bookmarked to a section on the symptoms of heart attacks. And earlier that spring a lifelong friend had died from the effects of nearly thirty years spent trying to lighten the weight of two tours in Vietnam with alcohol. All around me, it seemed, people I knew were being picked off with increasing frequency as accidents, disease, and old age closed in. Sometimes I cried and sometimes I didn't, but the sum of it all was disturbing.

At the market I hopped out of the truck and strode for the door, still intent on getting back to the building site as quickly as possible. It was the height of summer, the days were long, and a lot could get done if I moved fast and worked hard. I kept telling myself that the sooner my wife and I could move into the house, the sooner some of those bumps in our marriage would smooth out. Hurrying, I looked up just in time to catch a reflection in the market window of an older fellow moving toward the door and stopped, unbalanced for a moment by the realization that the reflection was me.

Puzzled, I stepped closer for a better look at the pale figure looking back at me. Silver, brush-cut hair ringed his balding scalp. Unshaven whiskers glittered on his cheeks. There was slack in his chin and something thin about his neck. Bags of exhaustion drooped under his eyes. He was a grizzled old coot and he was me.

"My god," I wondered out loud. "How'd I get so old?"

What I meant was that I'd thought I was younger.

What I really meant was that I'd thought I had more time.

After picking up the newspaper, I sat in the parking lot to read it. Sullivan had been despondent over his lack of insurance to cover the treatment of a spreading cancer.

Back out the road, with the truck unloaded, I took stock as I rushed up and down a ladder, boring holes and pulling wire. The auger bucked in my hands, and the way the bit chewed through the studs felt good, as did feeding the thick yellow cables through the holes and knitting them together into the complex web of a modern electric home. It was good work, satisfying in the way that things that have a clear purpose and a definite end often are, but I had to admit I was tired. I had been working hard, going eight, ten, sometimes eleven or twelve hours a day, seven days a week, for over a year, and my body was a catalog of aches and pains. Still, the realization that I had somehow drifted into middle age without noticing was a shock and a surprise. True, my knees hurt more or less all the time from the kneeling and crawling, the constant lifting and bending kept a permanent knot in my back, an accident with an excavator when I'd first started clearing the site had left me with a pinched nerve in my neck that had prevented me from sleeping well for months, and the fatigue often left me cranky, but these were things I felt would ease up after the house was finished and I could sit back and relax. And yet, sitting back—or rather its corollary, getting up again—had come to require a grunt of exertion and the use of my hands. So what was next? Grousing with the other old duffers about the size of my prostate? One of those pillboxes with compartments lettered for the days of the week like the ones Luisa jokingly referred to as her "Sun City castanets"?

In all probability, yes. The body is a Judas, and mine was starting to consider turning me in for the silver. I unbuckled my heavy tool belt and let it drop to the floor. Then I walked out the door and down the stairs. The site my wife and I had chosen to build our home on provides a fine view of what I consider heaven. To the east the forested humps and curves of the Herbert and Eagle river drainages wind out of a gash in the northern Coast Range. Both rivers spill from blue and white glaciers in the alpine. To the west is Lynn Canal, the world's longest fjord, where the passage of humpback whales, sea lions, and orcas is a daily occurrence. The far side of Lynn Canal is picketed by a series of 5,000-foot peaks. Beyond these lies one of the world's premier wilderness areas, Glacier Bay National Park and Preserve. Eagles and herons are as common around here as seagulls, and grizzlies and black bears amble through the surrounding forest on trails blazed by browsing deer. There is a stream less than half a mile away so rich in fish that during one recent summer commercial seiners working nearby harvested an astonishing twelve *million* pounds of salmon.

It was a fine day, and I wandered down a sloping path of crushed stone and stepped off into the forest on a faint trail that crosses a narrow gully and winds up a rise to a favorite overlook of mine above the cove. Once there, I forced my way through a thicket of huckleberry and blueberry bushes before settling on my haunches against a moss-padded stump. Below me, on a ledge just out of reach, glittered a patch of red salmonberries. There are days during Alaska's brief summer that are so soft and warm and rich that the smells alone make me want to live forever. And this was one of them. Thinking back, I realized the last time I had sat down to watch the clouds move or the sun set behind the mountains had been in early spring, during a brief respite between putting the last of the metal roofing on and starting on the siding. In the interim, eagle chicks had hatched and learned to fly, swarms of migrating shorebirds had passed through on their way north to the Arctic, and the seals had given birth to their pups. And all without my noticing.

I watched as a puff of wind swirled Lynn Canal into a pattern of sunny sparkles. Spruce needles pattered down on my head. If through some miracle of sustenance I could have sat there for the rest of my allotted years—say twenty, or forty if I was very lucky—the slow accumulation of needles and other forest litter would eventually have covered me entirely. For a minute I thought of how everything around me was in a constant state of change, even such seemingly immobile monuments as the mountains and glaciers. In the twenty years since I had arrived in the area, both Herbert Glacier and Eagle Glacier had receded several hundred yards. Over the two hundred–plus years since George Vancouver had first explored Alaska in 1794 and named Lynn Canal after his birthplace in King's Lynn, England, they had retreated several miles. Judging from the way I had aged without noticing, the amount of time I had left to sit and watch the tides roll up and down Lynn Canal or the salmon come and go was no more than a blink, especially when measured against the scale of my surroundings. I was fifty-two years old—though in the reflection I had looked sixty—and was not sure how much of my remaining blink I wanted to spend working like a Trojan.

A mile offshore, a whale rose and blew beside a submerged rock. In the distance the peaks of the Chilkat Range came and went behind drifting clouds. The whale dove, and I considered the fact that beyond the buoy marking the rock there were no more works of man. No roads, mines, electric lines, or lights for hundreds of miles. Behind the Chilkats lie the ice fields of Glacier Bay. On the other side of Glacier Bay the land rises and rises again until it reaches the summit of 15,300-foot Mount Fairweather, the fourth-highest peak in North America. Beyond Mount Fairweather the landscape drops steeply down to Lituya Bay, on the Gulf of Alaska, from where it is another sixty miles north along one of the wildest coasts in North America to a few scattered cabins at Dry Bay. And there is not a single man-made structure along the way. No construction projects eating up anyone's life.

But I did have a house to finish, which could easily take the rest of the year, then a shop and a carport to build, followed by a small guest cabin I envisioned for the spot upon which I was resting. The amount of time all this would take seemed overwhelming. Perhaps it was even more than I had to spare.

So I decided to take a walk instead.

CHAPTER 2

O N   A   M A P it looked easy. I could plant my thumb on Lituya Bay and cover the sixty miles to Dry Bay with an outstretched pinkie. At Dry Bay the Alsek River pours in from the east, running gray as cement from a burden of glacial silt gathered up by the river as it cuts through a range of granite mountains between Canada's Yukon Territory and Alaska. The Alsek serves as the northern boundary of Glacier Bay National Park and Preserve and runs north of Mount Fairweather. Mount Fairweather also marks the border between the Yukon and Alaska, not far from where the tumbling green water of a river called the Tatshenshini joins the Alsek. Several years earlier, a group of friends and I had carried in-flatable rafts north into the Yukon, thrown them into the Tatshenshini, and floated downstream to the Alsek. At the conjunction the two rivers combine to become a single throbbing monster with more than four times the volume of the Colorado River. Ten days and a staggering 140 miles of rapids and glaciers later, the silty giant had popped us out onto the coast beneath the largest nonpolar ice field in the world.

Since then, while working as a wilderness guide throughout Alaska, I had hiked, paddled, and boated the coast south and east of Mount Fairweather and sailed up the western side as far as Lituya Bay. Trekking north from Lituya Bay to the Alsek River, I told myself, would complete a circumnavigation of Mount Fairweather and close a circle around more than five thousand square miles contained within one of the world's wildest and most spectacular national parks. All I needed was a backpack and a pair of good boots to do it.

Of course, there would be obstacles. Several rivers would have to be crossed, along with a large tidal slough and a lake wedged between a tumbling waterfall and a glacier. There would be a five-hundred-foot-high moraine of glacial rubble to climb, and the weather along the coast can be frightful. Hurricane-force winds, storms that drop several inches of rain in an hour, and fog are all common. It is, as pioneering geologist Don Miller noted in a report to the U.S. Geological Service, "an area of bold contrasts," where a traveler will experience "every extreme of environment." For more than a hundred miles a belt of forest and underbrush as dense as any jungle on earth borders "a vast ice-covered land desolate and arctic in appearance."

Anyone traveling in Miller's footsteps would understand why the legends of the indigenous Tlingit Indians pinpoint the area as the site of Creation. Great plains of ice pool among the peaks, spilling deeply crevassed glaciers from every valley. To the Tlingit the glaciers were sentient beings that writhed and pulsed through the countryside, grinding and gnawing it into a land suitable for brutal gods. One of the most capricious gods is Kah-Lituya, a sullen, toad-like spirit that lives in a cave beneath the entrance to Lituya Bay. Kah-Lituya keeps a giant brown bear as his slave, and when angered, he orders it to seize the bay in its powerful jaws and shake it, creating giant waves.

Studies by Miller and other geologists have verified the Tlingit interpretation of the coast's geologic activity; their research shows that for millennia the glaciers have advanced and receded, carving the land into its given shape over aeons of successive ice ages. Lituya Bay also sits directly atop the Fairweather Fault, a 180-mile-long fracture in the earth's crust that geologists describe as a "strike-slip fault with lateral movement"—meaning that in Kah-Lituya's domain the entire North American continent grinds slowly along the plate underlying the Pacific, with results that can be catastrophic. In 1958 an earthquake measuring 8.3 in magnitude caused a mammoth rock slide to cascade into Lituya Bay, generating a wave that was the highest ever recorded on the planet. The tsunami surged 1,720 feet above sea level and scoured the mountain down to bedrock.* Incredibly, one of the three fishing boats anchored in the bay survived. This was one of several mega-tsunamis generated by Kah-Lituya's slave over the past 150 years.

But before I could concern myself with giant waves, I would have to get to Lituya Bay, which would require a sea voyage of 170 miles. My boat, the *Wilderness Swift*, is small and light and has a single engine. Its hull was designed for salmon fishermen working in sheltered waters. Cruising from Juneau to the outer coast would mean going north around Admiralty Island (the second-largest island in the United States), then west out Icy Strait to Cross Sound. Cross Sound broadens into open ocean at Cape Spencer. Past Cape Spencer, I would be exposed to the fury of the gulf for nearly fifty miles.

And crossing the open water to Lituya Bay was not even the riskiest part of the trip. It is getting *into* the bay that gives navigators nightmares. My copy of the *U.S. Coast Pilot* cautions mariners that tidal currents at the entrance to the bay can be as strong as twelve knots and warns that "the ebb currents, running out against a southwest swell, cause bad topping seas or combers across the entire entrance, through which no small vessel can hope to live."† In 1898, Lieutenant George Emmons of the U.S. Navy called it "the most justly feared harbor on the Pacific."

Lieutenant Emmons was not exaggerating. Since the French explorer Jean-François de Galoup, Comte de La Pérouse became the first European to enter Lituya Bay in 1786, the tide rips at the entrance have claimed dozens of vessels and more than one hundred lives. La Pérouse's expedition lost twenty-one men. After he was safe inside the harbor, the Tlingit occupying a village on the shore pantomimed to

---

* This is not a typo. The wave was 400 feet higher than the World Trade Center towers.
† The *Coast Pilot* is a compilation of navigation information, descriptions of bays and harbors, tide and current data, and meteorological tables published by the U.S. government. No prudent mariner would travel the coast of Alaska without one.

the adventurous Frenchman that shortly before his arrival they had suffered the loss of ten canoes carrying between seventy and a hundred people.

Drowning was a terrible fate for the Tlingit. If a body could not be recovered and cremated, a drowning victim might become a *kushtaka*, a half-man, half-otter changeling that occupies the realm between life and death. Like the toad Kah-Lituya, the *kushtaka* moves between land and water, and it has been known to take on the appearance of a beautiful, seductive woman or even a person's own loved one in order to lure him or her into deep water or away into the forest. People who get lost or disappear are often the unwitting victims of a *kushtaka*. Many become otter-men themselves.

When I asked a Tlingit friend about this, he just shook his head and looked away. The Tlingit memory is long, and stories of drowning and loss in Lituya Bay are common. The worst was the time Kah-Lituya swept away an entire village. Only a single woman, who was up on a ridge picking berries when the wave struck, survived.

Considering all this, I was not surprised by the reactions of my friends when I told them I was considering going by myself. Luisa just opened her eyes a bit wider and asked, "Alone?" Joel quietly recommended I take someone else. Jon, a friend who had shared his tent with me a decade earlier on the Tatshenshini River, just said, "You're nuts."

I did not argue. Luisa had recently had one cancer-riddled hip replaced and was already going skiing daily. Joel has filmed wild tigers at close quarters in India. Jon bicycled across Russia when he turned sixty, then trekked through Nepal and climbed to 18,000 feet in the Himalayas. Juneau is full of such adventurers, and I count among my friends people who have rafted wild rivers in Chile, wrangled sled dog teams in Antarctica, and climbed some of the world's highest peaks. Ed, the octogenarian from whom I'd bought the land I was building on, had been part of the climbing team that had made the first ascent of Mount Hess in the 1940s.

I valued their advice and concern, but hiking the coast did not seem to be an adventure on par with clawing one's way to the top of an unclimbed peak or skiing to the poles. Nor would it be a "first." The Tlingit Indians were certainly familiar with every step of the way, and I had located accounts of early gold miners and trappers who had made it through (one party had killed an extremely rare blue, or glacier, bear en route, and another had survived only because it had stolen a Native family's canoe). In modern times, several groups had covered the distance, although the last, which had attempted the trek the previous summer, had been stopped by a flooded river and forced to evacuate. That operation had resulted in two wrecked bush planes and the launch of a Coast Guard helicopter. But I could find no record of anyone having done it solo, largely, I imagined, because traveling with a group makes it easier to carry a boat of some sort for the water crossings. Doing it alone—and at my age—could prove difficult.

And yet, my age also provided a motive for going solo: Should the load I would have to carry, or the conditions, or the distance, prove too much, I could simply turn around and go home without having to dissuade a more gung ho companion. I tried to convince myself that the opposite was also true, that without a partner who might fizzle, I could go on as I pleased. But the truth is that after twenty years of guiding in Alaska, I have grown conservative when faced with the elemental power of the wilderness. To travel by boat to Lituya Bay and walk over a hundred miles up and down that wild coast would expose me to storms, geological chaos, and terrifying tide rips. And the thought of carrying a heavy pack all day made my back ache. Once on the ground, I might change my mind.

But the landscape alone should make the trip worth the effort. At Lituya Bay, Mount Crillon soars over 12,000 feet straight up from the water's edge. Beyond Lituya, a line of 15,000-foot peaks marches up the coast past Mount Fairweather. North of Mount Fairweather, Mount Saint Elias towers 18,000 feet above Malaspina Glacier.* Nowhere else on earth do such mountains rise so abruptly and vertically from sea level.

To persuade myself that it would be all right, I argued that I was not going to climb any mountains; I was going around them. I was just going for a walk on the beach, albeit a rather long one. As for Kah-Lituya, the odds of a major earthquake occurring while I was there were infinitesimal. Don Miller calculated the odds against a great wave happening on any given day at nine thousand to one (then fudged by adding that he believed the odds were actually much greater because of "a larger than average potential for slides resulting from the shaking and ground breaking associated with the 1958 earthquake"). And I presumed that the chance of encountering a *kushtaka* in the guise of either a beautiful woman or one of my own relatives was even smaller, because Miller also warned in his USGS report that within the region lie "thousands of square miles of wilderness counted among the least known and least frequented parts of Alaska." Trekking the coast would mean facing solitude of a sort rarely found on the planet. The only company I could count on was that of grizzlies. Lots of grizzlies. Southeast Alaska has one of the highest populations of brown bears in the world.[†]

My original reasoning—that stringing the beads of a dozen different trips into a necklace around Mount Fairweather and Glacier Bay National Park would somehow constitute a concrete accomplishment—was largely a rationalization designed to justify escaping the tiresome

---

* Compare this with Mount Everest, which rises slightly more than 11,000 feet from its base on a plateau at 17,575 feet to 29,000 feet at its summit.

† Though dozens and dozens of taxonomic subgroups were once used, biologists now agree that all brown bears and grizzlies—including European brown bears—belong to a single species, *Ursus arctos*. The names *grizzly bear* and *brown bear* are used interchangeably.

trials of construction and, even more important, allow me to find some breathing room to consider what to do about my ailing marriage. But beneath it whispered a nagging question: Could I still do it? Or had my abrupt entry into middle age reduced my physical abilities as thoroughly as it had turned me gray?

Throughout the summer the question grew louder, rising above the sound of power saws and hammers. Slowly, the wiring got done. The drywall was finished. I bought a dozen bags of plaster and forty gallons of paint. And every night as I popped the top off a bottle of aspirin to battle whatever ache was at the moment dominant and waited for my wife to come home, I thought of a long curve of beach stretching northwest between a range of ice-clad mountains and the sea.

CHAPTER 3

WINTER ARRIVED IN the form of small, dry snowflakes that came straight down out of a blue sky and hissed as they hit the ground. In early November the first of several howling winter storms slammed into the coast, dumping a trainload of moisture gathered up by the weather system as it moved along a storm track between Alaska and Japan. By Thanksgiving there was three feet of snow on the ground. As I worked—outside, under a tarp, with the shavings from a power planer flying out to mix with the blizzard—I kept tossing around what it really means to be middle-aged. The planks were from trees I had felled two years earlier, trucked to a small sawmill, and sawed into material for cabinets and flooring. Now I had two truckloads of lumber to mill, and it is no exaggeration to say that the shavings piled up faster than my insights into aging. According to U.S. census data, the average life expectancy for white males had increased from forty-eight years in 1900 to seventy-seven in 2007. The figures were skewed by turn-of-the-century infant-mortality rates, but nonetheless, fewer than two thirds of the twenty-year-olds alive in my grandfather's time could expect to reach my current age. Now, nine out of ten men live into their sixties, and nearly half reach eighty. In a little over a century—less time than it had taken for the trees I'd cut down to reach maturity—the odds of growing old had risen exponentially.

Feeding another plank into the planer's whirling cutterhead, I wondered what such statistics should mean to men like myself who don't spend much time fretting over things like retirement portfolios or risk management, or what they would have meant to someone like my grandfather, a West Texas rancher who climbed into a saddle when he was a young boy and stayed there until he dropped seventy years later. For generations my ancestors all worked the same patch of flint- and cactus-studded ground, and for such men—hardened by a relentless desert sun, two world wars, and a dust bowl—slowing down with age was never an option. (It was not until Franklin Roosevelt introduced his New Deal and social security in the 1930s that retirement became a possibility for any but the very rich. Now, thankfully, even those who make their living through sweat and labor are entitled to some leisure.)

Marveling at the way the spinning blades transformed raw wood into a finished surface, I sorted the emerging boards by color and quality while I wondered if all the aerobics and motorcycling engaged in by various men within my peer group were not just groping attempts to define middle age as an extension of youth, or if our society had simply changed so fast that we had not had time to develop a more appropriate approach to aging.

A board patterned with an attractive swirling grain emerged from the planer, and I set it aside for consideration. Throughout the building process, I had tried to pay attention to small details. If I could match the plank to others, they would make handsome panels in the cabinet doors. The woods I was using—spruce and hemlock for the cabinets, fir for the timbers and frame of the house, rot-resistant cedar for the outside decks and siding—were softwoods, without the defenses against marring offered by hardwoods like oak and maple or "engineered" products like laminated bamboo.

But this was part of the plan. In time, I hoped, day-to-day wear, weather, guests, and rambunctious children or grandchildren would eventually mark and smooth the various parts of the structure into what the Japanese call a *wabi-sabi* home. At its simplest, *sabi* can be defined as the beauty that comes to physical things with the passage of time, such as the way an old wooden door weathers into striking colors and patterns, or the grip of a tool develops a glowing patina after years of respectful use. *Wa*, the root of *wabi*, means "harmony" and connotes a life of ease within nature. When applied to objects, *wabi-sabi* implies the beauty of simple practicality. More important, the phrase carries a Zen overtone of living in the moment and accepting the inevitability of decay. It might take decades, but years of good living would transform the assemblage of wood and concrete into a comfortable *wabi-sabi* home, where my wife and I could grow old together graciously.

The planer growled and bogged down on a knot. I cranked a wheel to raise the cutterhead and tossed the plank aside. Some of the boards were so peppered with knots that they would serve only as firewood. In others, a well-placed knot or a twist in the grain brought the wood alive.

The next piece was a beauty, a chunk of mountain hemlock so perfectly free of defects that it ran through the planer like butter and came out the color of fresh cream. There are two species of hemlock in Southeast Alaska: western, which is larger and more common, and mountain, which is exceedingly slow growing. I remembered the tree the board had come from. A rise of bedrock on the ridge where the house was to be built had dictated that I cut it down before laying out the foundation. It was small, only ten inches in diameter, and as soon as it fell, I regretted it. The stump was a blur of growth rings packed so tightly together that it required a magnifying glass and a needle to count them.

The tree was 299 years old. It had taken three centuries to grow to the size of my leg. When it sprouted, Benjamin Franklin was an infant and Louis XIV was the king of France. Alaska was still firmly in the grip of the Little Ice Age, and the first Europeans would not arrive on the scene for another thirty-five years.

I turned the board over and ran it through the planer again, then turned it on edge to square it. The grain was perfect, quartersawn into a pattern of clean, straight lines arranged so closely together that they resembled the edge of a book.* If properly dried, the wood would have little tendency to cup or warp.

I flipped a switch to shut off the planer and removed my earplugs. The tarp over my head flapped in a gust of wind. Laying the plank across a sawhorse, I brushed away a litter of shavings and blew on my fingers to warm them. I knew what I wanted to do with this wood.

Thirty years earlier, during a pilgrimage to the now-deserted family ranch in Texas, I had hiked across the parched and stony land to the site of my family's original ranch house. The ranch had been vacant since 1958, abandoned after eleven years of drought. The house my great-great-grandfather had built in the nineteenth century was gone, except for a square of hand-cut limestone blocks outlining the foundation. Shards of weathered siding littered the ground. A jumble of old paint cans, nails, and rusty tools marked where the barn had once stood. Even in the best of times the house had been too humble to claim a living room or parlor, but growing out of the foundation of what had been the "front room" was a twisting, rough-barked tree. Mesquite trees yield wood that is blood-red and iron hard; it took me most of the morning to cut the tree down with a rusty saw I dug out of the wreckage of the barn. Afterward, I kept a few small boards from that mesquite log squirreled away, believing that someday I would turn them into a cabinet as a way of remembering my ancestors.

Eyeing the clean, white face of the mountain hemlock, I decided that combining it with the rosy hues of the Texas hardwood would create a beautiful contrast. And I liked the idea of a material connection between a tree grown within the foundation of my ancestral home and one sacrificed for the home I was building. In Japan many older houses have a tokonoma, an alcove or recess decorated with a simple

---

* *Quartersawn* describes lumber from a log that has been sawed into quarters lengthwise. Boards are sawed from each quarter by cutting at right angles to the annual growth rings, which then appear as parallel lines on the face of the board. Quartersawn wood is prized for its stability and resistance to warping.

scroll or a vase of flowers that is considered the spiritual center of the home. I imagined a small wall cabinet crafted from the hemlock and the mesquite serving the same purpose.

Unplugging the work lights, I drew a sheet of plastic over the planer, tucked the plank under my arm, and started toward the house. Halfway there I stopped to listen. It was perfectly quiet but for the sound of snow blowing through the trees. The wind smelled of fresh shavings. I thought again of the mesquite and the hemlock, and the passage of time they represented. It was dark, and snow hurtling out of the night stung my face. Kicking through a knee-deep snowdrift, I worked my way under the house and stored the plank in the crawl space. It would need to dry for a year or two before I could use it.

CHAPTER 4

WINTER JUST KEPT growing harder. Cold air flowing down from the glaciers pooled in the cove, and the temperature plummeted, falling so low that sawdust froze into a fist-sized knot around the spindle of the table saw, preventing me from raising or lowering the blade. Storm after storm sailed in from the gulf, until by Christmas nearly twenty feet of snow had fallen. It was the worst winter in Juneau's recorded history, and by January the land had begun to starve. Deer, driven from the forests, died by the dozen on the beaches. A hungry wolf took my neighbor's dog.

On the first day of March I began to write out a list of things I would need to hike the outer coast and started sorting equipment. A sleeping bag, a tent, rain gear, and extra clothing went into the "indispensable" stack, along with a cooking pot, a stove, and waterproof matches. A coil of strong, thin line would be important to hang my food from a tree at night to keep it out of the reach of bears. My camera and headlamp went onto a pile of things I wanted but could do without if necessary—carrying everything on my back made every ounce critical. And just as important was setting a date for departure. There were several factors to consider.

First was the bears. The grizzlies along the gulf come out of hibernation in late April and head for the coast, where new grass provides them with an excellent source of fresh protein. Throughout May patches of fresh beach rye needling up through the remains of the previous year's vegetation hold the bears' attention. In early spring every bear on the coast would be grazing on the beach, right where I planned to be walking. By June the snow cover would begin to melt in the higher altitudes, and the bears would move inland, following the snow line in pursuit of new vegetation. During summer, bears feed deep in the forest and up in the alpine until the salmon runs begin, in July, when they drop down to the coast and the rivers again. If I timed the trek for the period when the majority of the bears were away from the beach, it would decrease the chance of a confrontation.

The flip side of this was that the greening coast offered me the same advantage it gave the bears. In spring the stems and leaves of young "twisted stalk" plants are tender and edible, as are the tightly coiled fronds of the fiddlehead fern. Crisp beach asparagus and goose tongue pedicels push up through the soil, and the pale green buds of devil's club are tasty when lightly steamed. In other words, the foraging can be excellent. Combining wild greens with the salty meat of limpets and chitons pried from the rocks at low tide might reduce the amount of food I had to carry. In May an hour or two of picking and plucking every day could provide a decent meal.

My next consideration was the rivers. Poring over a map of the coast, I ticked off the thin blue line representing a watercourse in at least a dozen places. Judging by the size of the watershed each one drained, some would be little more than creeks. But even an ankle-deep rivulet can rise waist-high during one of the coast's infamous rainstorms. And by midsummer this would be compounded by runoff from melting snow in the higher altitudes. April and May are usually cool, with little runoff, but June's twenty-plus hours of daylight and warmer weather can bring on the perverse phenomenon of flooding caused by too much sunshine.

Last, but just as important as any other consideration, was the isolation. Early in the year, before the first salmon approach the coast from offshore, the cabins at Dry Bay are unoccupied. Not until mid-May do the fishermen who make their living there fly out to begin overhauling their nets. Likewise, very few fishing boats would be traveling the outer coast, and even fewer pleasure boats. I had a small handheld marine radio in the must-have equipment stack, but its range was limited to a few miles. If there were no vessels along the coast, I would be completely out of communication. In such a setting even a small accident can develop complications quickly. Taken to an unlikely extreme, a twisted ankle could mean starvation.

Three weeks later I was still moving gear from stack to stack and debating whether to eat better and face more bears, or avoid the flooding to make the water crossings easier and feel excommunicated. And all the time, the answer was falling from the sky, coming down in the form of intricately crystallized flakes of frozen moisture that fell one at a time, by the millions and the trillions, until the combined weight of their falling threatened to obliterate the world.

The calendar said the twenty-first of March was the first day of spring, but it was lying. There was four feet of snow on the ground, and more was coming. The forecast called for a warm front to roll in from offshore and drop another trainload of snow when it hit the coast. It would be worse if the warm front brought rain. The wind was already moaning through the mountains above Juneau, sweeping the existing snow into ever-deeper drifts along the lip of the avalanche chutes aimed at the city; even a light rain falling on the snowpack might loosen it enough to send a mile-wide slab of snow and ice thundering into the most vulnerable neighborhoods. Early that morning the Department of Transportation had used a howitzer to create a "controlled" avalanche south of town that plunged so wildly out of control down the mountain that when the powder blast finally cleared, it revealed a thousand-foot section of highway buried under twenty feet of debris. At two P.M. the city manager, working with the Southeast Alaska Avalanche Center, released the following bulletin:

"On a scale normally stretching from 1 to 4 (low, moderate, serious, high) an update from the Southeast Avalanche Center continues to call the avalanche danger 'extreme' or *off the scale.*"

"We do not normally use the fifth point of the U.S. scale," said

Bill Glude, director of the Avalanche Center, "but on those rare occasions when avalanche danger is so high that it is essentially off the scale and widespread natural avalanches are probable, the designator is 'extreme' or 'black.' Being anywhere near avalanche terrain or runout zones is not recommended."

To avoid being "anywhere near" avalanche terrain in Juneau would mean leaving town. The best the city could do was open a public facility on the edge of the black zone to those wishing to evacuate their homes. "They should bring with them all needed medications, pillows, sleeping bags or blankets, and vital papers," said the city manager. In other words, there would be nothing left of their homes if an avalanche occurred.

The city held its breath. The buttresses of snow overhead sagged and groaned. When it began to rain, every ear in town cocked heavenward for the first rumble of destruction. And still no one took the city up on its offer. The facility remained empty, perhaps because the bulletin also noted that pets could not be accommodated or because the refugees preferred to crowd in with friends living outside the danger zone. But it seemed like the reluctance of so many to evacuate also demonstrated the deeply human impulse to cling, when things get threatening, to the sheltering idea of "home," just as so many did at the approach of Hurricane Katrina or when smoke started boiling out of the nuclear reactor in Chernobyl, Russia.

For days, obliteration never seemed far away. And the sword hanging over the community's head made my decision for me. With the mountains under such a burden of snow, the likelihood of extreme levels of runoff when it started melting was inarguable. By summer, raging water would make the coast impassable, as it had for the expedition that had attempted the traverse two years earlier. My best bet was to go before that could happen. I decided to depart for Lituya Bay in early May.

CHAPTER 5

Gʀᴀʏ ᴡᴀᴠᴇs ʀᴏʟʟᴇᴅ toward me from a horizon streaked with bruised clouds. The boat bucked into an oncoming wave, pitched hard to one side, and righted. I was 120 miles out of Juneau on my way to Lituya Bay, and a mile to starboard I could see the swells exploding into spray against Cape Spencer. For a moment I considered turning back, but I decided against it because I had already turned back once before, gone timid a day earlier at the sight of ten-foot rollers leaping and tumbling in a tide rip that pours out of Cross Sound into the gulf beyond the cape. Besides, though the sea frightens me, the weather and choppy water matched my mood.

Through some miracle of adhesion—some fine, hair-thin agreement between a million tons of snow and the urgings of gravity—the slide hanging over Juneau had stayed in place, though the weather had thawed, frozen, and thawed again through an improbable temperature cycle that had wavered back and forth across a single degree. But whatever miracle had kept the avalanche aloft over the city had not held for everyone; four days before I left for Lituya Bay, Luisa died.

I was upstairs, installing a complicated shower valve in the half-finished bathroom, when her husband called. The instructions for the valve had apparently been written in Chinese, then translated into English by someone with a loose grip on both languages; I was frustrated by a number of small plastic pieces that did not do what they were said to do. But everything—Juneau's brush with destruction, the fatigue of laboring alone on the house for months through the record snowfall, and the lousy translation—became unimportant after I answered the phone.

Joel's voice shook as he struggled to speak. Luisa had stopped eating, he said. Then a fever had set in and she was dying. I should come right away if I wanted to say goodbye.

I cursed as I threw my tools into a bucket. After I hung up the phone, it felt like someone else was in charge of my body, and I watched, hearing only the sound of my own breathing, as that someone got into my truck, put the key in the ignition, and dropped the gearshift into reverse. A week earlier, spring had finally begun to edge winter aside, with the sound of geese overhead and water trickling from banks of rotting snow, but the day was cold, harsh, and windy. The light coming through the clouds was as thin and gray as poorhouse gruel. I am normally a cautious driver, but when I finally slipped back into my body, the speedometer said I was doing eighty.

I had to brake hard to make the turn to Joel and Luisa's beach house. The truck slewed to a stop at the top of a flight of stairs. The branches of an ancient spruce swayed in a gust of wind. A flock of crows rose tumbling and raucous as I passed, then settled again, shrieking. Twigs rained down on my head.

I stopped, reluctant to continue, and tried for a moment to decipher what message might be written in a hieroglyph of tiny branches and leaves at my feet, but there was nothing, just the crows and the wind. The metal stairs rang under my boots as I hurried down.

She was in the living room, propped up in an adjustable bed that a quartet of friends had carried down the long flight of stairs and into the house when it became clear there was nothing more to be done for her at the hospital. At the first sign of spring Joel had hung a sugar-water feeder on the porch, and the windows buzzed with rufous hummingbirds, dipping and swirling like spots of incandescent light. Beyond the hummingbirds the wind stirred the waters of Lynn Canal into tumbling whitecaps that hurried west toward Admiralty Island.

Luisa's breath was shallow and uneven as I sank to a stool beside her. We have never been the sort of people who speak of love easily, but I took her hand. We do not speak such words effortlessly or often because to do so risks watering them down. Instead, they are the last arrow out of the quiver, hoarded for critical moments such as these, because, to paraphrase the writer Annie Dillard, what *else* are you going to say to the dying that does not enrage with its triviality?

I leaned in and squeezed Luisa's hand. Her eyes were closed, but I knew she could hear me. At first all I could do was say how grateful I was to have had her in my life, and ramble back and forth over how our friendship had enriched me. Then I realized I was repeating myself and thought to say, "Don't be afraid," and "Don't worry about Joel. We'll take care of him."

Then I told her I loved her and said goodbye.

On my way out the crows were strangely silent. The wind overhead hissed and sighed. I climbed into my truck and started the engine. Then I rolled up the windows so no one would hear me howl.

A memorial was planned for the end of May. By then the wildflowers would be blooming, and the odds of good weather would be high. But the rivers on the outer coast might also be flooding, so I considered canceling. It could take a month to get to Lituya Bay, hike the outer coast, and return to Juneau, and I did not want to miss the service. There was no guarantee I could get back in time.

When I mentioned this to one of the friends who had carried Luisa from the hospital and down that long flight of stairs so she could spend her last days at home, he grew solemn. Jon is exceptionally quick-witted, with an infectious laugh that bursts out from his sternum, but since Luisa's death he had been grave. When he is serious—when he has something to say and thinks you should really *listen*—he tilts his head a few degrees and looks as stern as a deacon. This is what he did when I explained that I was thinking of canceling. We were in a bar. The waitress had just brought us drinks.

"I know what Luisa would say," he said, pausing to toy with a napkin before he picked up his drink and pointed it at me. "She'd say go."

He was right. Luisa had lugged heavy sound-recording equipment to the Arctic, Africa, and Greenland while producing films with her husband. They had built a log cabin in the interior of Alaska and spent summers canoeing wild rivers. In the twenty years I had known them, I had rarely known Luisa to decline an adventure. So I went home, dug out a small Buddhist prayer flag she had given me after a trip to Mongolia, and folded the Sanskrit-emblazoned banner into a pocket of my pack.

Now the pack and the flag were safely stowed in the hold, I was three days out of Juneau, and my shoulders were stiff with the tension that comes of being alone in a small boat on a very large and boisterous sea. But the early-morning weather report had promised decreasing winds and calmer seas by afternoon, so I decided to press on.

The *Swift* lurched over the top of another wave, and I braced myself for the impact at the bottom. The morning broadcast had also crackled with a one-sided conversation between the Coast Guard station in Juneau and a vessel in trouble in a fjord south of Juneau. From what I'd been able to make of the static-filled transmission, a rescue helicopter was under way. I scanned the horizon and wondered what the chances of any sort of rescue would be where I was going. There were no boats in sight.

I throttled back, lowering the boat's speed to decrease the violent motion. If I could claw offshore a few miles, I might find calmer water. The effects of tides and currents on the seas are more pronounced close to shore, and more "sea room," the distance between a boat and land, is always a sailor's friend. The farther offshore one is, the more time one has to deal with unexpected problems, mechanical or otherwise, before a disabled vessel can be swept onto the rocks.

A flock of pelagic cormorants flapped out of the way at the approach of the *Swift*. Soot-colored shearwaters soared along the backs of rolling waves. The currents that rage through Southeast Alaska flush a rich soup of nutrients from the depths that combines with sunlight at the surface to create masses of phytoplankton. Phytoplankton supports tiny animals like copepods and various larvae, which in turn become food for herring and krill. Everything from seabirds to whales feeds on herring and krill, and west of Cape Spencer, where the seabed disappears into an abyss, the sea and sky are always full of life.

A large shadow swept across the deck, and I glanced out the window just in time to catch a rare glimpse of a black-footed albatross, sweeping by on seven-foot wings. The black-footed albatross is a giant bird that breeds in Hawaii, then rides to Alaska in the summer on the winds that rotate around a static weather system called the North Pacific High, sleeping, it is said, on the wing, taking catnaps that can last a hundred miles. This one swooped, circled, and disappeared astern without moving a feather. In the distance rose the glistening back of a humpback whale.

A glance at the radar told me I had edged two miles outside of Cape Spencer. The foot of the cape was speckled with rocks and reefs. I reached for my cell phone and checked the signal—weak, but still strong enough for me to call my wife.

There was a single ring and a moment of static before the connection went straight to voice mail. She was too busy to talk.

"Call me back if you get this, will you, hon?" I said after a cheery recording of her voice invited me to leave a message. "I'm about to go out of range."

Beyond the cape there would be no cell phone or other means of communication. I cut the throttle back and waited. Without steerageway the hull rolled broadside to the waves. Throttling up to regain control, I idled forward, poking the bow into the chop.

Half an hour later the radar told me I was three miles beyond

Cape Spencer. I jogged into the waves for a few minutes, hoping the phone would ring, but it stayed silent. I spun the helm and turned northwest toward Lituya Bay.

Thirty miles and a couple thousand whitecaps later the clouds broke into rags and thinned. Silver sunlight poured across an iron-colored sea. White birds rose and fell between the waves. To starboard the blue-and-white tongue of La Perouse Glacier poured out of the mountains behind a surf-pummeled beach. There was no sign of humanity. No boats on the sea, no planes overhead. No activity in any direction. The radio had been silent for hours.

Through binoculars I could see the tops of trees rising from beyond the surf. The scene was identical to one Captain James Cook had noted while exploring this coast 230 years earlier, on a clear, fine day in May of 1778, as HMS *Resolution* and its sister ship *Discovery* crawled north in light winds over a rolling, glassy sea. Cook, writing in the staid, clear language preferred by the British Admiralty, recorded that the towering mountains in sight to starboard were "wholly covered with snow, from the highest summits down to the sea coast, some few places excepted where we could perceive trees, as it were, rising their heads out of the sea."

It was such a fine, almost balmy day that Cook was inspired to name the towering mountain behind the next headland he came to Mount Fair Weather. In choosing to commemorate the weather that allowed him to see the 15,000-foot peak from miles away, Cook was unknowingly acknowledging something the Tlingit Indians had known for centuries: When Na goot Ku, a friendly, birdlike spirit that lives on Fairweather's summit, lifts the clouds enough for "the paddler's mountain" to be visible, the weather will be calm enough to travel at sea by dugout canoe.

Na goot Ku was not as benevolent toward all of the early explorers

as he was toward Captain Cook. Alexei Chirikov, the Russian commander of the first European ship to approach North America from
the west, never saw Mount Fairweather. It was cloudy and close to
nightfall when a lookout aboard Chirikov's ship, the *St. Paul*, spotted
the coast on July 15, 1741. The *St. Paul* and a second ship, the *St. Peter*,
under the command of a Dane named Vitus Bering, were all that remained of what had once been the greatest army of exploration the
world has ever seen. When the Great Nordic Expedition had departed
Saint Petersburg under Bering's command in 1733, it had been ten
thousand strong, a swarming horde of soldiers, carpenters, hunters,
engineers, and scientists sent out by Peter the Great with orders to
map Siberia, build the city of Petropavlovsk, sail across the unexplored
reaches of the Bering Sea until they struck North America, then continue south to Mexico. Eight years later, by the time Chirikov's lookout spotted the faint outline of a tree-covered island looming out of
the night near what would one day be the border between Canada and
Alaska, the ambitious expedition had been winnowed down to two
worm-riddled hulks manned by tubercular, scurvied ghosts. Exhausted and in poor health, neither Bering nor Chirikov had the heart
for further exploration.* The *St. Paul* and the *St. Peter* had lost contact
with each other shortly after leaving Siberia, and Chirikov, leery of approaching the strange new coast without the support of another vessel, came cautiously about and stood offshore again.

On July 18, after three days of sailing north, a lookout at the *St.
Paul*'s masthead spotted what appeared to be an opening to a large bay.
Water was running low, so Chirikov ordered Fleetmaster Dementief to
go ashore in a small boat with a couple of empty casks to explore.

Dementief armed ten men with muskets and a small cannon,

---

* Vitus Bering, who is often credited with "discovering" Alaska, spotted land on July 16, a
day after Chirikov, when he saw Mount Saint Elias rising above the clouds approximately
200 miles north of Chirikov's position.

launched the larger of the *St. Paul*'s two longboats, and rowed ashore, mindful of Chirikov's instructions that he was to discern who lived in the bay and whether they possessed any valuable metals (i.e., gold). Chirikov had also given Dementief ten rubles to present to the bay's inhabitants and ordered him to build a large bonfire upon landing to signal his safe arrival.

Dementief and the others were never seen again. The *St. Paul* coasted back and forth watching for five days, but the boat never returned. On July 23 the *St. Paul* stood in toward shore, sailing as close to the land as Chirikov dared, but no closer than two or three miles. Smoke was seen rising from the beach, and he ordered that a signal cannon be fired. There was no response, and no boat came off. Again and again the cannon signal went unanswered. Fearing that Dementief's boat had somehow been damaged, Chirikov then sent in the ship's second—and last—small boat, manned by the *St. Paul*'s bosun, a carpenter, and two helpers, with materials for repairs. They, too, disappeared.

The next day the Russians made the Western world's first, fleeting contact with the coast's inhabitants. Two canoes were seen coming out of the bay, one large and one small.

"We naturally thought they were our boats," said Chirikov in his report, "and stood towards them."

There was very little wind. Chirikov ordered the sails taken in and the shrouds tightened, but when the small boat came closer, they became aware that it was not their boat, "for it had a sharp bow, and those in it did not row but paddled."

The larger of the two boats hung back in the distance, and the smaller one would not come close enough for those aboard the *St. Paul* to make out the four occupants clearly or see their faces.

The small boat's occupants stood up and began shouting, "*Agai! Agai!*" and waved for the *St. Paul* to follow them. Then they turned and paddled away.

"We could not pursue them," said Chirikov, "because in the first place there was no wind, in the second place the small boat went very fast, and the large one had stopped a considerable distance from us." The two canoes sped back into the bay, he continued, and "we became convinced that some misfortune had happened to our men, for it was the eighth day since [Dementief] had left us."

Chirikov decided that the failure of "the Americans" to approach his ship indicated that they had killed or detained his men. When evening came, he ordered the *St. Paul* to stand offshore, where they drifted, waiting for two more days before abandoning all hope of recovering the missing sailors. With the ship's carpenter lost, no boats on board, and no materials to build another, Chirikov had no way to get ashore. There was nothing more he could do. Low on water, and with fifteen of his crew missing, he had no choice but to order his remaining men to sail for home.

Scholars have debated exactly where Chirikov's men were lost for decades; navigation in the mid-1700s was often hit or miss, with errors of up to a hundred miles not uncommon. Various translations of Chirikov's reports give the *St. Paul*'s position as 57° 15' North, 57° 39' North, and 57° 50' North—a spread of thirty-five nautical miles, which is enough to place the ship in several locations that bear a resemblance to Chirikov's description.* Both Lisianski Strait, a few miles from Cape Spencer, and the entrance to Peril Strait, fifty miles farther south, are possibilities. Both are openings into the coast through which the current flows with sufficient strength to threaten the unwary. On the ebb, strong tide rips can occur at the mouth of each. But for my money, the modus operandi of the place that engulfed the Russians is pure Lituya Bay.

---

* Read, for example, as "Fifty-seven degrees, fifteen minutes north," 57° 15' North indicates a position fifteen nautical miles north of the fifty-seventh parallel in the northern hemisphere. Each "minute of arc" (equivalent to one sixtieth of a degree) measures one nautical mile, obtained by measuring the height of the sun above the horizon at noon.

Neither Lisianski nor Peril Strait is particularly threatening on the flood, when the sea is crowding the entrance (with the caveat that Sergius Narrows, a rockbound dogleg several miles into Peril Strait, is *exceedingly* dangerous during the flood, but lies far enough into the strait for an experienced seaman to notice the speed of the current increasing and pull ashore before his craft becomes endangered). In calm seas, the other dangers in both areas are readily apparent to anyone approaching from seaward and easily avoided.

The entrance to Lituya Bay, however, is deceptive. On the flood, from seaward, it appears wide and clear, with no visible obstructions. A stranger approaching from offshore sees a broad entrance marked only by a few current lines like those of a deep, swiftly flowing river. But just inside the entrance, running from right to left beneath the surface, lies a submarine berm of rocks and rubble bulldozed into place by the last advance of the glaciers. To pass through safely, a mariner must enter to starboard, on the right-hand side of the opening, then steer hard to port, crabbing and clawing across the swift current to remain within a narrow, safe channel that runs at an oblique angle inside the left-hand shore. To do otherwise—to follow one's natural inclination and steer with the current—means being thrown against the hidden rocks.

Beating through the waves as La Perouse Glacier fell behind me, I needed no great imagination to envision this happening to Chirikov's shore party. Under the circumstances, it was nearly impossible to imagine the scene unfolding otherwise. It would require seamanship of a fairly amateurish sort to be drawn into and destroyed by the flood at the entrance to either Lisianski or Peril Strait, although the ebb, or outflowing, current can be dangerous at all three locations. And under conditions such as those the *St. Paul* met when it approached the coast (light winds and a smooth, glassy sea rolling in from the west), a tide rip of any magnitude or breakers over a reef would have been visible from a distance and easy to avoid. The crew of a small, oar-powered vessel approaching from seaward would have had to work exceedingly hard to row *into* a tide rip, as the current would have been working to thrust them *out*.*

Nor, I told myself as a fusillade of salt spray broke across the *Swift*'s windows, was it likely that the Tlingit killed or detained Chirikov's men. While a violent, warlike people, the Tlingit were also avid traders. Time after time, when encountering strangers, they would prove to be more interested in doing business than in attacking. During the 120 years in which Russia occupied Alaska, the Tlingit would repeatedly harry, burn, and slaughter the invaders in response to their thieving brutality, sometimes seizing the Russians' own guns and cannons and using the weaponry against them. But a first encounter with musket-toting, cannon-firing strangers would have terrorized even the boldest warrior unfamiliar with the murderous thunder of gunpowder.

More likely is a scenario wherein the crews of both Russian boats found themselves stunned and helpless as the current running into Lituya Bay seized their boats, splintered them against the rocks, and drowned the men. The Tlingit, watching from on shore as the trage-dies unfolded and not wishing the drowned strangers to become *kush-taka* otter-men, would have done their best to recover the bodies for cremation. Slack water—that period of relative calm when the inrush-ing tide slows and prepares to reverse itself and run out again—lasts only ten to twenty minutes at Lituya Bay, which might explain the Na-tives' haste when they yelled for Chirikov to join them; to tarry would have meant being trapped outside by the current.†

---

* The scholar Allan Engstrom makes a strong argument for Chirikov's men having landed at Surge Bay, on the southern shore of Cross Sound. According to local fishermen, Surge Bay can be dangerous during westerly seas. Engstrom's hypothesis is also strengthened by the recent discovery of a stone petroglyph, carved by an unknown Tlingit artist, that appears to represent a two-masted ship resembling the *St. Paul*.

† Frederica de Laguna, one of the foremost ethnographers of the Tlingit culture, has postulated that the cries of "*Agai!*" that Chirikov heard were the Natives saying, "*Haa·déi!*," or "Come down! Over here!," a phrase used to summon visitors to traditional ceremonies.

A wave larger and more threatening than the rest reared up off the bow of the *Swift*, and I throttled back to meet it. Sunlight glittered across its face. There was a moment of silence, followed by a brief weightless feeling as the *Swift* dropped into the trough preceding it. I held my breath as the wave slammed into the bow. It broke like a dam collapsing. The sea and sky disappeared in a barrage of foam.

The next wave jarred my spine. A third rattled the coffee cups on their hooks and banged a skillet to the floor. I flicked on the wipers to clear the spray from the windows and looked west, where the swells were coming from; streaks of pale haze filled the sky.

I braced myself for the next lurching wave and tuned the radio to the weather channel. Recent upgrades to the marine weather-reporting system have made it possible to receive updates in most locations along the coast, and though I was beyond the transmission range of my boat's low-powered radio, the digital voice of the automated forecast came through loud and clear. What it had to say made my stomach jump; instead of the decreasing winds that the early-morning forecast had promised, strong winds were now forecast to hit the coast that night.

I pulled out a chart and spread it on the galley table to measure the distance to Lituya Bay. The *Swift* is equipped with a modern GPS, or global positioning system, but I prefer paper charts. Many of mine have been with me for decades. Some I have owned since I first went to sea on commercial fishing boats in my twenties, and they have accompanied me on a variety of sailing vessels, yachts, and tugs since, until winding up as an essential tool aboard the *Swift*. They are soft from years of handling, tattered along the folds, and stained with sea spray and drops of coffee. The margins are full of penciled notes— characteristics, I suppose, that may constitute *wabi-sabi* of a nautical, personal sort, but I know I should replace them, if for no other reason than that I may someday mistake a spot of mildew for a nonexistent rock. Still, they feel like old friends and can be trusted not to lie to me.

What chart number 16720 now told me was that I was still twenty miles from Lituya Bay, and the weather was deteriorating.

I did a quick calculation to estimate my time of arrival at the entrance. The battering chop had slowed me down. If I missed slack water, the ebb running from the bay could turn the swells into combers that would prevent the *Swift* from entering. Then I could either wait for the next period of slack water, jogging into the waves for six hours as the weather worsened, or turn tail and run, hoping to reach Cape Spencer before the gale struck. My mouth went dry as I tried to decide.

An image of the *Swift* capsizing in a thundering breaker in the entrance to Lituya Bay flashed through my brain, and I felt my chest tighten. Then I imagined the anxiety the Tlingit must have felt when the *St. Paul* appeared on the horizon; what the strange white-winged apparition must have meant to their universe; how they must have wondered, with their hearts in their throats, what changes were coming as they watched the phantasm divest itself of canoes unlike any they had ever seen, manned by creatures who sat facing aft, pulling oars, instead of facing forward and paddling; then the horror of seeing the alien craft swept into the current and upended to the sound of screams in an unknown language.

I thought of the courage it would have taken for the villagers to recover the bodies; of what trembling, willful hearts it would have required to handle the remains of such oddly dressed, lavishly bearded strangers in order to prevent their souls from becoming *kushtaka*; and of the terror of those who may have already been convinced the men were creatures from another world. And I wondered at the fortitude of the warriors who paddled out to the specter of Chirikov's ship as it coasted back and forth on the horizon belching thunder.

Taking a deep breath, I tried to relax my shoulders. The sea was pale green and the mountains a breathless white. I rolled my neck and considered the early explorers: Vitus Bering never made it home to Russia. The leader of the Great Nordic Expedition died of exhaustion, huddled in the remains of the shipwrecked *St. Peter* on a small island off the coast of Siberia. He was sixty-two years old when he died. Chirikov was forty-four when he succumbed to consumption in Saint Petersburg. Captain Cook was murdered by the natives of Hawaii at fifty-one.

I would turn fifty-three in a month.

A feeling of doubt rose within me, and for a moment it was easy to imagine myself in Chirikov's boots, with the question of what I was doing so far from home washing over me, rising and falling to the rhythm of the waves. My internal bearings grew as hazy and uncertain as the Russian commander's navigation; how, I wondered, had the early explorers traveled into the unknown for years on end without yielding to the gnawing hunger of homesickness? When Napoléon retreated from Moscow, half his army died trying to claw its way out of the bitter Russian winter, and many of the deaths were attributed to *nostalgia*, or "home-ache." The exhausted, disheartened soldiers simply gave up and lay down by the road to die.

I watched the waves roll toward me and considered turning back again. Running southeast toward Cape Spencer with the seas behind me would eliminate the incessant pounding, and home was calling. I thought a bit longer, then put my hand on the throttle and eased it forward; I could still reach Lituya Bay by slack tide.

CHAPTER 6

Two hundred and twenty years before I waited, pitching and rolling in the chop off the mouth of Lituya Bay, for the tide to turn, a group of young Tlingit hunters on the shore near the mouth spotted something unusual far out to sea. Inside the bay nearly three hundred people were picking berries, catching halibut, and hunting seals, working to put away enough food for the coming winter. Unlike on the day I arrived, the sea the young hunters walked beside was smooth and glassy. A gentle breeze blew in from the west. But the people occupying the temporary summer camp inside the bay were already on edge. Only a few days earlier a group of four canoes arriving from Kaax'noowu, a village one hundred miles away on Icy Strait, had been caught in the tidal maelstrom at the entrance and had overturned. Several people had drowned, including a prominent chief. And not long before that disaster a flotilla of seven trading canoes paddling south from the land of the Aglegmute and Chugatsch Eskimos, west of Yakutat, had been swamped, again with a terrible loss of life. With so many recently severed souls to mourn and the increased threat of *kushtaka* lurking in the area, it did not take long for alarm to spread when the young men ran toward their uncle's hut shouting, "Come quick! There is something on the horizon we have never seen before!"

The uncle, Yeahlth-kan, was a wise man, one of the camp's leaders, and he rose from where he was sitting in front of his family's simple shelter and followed his nephews to the water's edge. What he saw there disturbed him: An enormous black being with broad white wings was moving slowly along the horizon, traveling first in one direction, then in another with a flap of its great wings. In a flash he decided it must be Yéil—Yéil, the Creator, who in the form of a raven had brought light to the world and created all living things. After creating the world, Yéil had flown away, but only after promising to return someday from the direction of the setting sun. And now here he was, flying southeast on wings that flapped and rose with every puff of the western breeze.

Panic broke out among the people. Men with guilty consciences drove copper blades through the skin of their breasts and stood rigid, awaiting Yéil's judgment. Others with less to fear ran to clean their houses and paint their faces to be ready to receive him. Fires were built and covered with sweet grasses in order that the children might be passed through the smoke and purified. It was well known that looking directly upon Yéil's radiance could turn a person to stone, so the uncle instructed everyone to cut skunk cabbage leaves, roll them into tubes, and use these to view Yéil safely.

The alarm and confusion that raced through the Tlingit camp are understandable, but in truth they had little to fear; it wasn't a vengeful Maker of the Universe coming over the horizon but a short, rather pudgy Frenchman bearing the melodious though somewhat cumbersome title of Jean-François de Galoup, Comte de La Pérouse, a rear admiral of the royal French navy. The two ships under his command were the entirety of an expedition billed by its patron, Louis XVI, as "the Greatest of All Voyages." It was July 3, 1786, and La Pérouse's ship, the *Boussole*, and its consort, the *Astrolabe*, captained by La Pérouse's good friend Fleuriot de Langle, had departed Brest eleven months earlier on a mission to discover new lands and economic opportunities for France. The king was a fan of the Romantic notion, often attributed to the Swiss philosopher Jean-Jacques Rousseau, that held that primitive peoples, uncorrupted by the pressures of modern society, existed in a state of natural grace, and among his more than two hundred pages of excruciatingly detailed instructions to La Pérouse was a mandate that the commander and his crew were to pursue a policy of

pacifique, or "peaceful," relations with whatever natives they encountered.* All contact was to remain as friendly as possible and be of benefit to the *indigènes*. In a further doff of his crown to the growing
humanitarianism of the Age of Reason, the king also insisted that there
be no deaths from either violence or disease among the *Boussole*'s and
Astrolabe's crews, which was a remarkable policy given that for the
past two centuries the English, Portuguese, Dutch, Spanish, and Russian expeditions spanning out to claim the globe had often suffered
casualty rates as high as 75 percent.

So far the king's enlightened policies had paid off; in the ten
months since the *Boussole* and the *Astrolabe* had left France, the expedition had not lost a single man, and La Pérouse had won the undying
affection of his men for his concern for their welfare.

In short, he wasn't the sort of person to turn anyone into stone.
When a lookout saw the columns of smoke from the purifying fires
onshore, he ordered the ships to tack and head in. As they drew nearer,
the outline of Lituya Bay became clear, and at two o'clock in the afternoon the entrance was spotted between a cluster of rocks awash in
rolling surf on one side and a low, boulder-covered spit on the other.
Behind the spit, La Pérouse noted in his journal, lay a "very fine bay,"
so large that "nature seemed to have constructed in the remotest part
of America a harbour resembling that of Toulon, but on a gigantic
scale, adapted to her ampler powers."

This was exactly what he had been hoping for ever since they had
popped out of the fog and spotted the hulking white tower of Mount
Saint Elias north of Yakutat on June 23, ten days earlier. Turning

---

* There is irony in this, in that Rousseau did not in fact equate the state of "natural man"
with that of the "noble savage," as has so often—and so mistakenly—been claimed. For
Rousseau, the "goodness" of uncivilized man was that of behaving according to his true
nature, rather than one codified by artificial notions of virtue and morality. Rousseau's
political philosophy also greatly influenced the French Revolution, which led to Louis
XVI's being guillotined. The king is said to have asked, "Is there any word of La
Pérouse?" on the way to his execution.

southeast to parallel the coast, they had tried twice to send boats
ashore for wood and fresh water—once, it is now presumed, near the
southern entrance to Yakutat Bay and again at the mouth of a large,
shallow body of water filled with breakers that La Pérouse dubbed the
"Behring River," which was almost certainly the mouth of the Alsek
River, at Dry Bay. Both efforts had been foiled by fog and dangerous
surf. Now the calm water he could see behind the low spit appeared to
offer an opportunity to refill the water casks and gather firewood in
safety.

What the Tlingit saw was Yéil turning slowly toward them as if
drawn by the smoke of their fires. The ships tacked, their sails flapping
like great wings, and Yéil crept closer. To the watching Natives, the sea-
men climbing through the rigging in response to the whistled signals
of the bosun's pipe looked and sounded like capering crows. Most of
the Tlingit fled into the forest; only a few stayed behind to snatch awestruck glances through their viewing tubes.

It must have been torturous for Tlingit and Frenchmen alike to
have the *Boussole* and the *Astrolabe* creep to the entrance in the light
winds, only to see the tide change and the current that suddenly began
flowing from Lituya Bay thrust the ships back out to sea again. Alarmed
by the speed with which the current had arisen, La Pérouse began to
worry that if his ships *did* get into the bay, they might have difficulty
getting out. The harbor could be a trap, requiring an unlikely combination of wind and tide to escape. The cataract pouring from the entrance, he admitted, "abated my eagerness to put into the harbor," and
he ordered the ships to stand out to sea again.

Throughout the night the *Boussole* and the *Astrolabe* stayed side
by side as La Pérouse and de Langle conferred back and forth on a
course of action. By morning de Langle and La Pérouse's other officers
had convinced him that this was a chance for French glory; the bay
was on none of the maps drawn by Captain Cook, and it would be the

expedition's own discovery. An exultant La Pérouse promptly named it Port des Français.

At six in the morning both ships stood in toward shore, timing their arrival at the entrance to coincide with high tide. Boats were put over the side with orders to take up stations on each side of the channel. The wind was steady from the west and southwest, perfect for a broad reach into the north-and-south-running entrance. The inrush of the flood was easing just as the *Astrolabe* pushed into the opening.

Then the wind suddenly veered ninety degrees, chopping around to the northwest, and, in La Pérouse's words, "it became necessary to throw the ship up in the wind and lay all aback," meaning that the only way to avoid being driven onto the rocks by the sudden shift in the wind was to turn upwind and allow the sails to blow back against the rigging in a desperate attempt to turn the ships around within the narrow confines of the channel. But with the sails pinned against the shrouds, both ships lost all steerageway. Caught in the current, the *Boussole* and the *Astrolabe* spun out of control.

From my position outside Lituya Bay I could see the point at which La Pérouse's ships had faltered and begun to stagger toward disaster. On the eastern side of the entrance a dozen tawny sea lions sprawled atop Cormorant Rock, lorded over by a bull the size of a small forklift. By my calculations high tide was due, but I could still see swirls of current in the channel.

The Fathometer said there was twelve fathoms of water under me, but as I idled the *Swift* ahead, it jumped suddenly to eight, then five; the tide was still flooding in from the west, pushing me into the bay at a right angle to the entrance. Fishermen familiar with the bay and its entrance had warned me that a variety of influences could alter the calculated time of slack water by as much as an hour, and this seemed to be happening now.

I spun the helm and came about to move offshore again, growing impatient; I was tired of the pounding seas, and my hands were starting to cramp from gripping the wheel, but it was easy to imagine the panic on board the *Boussole* and the *Astrolabe* as the ships stalled and began to slide toward the foaming rocks. I decided to wait another half an hour, then try again.

Then out of nowhere came a sea that slammed into the *Swift* at an angle slightly different from the rest, a slab of water that seemed to pick the boat up and drop it like a football player performing a drop-kick. The boat corkscrewed under me, slid sideways, and banged into the trough. Water gushed through the scuppers, and I cursed as I grabbed for a handhold to avoid being thrown to the deck. Behind me, the calm water inside the bay beckoned.

A minute later I was jockeying into position to make a run for the entrance. Lining up on a navigation aid installed by the Coast Guard after a series of accidents had left the broken remnants of several fishing vessels scattered along the spit near the mouth, I threw a last glance at the chart, where the blue delineating shallow water on each side of the channel was peppered with shoals marked "foul." Then I eased the throttle forward and started in. The motion of the waves eased as the boat gained speed, running on the same "broad reach," or right angle to the wind, that La Pérouse had enjoyed as he had approached the entrance.

The seabed climbed quickly, the Fathometer's flashing orange light indicating that I had crossed the ten-fathom line, then rising to seven fathoms, six, five . . . if I strayed into less than three fathoms of water, I would be in trouble. I could see water foaming and swirling over submerged rocks on both sides.

Once the *Swift* was into the entrance, the chop settled into a smooth laminar flow with the appearance of calm water, but I could still feel the current wrestling for control of the helm. I had to adjust the steering constantly, first to port, then to starboard, then back to port again, to counter sucking, whirlpool hydraulics that had overwhelmed far larger and stronger vessels in the past and destroyed them. (It isn't for nothing that Alaska's fishermen call the entrance to Lituya Bay the Chopper; the body count in the twentieth century was in the dozens.) Even with enough power and speed to stem the current, I could feel the *Swift*'s hull squirming from side to side as if it were in the grip of a living thing.

La Pérouse had gotten lucky at the last minute. With the drifting *Boussole* only "half a pistol shot," or twenty-five yards, from the rocks on the eastern point, an unexpected surge of countercurrent caroming off the right-hand shore had miraculously pushed both ships back into the channel and through the entrance. "During the thirty years that I have followed the sea," he later wrote, "I never saw two vessels so near being lost; and to have experienced such an event at the verge of the world would have enhanced our misfortune."

Just as I thought that I, too, had pushed safely through the entrance, there was a jolting impact that bounced me in my seat, and my heart leaped into my throat. For a moment I was certain I had struck a rock. Craning my head to look back at the boat's wake, I saw that I had instead encountered a phenomenon I had been warned about by a fisherman. Lituya Bay is a bit less than nine miles long and two miles across at its widest point, with a surface area of approximately eighteen square miles. This means that during a fourteen-foot tide more than seven *billion* cubic feet of water must force its way through the channel in six hours.* During the peak of the tide the current runs at close to thirty million cubic feet per minute, and even during the last hour of

---

* Alaska has semidiurnal tides, meaning there are two complete cycles from high to low in every twenty-four-hour period. More accurately, each rise or fall takes a bit more than six hours, causing both highs and lows to occur approximately forty minutes to an hour later every day.

the flood, as the tide slows in preparation for the brief period of calm before it reverses and starts out again, the flow averages ten million cubic feet per minute, or the equivalent of 1.25 million gallons every second.* With so much water trying to force its way over the shallows at the entrance, there are periods when the water level outside the harbor is appreciably—and abruptly—higher than that within the bay. The jolt I had felt was the *Swift* hurtling off this "step." Looking back, I had the dizzying experience of looking *up* at sea level outside the bay.

Drifting aboard the heavily loaded *Boussole*, La Pérouse might not have noticed the phenomenon—he makes no mention of it in his writing—but with the *Swift*'s engine at three-quarters speed I was traveling at several knots, and just as suddenly as the leap off the lip of the tide had startled me, I was out of the current; within a few dozen yards I was in calm water, inside the bay.†

The contrast between the roiling, open sea and the sheltered water inside the bay was breathtaking. Ahead of me lay a sheet of silver mercury so perfectly polished that it reflected the inverted image of the mountains ringing the head of the bay with a precision that might have induced vertigo were it not for the ripples of my own wake, which curved past me and shattered the mirrored surface into sparkling shards as I throttled down. La Pérouse was so exultant at his expedition's survival and the scene before him that he called what I was looking at "perhaps the most extraordinary place in the world."

"To form an idea of it," he wrote that evening, "it is necessary to conceive a basin of water, of unfathomable depth in the middle, bordered by peaked mountains of great height, covered with snow, and

---

* By comparison, Niagara Falls flows at approximately 100,000 cubic feet per second. The Colorado River's average flow through the Grand Canyon is 30,000 cubic feet per second, and the Colorado is considered one of the premier white-water rivers in the world.

† Ten years after La Pérouse visited Lituya Bay, the master of a Russian vessel entering the harbor recorded a drop of "one and a half fathoms," or nine feet, at the entrance, which his vessel shot "with irresistible speed and great danger." The drop the *Swift* went over was much less than that.

without one blade of grass to decorate this vast heap of rocks, condemned by nature to eternal sterility."

There was not a breath of wind to ruffle the surface, he wrote, and "nothing disturbs it but the fall of enormous masses of ice, which frequently separate from five different glaciers, while the sound is re-echoed by the distant mountains. The air is so calm, and the silence so profound, that the single voice of a man may be heard half a league [away], as may the cries of a few sea-fowl, which deposit their eggs in the hollows of the rocks."

Two centuries later the "eternal sterility" that so moved the French explorer has been covered by an unruly green forest, but the eternal silence remains; when I stopped the boat and switched off the engine to go on deck and take in the scene, the air was so still I could hear the keening calls of a black-legged kittiwake colony on the side of Cenotaph Island, two miles away.

I took a deep breath, then another, and felt the strain of the passage across the gulf start to drain away. After the chaos of the open ocean the bay seemed a cozy sanctuary, even though the snow-covered flanks of the mountains embracing it were veined and smeared with the muddy tracks of avalanches and rock slides. Under the moderating influence of the sea, spring was more advanced here than it had been back in Juneau, and I caught a whiff of something new and green curling out from the band of alders and willows crowded between the forest and the water's edge onshore. Behind me the boom of the surf was a muffled susurration.

I don't know how long I drifted, just breathing and listening and letting the peace of the place ease into me. I spent a few minutes willing the knotted muscles of my shoulders to relax and the tension of the run from Cape Spencer to melt away, but for most of that time I was empty, my mind stalled, with no thought of what should come next. It wasn't until hunger poked a bony finger at my stomach that I thought to get moving. I had not eaten since the small hours of the morning—ten hours, fifty miles, several thousand waves, and a gale warning earlier.

There was a piece of fresh king salmon in the ice chest and a sack of rice in a galley locker, so I started the engine, took a last look at the entrance, and headed deeper into the bay to find an anchorage.

CHAPTER 7

THE ANCHOR RATTLED over the bow, and I measured out 150 feet of chain and line before reversing the engine to drag the flukes into the muddy bottom. A lone sea lion rolled to the surface fifty yards from the boat, huffed at the commotion, and went down again. When he did not resurface, I tugged on the anchor line to make sure it was set before stepping into the cabin to shut off the engine and power down the radar, leaving the Fathometer running. Its readout said I was in six fathoms of water, fifty yards off the eastern shore of Cenotaph Island, in almost the exact spot where La Pérouse, after a brief stop near the entrance, had decided to shelter his ships for the duration of his stay. If the strong winds predicted to hit the coast that night arrived, the *Swift* and I would be protected. According to one Tlingit account of La Pérouse's arrival in the bay, after Yéil came to a stop and folded his wings, the sound of the *Astrolabe*'s and the *Boussole*'s heavy anchor chains going over the side created a noise so harsh and grating that it "drove terror into the hearts of the wicked, but the good felt greater joy."

Amid the fear and excitement of Yéil's arrival, Yeahlth-kan, the wise uncle, decided that preparations must be made to go out and greet him.* Calling the people in from their hiding places, he sent the women

---

* The name of the elder varies among traditional Tlingit oral accounts of La Pérouse's arrival. In some he is called L'eiwkut or Yeahlth-kan, while in others he is referred to only as "an old man." Other details vary slightly as well, but the gist of the story has been handed down with remarkable consistency for over two hundred years. In choosing to use Yeahlth-kan as the elder's name, I mean no disrespect to those who relate the account using other names.

to one clan house and gathered the men in another. Then he dismissed any of the men who had lain with a woman within the last four days. This left only a handful of young men, and he selected four of the bravest to accompany him. Together they purified a canoe, put on coats of heavy leather with wooden collars, donned fighting headdresses, and armed themselves with spears and copper knives. But no sooner had the delegation shoved off from the beach than a cloud of smoke arose from Yéil's great body, followed by a thunderous boom. The smoke and noise of the signal cannon La Pérouse fired to salute the young warriors terrified them so much that their canoe overturned.

As told by Kaawa.ee, a Tlingit chief from the Juneau area who later heard the story from the immediate descendants of the clans who were there, after the canoe overturned, "one nearly blind old warrior [Yeahlth-kan] gathered the people together, and said that his life was far behind him and for the common good he would [go alone] to see if Yéil would turn his children to stone. So he told his slaves to prepare his canoe, and putting on a robe of sea otter fur, he embarked and paddled out."

To the Tlingit onshore, it appeared as if the old man was magically taken up into the air when the crewmen on board the *Boussole* lowered ropes and hoisted him and his canoe onto the ship's deck.

Once he was on board, the old man and the French sailors began sizing each other up. The old man was puzzled that Yéil could have a white face and go about in bare feet, or have eyes that were gray or blue, until someone wearing finer clothes and carrying himself with the bearing of a chief came on deck. Thinking that this might be Yéil, the old man stretched out his arms and asked that mercy be accorded to his family and friends onshore.

The officer responded by speaking in a strange language to a sailor standing nearby, who hurried off and came back a minute later with a plate of ship's biscuit, or pilot bread—a type of large, dry cracker that could be stored for months and remain edible. The old man, thinking the pilot bread looked like something made from human skulls, refused to take it. Again the sailor was sent to the galley, and he came back with a bowl of rice. This the old man also refused, thinking it was a bowl of maggots. A tumbler of wine he rejected as blood.

Finally a man dressed all in white appeared, carrying a brass bell, which he rang a time or two before presenting it to the old man. Then the man in white crossed his hands twice in the air, making the universally recognized sign for trade, and all of the old man's trepidation disappeared; gods, after all, seldom indulge in simple business transactions. These beings, though strangely colored and oddly dressed, were only people like himself.

In short order, the old man had traded his sea otter cap for the bell and his robe for a metal plate and a strap of iron, which could be forged into a knife superior to the one he carried, made of soft copper. Stark naked, he went over the side in his canoe and paddled ashore, carrying his prizes and a bucket of rice the men had insisted he take to share with his people. None of his family or friends would eat the rice either.*

My own rice was fine. It came off the stove just as the king salmon was ready in the oven. I heaped food on a plate and went on deck to enjoy it, grabbing a beer from the cooler as I went. The salmon fell into buttery flakes at the touch of a fork, and the beer was the perfect temperature. I ate slowly, leaning against the rail and losing myself in the immense solitude of the scene, savoring the flavor of the lightly herbed and buttered salmon. As soon as Yeahlth-kan had returned to shore, after all of his people had touched him to be sure he had not been turned to stone and had inspected his invaluable piece of iron,

---

* In 1937 a Tlingit man of the Wooshkeetaan clan that claims traditional use of lands north of Juneau told a game warden for the Territory of Alaska that he still had the bell, saying that at that time it had been in his family for eight generations.

a tremendous trading frenzy had broken out between the Tlingit and La Pérouse's expedition. At first salmon was a major commodity. The fish was a godsend to the Frenchmen, who had been without fresh provisions (or as La Pérouse put it, "salubrious and agreeable items") since the last of their pigs had died three weeks after they'd left Hawaii.

From where the *Swift* lay at anchor, I could see the mouth of a small creek that would be plugged with salmon by July. This would draw bears, eagles, seals, and sea lions to feed on the spawning fish, but in early May little was stirring within the bay with the exception of an abundance of seabirds. Harlequin ducks and kittiwakes dove and fluttered around the boat nonstop. It was almost nine o'clock at night, but I was at latitude fifty-eight degrees north, eight degrees short of the Arctic Circle, and twilight would not set in until after ten.

The air was preternaturally still, and it was easy to imagine La Pérouse's ships, appearing puny against the backdrop of towering mountains, with a stream of canoes hurrying back and forth in pursuit of trade. "We were," wrote La Pérouse, "constantly surrounded by the canoes of the savages, who in exchange for our iron, offered us fish, otter skins, and various small articles of their apparel." Unaware that the Tlingit were accustomed to trading—and raiding—as far south as what is now the coast of Washington, Oregon, and perhaps even California, and in the interior of Canada, he added that "to our great astonishment, they appeared perfectly accustomed to traffic, and made their bargains with as much address as the most able dealers of Europe."*

He was amazed that the Tlingit had no interest in the glass beads, tin pots, and other knickknacks that explorers had long been used to

---

* The Tlingit already possessed a few pieces of iron when La Pérouse arrived, possibly from trading with the Eskimos of Prince William Sound and the inhabitants of Kodiak Island and the Aleutian Islands, more than 500 miles to the west, who were already under the sway of the Russians. There is also evidence that the ocean currents of the North Pacific had on occasion deposited the hulks of disabled fishing boats from China and Japan on Alaska's shores. The iron fittings from such shipwrecks would have been priceless.

pawning off on various bands of Natives; iron was paramount, "gold itself [being] not more eagerly desired among Europeans than iron in this part of America." For their own part, after a few meals of fresh salmon and halibut, the Frenchmen cared for nothing but sea otter skins, which they planned to exchange for a fortune in China. Only a year earlier a sixty-ton brig under the command of an Englishman named James Hanna had sailed from Nootka Sound, on the rugged outer coast of Vancouver Island, to Macao with a cargo of five hundred sea otter hides that had earned him the enormous sum of twenty thousand dollars.

In the 1700s the Pacific Coast of North America teemed with sea otters. From California to the distant reaches of the Aleutian Islands and the coast of Siberia, hundreds of thousands of this largest member of the weasel tribe fed and swam. The tremendous commercial potential of the animals' thick, gleaming fur was not truly realized until Captain Cook's third and last voyage, in 1780, when members of his crew traded with the natives of British Columbia for a few skins that they subsequently peddled for a handsome sum when they made port in Canton, China. After word of Hanna's enormously profitable voyage spread, the market exploded so rapidly and voraciously that by the time La Pérouse reached the Pacific, the Spanish were already pushing north from California toward British Columbia, plundering as they went, and the Russian fur traders, or *promyshlenniki*, were swarming into Alaska from the west, murdering and enslaving the local tribes as they encountered them.*

La Pérouse's "Port des Français" lay squarely in the middle of the only unexploited region left. In his report to Louis XVI the explorer

---

* A century later Henry W. Elliott, who visited Alaska in 1882 as an agent of the U.S. Treasury Department, noted the continuing effect of the Russians' "brutal orgies" against Alaska's Natives, writing in his report to the government that "the wild, savage life which the Russians led in the early days of their possession of this new land . . . beggars description, and seem[s] well-nigh incredible to the trader or traveler who sojourns in Alaska today."

stated that he "would not be surprised if a factory, extending its commerce only about forty or fifty leagues along the coast, should collect annually 10,000 skins of that animal."

Within days the trading reached a fever pitch as word of the French ships and their barrels of nails, iron, and metal fittings spread along the coast. La Pérouse estimated the number of Tlingit residing along the bay on his arrival at three hundred, but concluded that during the expedition's stay the *Boussole* and the *Astrolabe* were visited by at least five hundred more. The weather was so settled, he noted, that canoes were constantly coming and going through the entrance with every tide.

"Every day we observe a fresh succession of canoes entering the bay," he wrote in his journal, "and ever day we beheld [*sic*] entire villages remove, and yield their place to others. The Indians apparently dread the channel, and never trusted themselves but at slack water; and we could distinctly perceive with our glasses, that when they arrived between the two points, their Chief, or at least the most considerable personage among them, rose up and stretched his arms toward the sun, as if addressing a prayer to him, while the rest paddled with all their strength."

In ten days the expedition managed to acquire 3,231 hides, pieces of skin, tails, and garments made of sea otter fur—a silken haul that La Pérouse estimated would bring the crew 41,063 Spanish piastres in China.*

In the end, however, the "savages" proved to be the sharper traders; the *Astrolabe* and the *Boussole* were lighter by several hundred pounds from the loss of iron when they departed, but when the Frenchmen sold their furs in China, the majority of the skins turned

---

* Why La Pérouse made his estimate in Spanish piastres is a puzzle, but it may have been because gold was relatively scarce in the eighteenth and early nineteenth centuries, and silver, which the Spanish possessed in abundance from their mines in South America, was commonly used in matters involving foreign exchange.

out to be inferior. The entire trove brought only ten thousand dollars. A few of the best were sent from Macao to France, where they were presented as a gift to Marie Antoinette.

After finishing my dinner, I scraped the remains of the glittering fish skin and bones over the side and watched them turn aqua white, then dark blue as they sank out of sight in the dark water. I watched as a lone sea otter paddled by a hundred yards away, lying on its back, whiskers twitching, the thick rudder of its tail propelling the sixty-pound animal along with an easy, sinuous wake. It was the only otter I could see anywhere in the bay. It had not taken long after the Frenchmen had left for the Russian, British, American, and Spanish fur hunters to converge on "Port des Français" and decimate the great rafts of sea otters. Within a few decades they were entirely gone. The lone paddler I was watching was probably an heir to a reintroduction program undertaken by the federal government in the 1970s.* The sea otters had disappeared, as had the Tlingit living and hunting in the area. The latter had made a fine profit off the Frenchmen, but in the end it had proved a devil's bargain, cracking open their world as it had to new diseases, alcohol, and a near deathblow to centuries of tradition. Gone, too, was the immense herd of harbor seals that had once thrived in the bay and fed the Tlingit. Harbor seals haul out on icebergs for protection from predators and to bear their pups in spring; as Lituya Bay's

---

* It is an interesting footnote that the survival of the sea otter in Alaska can be attributed to the rise of nuclear weapons and the advent of the Cold War. The animal had been wiped out across most of its range by the end of the 1800s, and the only viable population remaining was located near Amchitka Island, in the remote Aleutians. When the Atomic Energy Commission announced that it planned to perform nuclear tests on Amchitka Island in the 1970s, the resulting uproar over the threat to the sea otters resulted in the AEC's funding the research that made transplanting the little-studied and poorly understood otters—whose sensitive physiology had turned every effort to reintroduce them to Southeast Alaska and British Columbia into a disaster—viable.

glaciers had retreated and gone stagnant, the seals had been left without refuge, and their numbers had plummeted.

I rolled out my sleeping bag and prepared to climb into my bunk. Without the sea otters, seals, and Tlingit, Lituya Bay was as silent as it has ever been in history. Glaciers advance, recede, and grow still; great nations of animals and men rise and fall. The last thing I remember thinking about before I fell asleep was how the world can change irrevocably in a moment, suddenly, beneath our very feet.

CHAPTER 8

THE NEXT MORNING I rose early to sit on the deck and drink a cup of coffee in the vivid morning air. I was tired, but the sky was clear; the weather front predicted to roll ashore in the night had veered and gone south of Cape Spencer, leaving in its place a crisp spring day that was warm in the sun but cold in the shade. I wanted to do some exploring, so I slipped a kayak over the side and tethered it to a cleat before finishing the leftover salmon and rice for breakfast and pouring a second cup of coffee. The days and distance of the journey from Juneau to Lituya Bay seemed to be slowly easing the knot left in my chest by Luisa's death and the strain of my marriage.

While I sipped at the coffee, I did nothing but watch a barn swallow flutter out from shore and circle the boat. Time after time the sparrow-sized bird flew out from the beach, skimming just above the water, then rose in a graceful arching loop that carried it past the *Swift* only a few feet away. I had been working seven days a week for over a year, and with nothing pressing—no materials to order, no subcontractors to schedule, none of a thousand never-ending details to see to—watching the fluid, agile flight of the fork-tailed bird seemed enough to attend to.

As I watched, I grew curious about what it was doing; swallows are insect feeders, with demanding metabolisms, and this one had probably just arrived from its wintering grounds in South America. Some of Alaska's swallows make a 14,000-mile round-trip to Argentina and back, and it seemed puzzling that after such an energy-sapping undertaking, it wasn't feeding, but instead seemed intent on inspecting the *Swift* as closely as possible. Swallows have been known to starve to death when inclement weather drives their insect prey under cover for even short periods, yet this one, which had almost certainly depleted the bulk of its reserves, was finding a fiberglass boat hull more interesting than the swarms of midges and gnats I knew the sun would be bringing out of the brush onshore. Over and over it returned to the boat, flying around and around before darting off a few yards and then heading back. And each time it would break into a hover at the starboard scupper, suspending itself on rapidly beating wings a few inches from the opening. The feathers on its back were iridescent blue black, streaked with green in the morning sun.

It seemed to have no fear of me. Each time it hovered to inspect the scupper, it cocked its head to peer up at me as I leaned over the side to watch. The blink of a nictitating membrane across its tiny black eye seemed to give it a questioning look, as though it were asking for permission to enter the hole.* After fifteen or twenty minutes of this (or however long it takes a lethargic man to drink a cup of coffee and a swallow to fly back and forth from an anchored boat to a beach a dozen times) it rattled off a staccato of high-pitched chirps and sped away.

Alone again, I dipped my cup over the side to rinse it, then looked around at the mountains spanning the fjord. They were dazzling white in the sun and streaked with dark faces of rock too broken and precipitous to carry snow. Towered over by peaks that rose more than two miles above sea level yet were in their turn diminished by the size of the sky over the open ocean, the scale of the landscape felt so vast that I could gain no perspective of my own place in the universe of ice, water, firmament, and stone except to feel spectacularly unimportant and alone; for a moment I wished the curious swallow would return.

---

* Birds do not blink like humans do. They have three eyelids: one upper, one lower, and a nictitating membrane that lies between the other two and the cornea. The nictitating membrane has a lubricating duct and is used to clean and protect the eye. And when a bird wants to close its eyes, the lower lids move instead of the upper ones.

When it didn't, I pulled the kayak alongside and started assembling my gear. First came the paddle, a lightweight composite of carbon and hard plastic, then a spray skirt and a bulky purple life jacket. (A spray skirt is a cone of waterproof material that fits tightly around a paddler's body. The hem is fastened over a lip around the cockpit with an elastic drawstring to prevent water from entering the kayak if it becomes necessary to paddle in breaking waves.)

The water was so calm that I could see the faint dimples and rings of salmon smolt that had recently out-migrated from their natal streams and were rising to feed on copepods and other tiny invertebrates beneath the surface a hundred yards away. But the weather in fjords like Lituya Bay can change so rapidly that any venture away from the shelter of the boat had to be treated as if I might be gone for days. On a clear day like today, warm air rising above the sun-drenched forests and surface ocean waters might leave a vacuum in its place that would draw colder air down from the upper reaches of the mountains. The glaciers that feed into Lituya Bay are part of a complex system of ice fields and glaciers that sprawls over more than a thousand square miles, and when the cold, dense air of this wintry alpine kingdom begins to flow downhill, the wind may rise quickly. The narrow fjords create a natural Venturi effect that can squeeze and accelerate the moving air in a manner not unlike that of the furious rush of fuel and oxygen through a hot rod's carburetor. When these outflow winds strike, it can be the meteorological equivalent of going from zero to sixty in a few seconds.

Watching a wisp of cloud that hung without moving near the summit of a peak at the back of the bay, I thought such a thing unlikely, but I dug around in the hold until I found a paddle float anyway. A paddle float is an inflatable ring that can be slipped over the blade of a paddle to create extra stability if a paddler is dumped from a kayak. Braced at a right angle to the hull, the paddle and float create an outrigger that allows a paddler to climb back into the kayak without tipping over again. I tucked the float under a net of shock cords fastened to the kayak's foredeck along with a spare paddle, so both would be in easy reach, then searched through the jumble of packs, boxes of food, and boat gear in the *Swift*'s hold for a waterproof vinyl bag. Matches, a tube of fire-starting paste, and the handheld radio went in first, followed by a chocolate bar and a metal cup stuffed with four or five packages of dried soup mix. A pile jacket and an extra set of polypropylene long underwear went into a second bag along with a square of lightweight waterproof material I had been using for years as a tent ground cloth. With fire, food, dry clothes, and the means to create a shelter tucked into the kayak's watertight hold, I should be okay if I somehow wound up wet and marooned by bad weather for a few days. I was already in the kayak and about to shove off when I remembered the bear spray. Bear spray, or repellent, is a pressurized aerosol containing a concentration of oleoresin capsicum, the oily inflammatory ingredient found in red-hot chili peppers. Thumbing a trigger mounted on top of the six-inch can is a bit like firing a small fire extinguisher; it releases a jet of intensely irritating spray that creates a burning sensation in the eyes, nose, and respiratory system of anything encountering it.

I did not expect to need it. Bear spray has proved to be relatively effective in countering aggression, and I usually carry it when traveling in bear country, plus a twelve-gauge shotgun if circumstances warrant, but in the twenty years I have been guiding in Alaska, I have never used either. Bears—both black and grizzly—are generally much better behaved than we give them credit for. The bulk of my guiding work has been with wildlife photographers and natural history film crews, which frequently requires spending days or even weeks at a time in close proximity to grizzlies, but I had come to believe that with enough caution the risk could be greatly reduced, if not eliminated. During an estimated two or three hundred close—and sometimes *very* close—encounters with grizzlies and black bears, neither I nor any of my clients had ever been seriously threatened or injured.

This is not to say that bears are not dangerous. On average, one person is killed by a bear in Alaska every year, and five or six more are injured. Two thirds of the victims are hunters who surprised a bear in thick brush. Such "defensive" attacks occur when a startled bear responds to something it perceives as a threat, or a female bear feels her cubs are at risk, or an animal is defending a source of food such as a moose kill. The victims of defensive attacks are often clawed or bitten badly, but the attack usually ceases when the bear believes the threat has been eliminated. "Playing dead" by not resisting can be an effective method of surviving a defensive onslaught.

On the more horrific end of the spectrum are "predacious" attacks, when a bear actively targets a human as prey. Predacious attacks seldom occur spontaneously and are usually presaged by escalating aggression; the bear may circle, move in, retreat, then return again, as if probing its target or working up the nerve to attack. A bear's becoming increasingly less responsive to the shouts, pot banging, gunshots, or other loud noises that would usually repel it is a hallmark of an impending predatory event.

In the past ten years I had lost two friends to grizzlies, but in spite of this I knew that predatory attacks are in truth extremely rare; after forty years in Alaska, I could count the number of purely predacious attacks I knew of on the fingers of one hand. As a spokesman for the Alaska Department of Fish and Game once noted, with thirty thousand brown bears roaming the state and more than a hundred thousand black bears, "if bears really wanted to eat people, they would . . . We'd lose somebody every day."

Nonetheless, I kicked the rudder to the side and dipped the paddle to swing the kayak back alongside the boat, then grabbed the bowline and hoisted myself out to retrieve the bear spray. I was not planning to take any long hikes into thick brush that day, but I am cautious by nature and would feel better taking it along.

Easing back into the kayak, I snapped the spray skirt into place and shifted my hips to settle my weight. I was bending forward to se-cure the bowline when I heard a familiar chirring—the swallow was back, hovering again in front of the scupper; only this time a second bird had joined him. They took turns fluttering up to the very edge of the opening, then backing out so the other could move in to take a look.

"I'll be damned," I said as one of the apparently fearless birds landed on the lip of the scupper and tilted its head to peer inside. Barn swallows nest in hollow trees or on sheltered ledges, where they can build cup-shaped nests of mud and grass, and now I understood that the first swallow to circle the *Swift* that morning was probably a male reconnoitering a potential nest site; the second bird was a prospec-tive mate. I may have laughed out loud as the male fluttered up to the perched female making a *chirk-chirk-chirk* sound, as if asking her opinion. *It's waterfront!* he seemed to say. *A sun-drenched opening, just perfect for a home!* When I dipped my paddle to back the kayak up a bit, the female tipped off the edge of the scupper and flew away. The male followed, chattering.

The water was so calm that a few paddle strokes were enough to get the kayak up to speed. Within a hundred yards I was growing warm as the chill of the early morning gave way to the repetitive reach-and-pull of the paddle. The only sound was that of water trickling off the blade. I was stiff and sore from bracing myself against the tossing waves the day before, but it felt good to be doing something with my body besides carrying planks and lifting sacks of concrete. The pinched nerve in my neck from the excavator injury two years earlier was bothering me, creating a slight numbness in my arm, but the kayak slipped so smoothly and musically through the water that I con-vinced myself that a few hours of paddling would be okay, or per-haps even therapeutic.

In fifteen minutes the *Swift* was half a mile behind me; in twenty minutes I could barely make out its shape against Cenotaph Island. By seven thirty, sunlight pouring over the mountains had washed away the last shadows on the walls of the fjord and turned a waning moon overhead pale white. It was a perfect morning, but I couldn't shake the feeling that I was leaving something important behind.

As the day grew warmer, a sweet odor filled the air. For five miles along the edge of the fjord, from a steep rocky point just ahead to the bay's entrance off my stern, a band of cottonwood trees lined the shore. Every twig and branch on the rough-barked trees was tipped with a pale green bud. The ripe, heady scent was the smell of a resinous secretion known as balm of Gilead, drawn to the surface of the nascent, tightly coiled cottonwood leaves by the sun.

The closer I got to shore, the thicker the smell grew, and I stopped paddling so I could just drift in the sunlight and perfume. The cottonwoods spread a quarter of a mile inland from the water's edge to an abrupt border with an ancient spruce and hemlock forest, where the new green buds presented a stark contrast to the darkness of the evergreens.

As I drifted, a low, distant roar mumbled across the fjord. I could not see where it came from, but I could tell from the sound that somewhere up among the alpine ridges at the back of the fjord, cornices of snow carved into the shape of breaking waves by the passing winter's winds had begun to sag under the weight of the sun's warmth and succumb to gravity. Again and again the rumble of faraway avalanches muttered across the water, and as I breathed in the balm of the cottonwoods and floated in the sun beneath the walls of doomed snow, I marveled that I had arrived at the exact point in time when the land was beginning to heave and writhe beneath its winter coat and burst into life with the sounds and smells of spring. It was a fleeting moment, I knew, because by evening—or at most within a day or two—the surge of photosynthesis and rising sap generated by the cascade of sunlight would begin to explode the cottonwood buds into small but full-fledged leaves, signaling that the grove's embryonic stage of life had passed and the work of procreation had begun. After the persistence of the preceding winter, with its never-ending threat of destructive avalanches and record snowfall, this seemed like a miracle, so I dipped the paddle and pulled for shore.

The tide was rising, and I hoisted the kayak onto one shoulder to carry it up the beach, moving carefully to avoid losing my footing on the algae-covered boulders. At the high tide mark I eased the kayak to the ground and tied the bowline to a drift log. I wasn't planning to go far, but more than one careless kayaker has been marooned in Southeast Alaska when the region's oversize tides sneaked up and stole an unsecured kayak away.

The cottonwoods were rimmed with a thick line of alders. A mat of last year's beach grass lay in a dense tangle on the shore, stippled along its outer edge with needles of new growth. I could see where an area of sedge grass sprouting along the banks of a small seep of melting snow and rainwater had been cropped by a browsing bear. With patches of rotting snow still lying in the shadows beneath the alders, the fresh sedge had probably been the bear's only source of protein. There were thin straws of twisted stalk starting to protrude here and there, bunch-berry leaves poking up in tightly wound spirals, and tiny buds as soft and furry as a kitten's paw on a stand of willows growing along the seep. Even with the rampant sunshine to hurry things along, it looked like it could be a week or more before there would be enough plant life to meet a bear's needs. Every bear on the coast would be on the move, traveling constantly in search of food.

I checked the bear spray on my hip, snapping the holster open and closed a few times to make sure it was working smoothly, adjusted it on my belt so it would fall naturally under my hand if I had to reach for it without looking, then practiced a couple of "quick draws" to prove it. The gunslinger posturing would have felt foolish if there had been anyone around to witness it, but it reassured me enough to push through the alders and into the cottonwoods.

The smell was enough to get drunk on. Balm of Gilead got its name from a biblical passage, in Genesis, in which the caravan that carries Joseph away into slavery is also transporting a cargo of medicinal balsam. The caravan had come from the ancient city of Gilead, east of the Jordan River. After being soaked in olive oil, the resin emitted by cottonwood buds emulsifies into a salve that is reputed to have analgesic properties, so I thumbed a few buds off a branch into the palm of my hand and squeezed them, hoping to force out enough resin to ease the burn of the pinched nerve in my neck. The buds crumbled into a pulp that left my hand sticky and sweet smelling. After the accident with the excavator, I had never taken time off to let the injury heal, and now, as I rubbed the crushed buds into my neck and shoulder, I wondered how a balm carried by a slave-trading caravan had become a symbol of delivery from overwork and suffering.

The thought was interrupted by the *koowk* of a raven calling from farther inland, then an answering *ka-hoowk!* from a second bird behind me near the shore. Given their documented vocabulary of more than thirty vocalizations and their well-deserved reputation for problem-solving skills and pranks, it is easy to understand why the Tlingit revere the big-brained raven as a symbol of the Creator. And it seemed fitting to have their company as I wandered through the cottonwoods, awash in the scent of salvation at the end of a vicious winter. There on the cusp of spring, with the past year's troubles beginning to seem far away, I realized that for the first time in months I was feeling almost relaxed, and I sent an imitative *kawk!* in response.

Raven's answer was to send another emissary from the feathered spirit world, a small ruby of light that zoomed past my head and dropped in to hover at a cluster of western columbines a few feet away. The flowers themselves seemed a small phenomenon; back in Juneau, where the snow was still two feet deep in places, the rufous hummingbird with the scarlet throat patch bobbing in and out of the delicate orange and yellow blossoms would have been hard-pressed to find a bloom. Shortly before I'd left for Lituya Bay, I had kicked through a mound of crusted snow and been amazed to find the tiny pink bells of blueberry flowers already fully formed beneath the snow; so rigid is nature's timetable in certain matters, and so strong is the rush to life, that the flower, which is perhaps the single most critical factor in the hummingbird's survival during Alaska's brief spring, had somehow known to bloom while still trapped beneath a layer of solid ice. Why this small cluster of columbines had chosen to bloom so unseasonably early was a mystery too.

The hummingbird hung above the columbine, probing with its bill. As I watched, the ache of losing Luisa began to creep back into my chest. The lone hummingbird reminded me of the dozen tiny, bobbing birds that had appeared at the feeder Joel had hung outside the window beside her bed, darting and hovering until the feeder looked like a hive of scarlet bees. Some appeared not to feed at all, but only floated, wings blurring, in front of the window, looking in at Luisa as she lay curled on her side under a blanket.

In some Buddhist traditions it is believed that at the moment of death the departing soul enters the body of a nearby animal; shortly after Luisa stopped breathing, the hummingbirds flew away.

The raven on the beach behind me called once, then again, and its mate answered. I could tell by the sound of the calls that they were moving away. The hummingbird's throat patch flashed, creating a fiery red burst among the orange and yellow flowers before the bird buzzed straight up into the canopy and disappeared, leaving in its place only the slowly nodding columbine and a hollow feeling in my chest that I tried to fill by taking a deep breath and letting it out as a sigh.

I was back out on the beach, untying the kayak and listening to the back-and-forth calls of the retreating ravens, when a half-remembered line from Edgar Allan Poe's "The Raven" muddled through my head: The protagonist laments the death of a loved one, crying out, "Is there no Balm in Gilead?," only to be answered by the raven's famously dark

"Nevermore." Then I considered how the cottonwoods, with their acres of new green buds and balmy perfume, were not only an example of the miraculous transmutation of water and sunlight into the wonder of spring, but a signature of cataclysm as well; not one of the tall, straight cottonwoods was over fifty years old, yet if I walked a mere quarter of a mile inland, to the line of dark hemlocks, spruces, and cedars that provided such a sudden contrast to the green cottonwoods, I would find trees that had been alive for a thousand years. The suddenness of the transition would certainly be noticed by anyone encountering it, and of interest to any curious naturalist, but to anyone familiar with the history of Lituya Bay, it would be a clear—and frightening—reminder of one of the most staggering geological incidents of the twentieth century.

CHAPTER 9

Lɪᴛᴜʏᴀ ʙᴀʏ ɪꜱ shaped like a T, with the tidal entrance at the bottom and Cenotaph Island halfway up the vertical stem. At the top of the T, to the right, is Crillon Inlet, which trends southeast for approximately a mile and a half. Gilbert Inlet runs to the left and terminates at the face of Lituya Glacier, which flows down the slopes of 12,700-foot Mount Crillon. Beyond Lituya Glacier lies Desolation Valley, which abuts Fairweather Glacier twelve miles farther north. Draw a line across Fairweather Glacier, down the middle of Desolation Valley, and along the Lituya T and you have mapped a small portion of the Fairweather Fault, where a great slab of the earth's rocky skin known as the North American Plate (which underlies all of North America, Greenland, and parts of Siberia) grinds up against its eponymous counterpart, the Pacific Plate. The Fairweather Fault runs southeast for more than a hundred miles from up near Yakutat to Cape Spencer, where it links into a jagged system of cracks and fractures that reaches all the way through British Columbia, Washington, Oregon, and into California. The surfaces of the fault are vertical and the motion of the tectonic plates is horizontal, which in turn means that the pressure that inevitably builds up between the North American Plate and the Pacific Plate as the two circle each other like a pair of grappling sumo wrestlers must sooner or later be released in the form of a jarring earthquake. When Howard Ulrich, a fisherman from the village of Pelican, seventy miles to the south, entered Lituya Bay on the evening of July 9, 1958, aboard his thirty-eight-foot wooden troller, the *Edrie*, he had no idea the Fairweather Fault was about to strike.

It was eight P.M. and the weather was clear. Ulrich had crossed the bar at the end of the flood with no problem. The sea outside was glassy, with a low swell rolling in from the west. There was no wind, and Ulrich's eight-year-old son, Howard Jr.—or Sonny, as he preferred to be called—was ready to help anchor the *Edrie*. Sonny was the spitting image of his dad; in an old photograph both wear plaid work shirts, heavy boots, and denim pants. The father stands with one hand on his son's shoulder, the boy smiling straight into the lens. Both are built square across the shoulders, like they were made to hold their ground.

All up and down the coast, mariners were making the most of the settled weather. A fleet of trollers was working the tide rips and rocks near Cape Spencer. A few had taken advantage of the calm seas to run fifty miles offshore to the Fairweather Grounds, where a series of seamounts were known to provide good fishing when good weather allowed. The crews of fish-buying scows in small shelters like Thistle Cove and Dixon Harbor, north of Cape Spencer, were sitting on deck in the sun, waiting for the salmon boats to come in for the evening, and a hundred miles north, up in Yakutat, the postmaster, John Williams, and his wife, Dora, had decided the best way to spend the beautiful evening was picking berries and having a picnic with friends on Khantaak Island, just offshore from the town.

After crossing the bar, Ulrich turned to starboard and made for a small bight about a mile inside the bay on the eastern shore. From where he dropped anchor, he could not see the entrance, so he was unaware, as he and Sonny cooked dinner and prepared to turn in for the night, that a second boat, the *Sunmore*, owned and operated by a young couple named Orville and Mickey Wagner, had come in and anchored on the opposite side of the entrance. At nine P.M. a third boat, the *Badger*, with Bill and Vivian Swanson on board, bucked the start of the ebb tide to get in.

The Swansons first thought to anchor near Cenotaph Island, and at the sound of their engine Sonny rolled out of his bunk and went up into the wheelhouse to see who it was. The trollers who work the off-shore grounds and coastline near Lituya Bay are a close-knit community and keep tabs on each other's comings and goings. After watching for a bit, Sonny went back below to tell his dozing father who their companions were.

After Sonny went below, the Swansons decided against anchoring near Cenotaph Island and turned around to go back and anchor near the Wagners, but not before noticing that the colony of black-legged kittiwakes that nest on the steep southern side of the island seemed unusually loud and nervous. People up in Yakutat also later reported that the gulls and terns were acting strange, constantly taking flight and circling, settling down, and lifting off again amid a cacophony of alarm calls.

By ten P.M., Lituya Bay was bathed in the lingering twilight of a summer sunset, and the crews of the *Sunmore*, the *Badger*, and the *Edrie* had settled in for the evening. Howard and Sonny Ulrich were already asleep. On the *Badger*, the Swansons were in their bunks. Up in Yakutat, Postmaster Williams and his wife decided it was time to head for home, so they launched their skiff and pulled away from Khantaak Island after saying goodbye to their friends.

At ten sixteen, an earthquake of almost unimaginable intensity struck. A deep rumbling welled up from underground, and the waters of the bay began churning and tossing so wildly that Bill Swanson tumbled out of his bunk. The *Edrie* rolled so hard that Howard Ulrich leaped out of bed and ran to the wheelhouse, thinking the anchor had come loose and the boat was being sucked across the bar by the ebb. Finding the boat still in the same place, but leaping and tugging at its anchor chain, he hurried Sonny up on deck, where they stood transfixed by what they saw. The peaks at the back of the fjord were, in Ulrich's word, "heaving."

"Have you ever seen a 15,000-foot mountain twist and shake and dance?" he later asked a writer for *Alaska Sportsman* magazine. The mountains looked as if they were suffering "unbearable internal tortures."

It was an apt description. Avalanches of rock and snow were breaking loose all across the faces of the mountains, raising clouds of dust that made the peaks and faces appear to be smoking. A thousand miles away at the University of Washington in Seattle, the needle was knocked off the seismograph. For four long minutes the west side of the Fairweather Fault lurched, slid, and ground northwest, dragging the entire 115 miles of coastline between Cape Spencer and Yakutat along the ragged edge of the North American continent. The Fairweather Range responded with a series of violent leaps and jerks.

The noise was frightful. On the *Badger*, Bill Swanson scrambled up into the wheelhouse and looked toward the head of the bay, where the sound was coming from. "The mountains were shaking something awful," he later said, "but what I noticed mostly was . . . Lituya Glacier.

"I know you can't ordinarily see that glacier from where I was anchored, and people shake their heads when I tell them what I saw that night, but I can't help it if they don't believe me. I know the glacier is hidden by the point [of Gilbert Inlet], but I know what I saw that night, too.

"The glacier had risen in the air and moved forward so it was in sight. It must have risen several hundred feet. I don't mean it was just hanging in the air. It seemed to be solid, but it was jumping and shaking like crazy. Big chunks of ice were falling off the face of it and down into the water. That was six miles away and they still looked like big chunks. They came off the glacier like a big load of rocks spilling out of a dump truck."

Thirteen hundred feet of the glacier's face sheared off. But as the earthquake continued, things got even worse. Between a minute and two and a half minutes into the earthquake, the entire flank of a 5,000-foot peak on the northeast side of Gilbert Inlet sheared off, releasing a crumbling slab of rock 300 feet thick, 2,300 feet wide, and

3,000 feet across. Approximately forty million cubic yards of stone, ice, and soil weighing an estimated ninety million tons fell more than half a mile down the vertical face of the peak into Gilbert Inlet.

"During all this," said Howard Ulrich, "I was literally petrified, rooted to the deck. It was not fright, but a kind of stunned amazement. I do not think I thought of it as something that was going to affect me."

The next thing he saw, as he described it a few years later, was "like an atomic explosion," and "after this big flash came a huge wave. It looked like just a big wall of water."

Swanson used the same words, saying that after the glacier dropped back out of sight, there was "a big wall of water coming over the point."

"Big" hardly begins to describe it. The "point" he spoke of was the shoulder of an unnamed 3,400-foot mountain that forms the western side of Gilbert Inlet. The wave was over 1,700 feet high.

"To call the scene awe-inspiring is a puny attempt to describe what was happening," Ulrich later remembered. "As far as I am concerned, suitable words do not exist."

While the Swansons and the Ulrichs stood transfixed on the decks of their boats and watched the wave crash over the mountain, hell was breaking loose all the way from Yakutat down to Cape Spencer. Postmaster Williams and his wife, Dora, watched in horror as the end of Khantaak Island, where their friends were still picking berries, lurched twenty feet into the air, then dropped beneath the surface of the boiling water.

A huge water tank at the Yakutat cannery collapsed, destroying two wharves. South of Lituya Bay, near Cape Spencer, the entire fleet of trollers was jolted by shock after shock emanating from the grinding fault line. A woman was heard wailing into a radio, "My god, how much more can our boat stand?" At Point Astrolabe, a crewman on the troller *Cameo* shouted, "We just saw a whole mountain come down!"

For 150 miles along the coast, one of the bulkiest mountain ranges in the world was shaking and heaving, collapsing in a writhing cloud of dust that turned orange and red in the fading twilight. A twenty-foot wave tore a fish-buying scow loose from its moorings in Dixon Harbor amid geysers of water that shot hundreds of feet in the air. The quake was felt 500 miles away in Anchorage. A thousand miles south in Seattle, musicians in a floating orchestra pit were knocked from their chairs by a tremor. But Ulrich, who could see no other boats from his anchorage, later admitted (with remarkable understatement) that despite the presence of Sonny he felt "very much alone" as he watched the giant wave crest over the point, then roar across the head of the bay and bounce off the southern shore before it began surging toward Cenotaph Island,

The Ulrichs and the Swansons all stood watching as the wave ripped the timber off the ridge above Gilbert Inlet to a height of 1,720 feet with a force that was later calculated at twenty-five million pounds per square foot, which was sufficient to instantly strip all the bark off the tumbling tree trunks and tear away their branches. Then it rebounded to the eastern shore below Crillon Inlet, flaying the mountainside up to 500 feet above sea level; it struck so hard that every tree, shrub, tuft of grass, and bit of vegetation was wiped away down to naked bedrock. It was only after the wave lashed over 320-foot-high Cenotaph Island and tore a swath through its middle that Ulrich came to his senses. Seeing the wave rolling down the eastern shore toward them, he said, "I began to move and I moved fast."

According to Sonny, the first thing Ulrich did was throw a life jacket on his boy and say, "Start praying." Then he fired up the *Edrie*'s engine and engaged the hydraulics to get the anchor up. Because waves break hardest near shore, his best hope of surviving was to head for deep water in the middle of the bay, where the *Edrie* might have some slim chance of being able to ride up and over the wave.

Neither he nor the Swansons had time to think about it, but the geology and form of Lituya Bay were working in their favor. Scientists at the Swiss Federal Institute of Technology later modeled a highly sophisticated miniature reproduction of the bay and the wave to understand exactly what had happened, building on work performed by the U.S. Geological Service's Don Miller, who was the first scientist on the scene after the cataclysm occurred. What they discovered was that a high-speed landslide (such as happens when ninety million tons of rock fall a vertical half mile) impacts the water so hard that the water moves away so quickly that it cannot flow back *behind* the landslide. This in turn creates an immense air cavity, which displaces even more water than the landslide itself, and the combination of the two forces is sufficient to create a wave of such size and force that in mass and energy it becomes greater than the sum of its parts. In Lituya Bay this meant the wave initially surged—or "blew"—more than half a kilometer high.

As the wave ricocheted back and forth between the fjord's steep walls, its unimaginable energy dissipated relatively quickly; the wall of water was "only" 500 feet high when it surged up the shore below Crillon Inlet, and it continued to drop as it curved back toward Cenotaph Island. Below the crossbar of the T, the topography around Lituya Bay loses altitude quickly, dropping from 3,000 feet at the peaks of the mountains on the seaward sides of both inlets, then down to a thousand or so feet opposite Cenotaph Island. Beyond Cenotaph, the terrain flattens quickly into low hills that slope into flats along the shore.

As the wave burst free of its containment between the steep rear walls of the fjord, it spread out and dropped rapidly. What Ulrich saw speeding toward him from behind Cenotaph Island as he desperately tried to raise the anchor was a solid wall of water that Miller later calculated to be 100 feet high, traveling at approximately 130 miles an hour.

And the anchor would not budge. With the engine roaring and the hydraulics squealing, Ulrich tried again and again to lift it, but it would not come. "Either the earthquake had wrapped the chain around a boulder on the bottom," he said later, "or a crevice had opened and swallowed the anchor."

Thinking quickly, he let the anchor chain run, paying out all that was left on the winch drum in order to gain some maneuverability with the engine and rudder. He hoped that maybe—just maybe—the anchor would hold and keep the *Edrie* from being thrown ashore. He gunned the engine and turned to meet the wave.

On the *Badger* the Swansons were still at anchor, in their nightclothes, watching the wave roll toward them. Bill looked away from the wave just long enough to see the *Sunmore* running at full speed for the entrance.

The wave was black and appeared to be nearly vertical. In its rush along the shore it had torn thousands of trees out by their roots, and these were being rolled, tumbled, and pitched like so many great spears across its face. It is impossible to know which boat was struck first, but Swanson said that no sooner had he thrown a last look at the fleeing *Sunmore* than the *Badger* was snatched up, lifted high into the air, and thrown backward, completely across the spit.

"We were way up over the trees," he said, "and I looked down on rocks as big as an ordinary house as we crossed the spit. We were way up above them. It felt like we were in a tin can and somebody was shaking it."

The *Badger* surfed 300 yards backward across the spit, then slammed violently stern-first into the ocean as the wave broke. The lazarette and fish hold probably filled immediately, because the troller never resurfaced, only floating with its wheelhouse and bow in the air and then sinking slowly as it was struck again and again by trees swept along in the rush of the tsunami. A log smashed through the wheelhouse door and struck Swanson in the chest, breaking some of his ribs, then washed out again. Working frantically, he still managed to fight his way out onto the deck, untie the *Badger*'s eight-foot dinghy, and launch it over the side. The oars had been washed away, and he was forced to pry a thwart loose to use as a paddle. The crippled troller sank out from under him and his wife just as they leaped into the wildly tossing dinghy, landing in frigid water up to their waists.

A mile to the east, the Ulrichs hung on for dear life as the *Edrie* shot to the top of the wave, rising so fast that the thick anchor chain snapped and whipped back around the pilothouse, smashing a window. Then the wave swept the little troller up onto what until moments before had been the heavily timbered shoreline but was now a boiling uproar of muddy water.

"I was sure that the end of the world had come for Sonny and me and our boat," said Ulrich. "I wanted my wife back in Pelican to know where and how her husband and first-born son had been lost, so I grabbed the handset of my radiotelephone and yelled into it: 'Mayday! Mayday! This is the *Edrie* in Lituya Bay. All hell has broken loose in here.'" Then he faltered a bit before adding, "I think we've had it. Goodbye."

The wave surged up the base of a hill behind Ulrich's anchorage, then poured back into the bay, carrying the *Edrie* along with it as it changed directions and began sweeping toward the western shore. Icebergs, trees, and debris clogged the surface; even with the engine at full power it was all Ulrich could do to bring the boat around and avoid being washed into an even thicker mess he could see in the fading twilight along the western shore. It was almost impossible to tell the water from the land; in a matter of minutes the wave had torn *four square miles* of timber from the shores of Lituya Bay and pounded it into a jumbled mass that continued to slide back and forth across the bay as the wave rebounded from side to side. For what seemed an eternity, the normally placid waters of the bay leaped and boiled with twenty-foot seas coming from every direction, each one bristling with icebergs and hull-crushing logs.

After a few minutes the chaos seemed to be subsiding, and Ulrich, thinking they had perhaps weathered the worst of it, reached again for the radio. "I wasn't sure, of course, that either of my [earlier] transmissions had been picked up," he said, but as soon as he spoke into the microphone, the airways burst to life. All up and down the coast frantic boat operators began shooting questions at Ulrich and each other, asking who was okay and who was missing. Did anybody know where so-and-so had last been seen? Was anyone else in Lituya Bay?

While the stunned trolling fleet began its dreadful inventory, Ulrich realized he had to make a decision. The debris was closing in around the *Edrie*, and in a few minutes it would be completely dark. There were strange currents and eddies full of grinding wreckage moving around the bay. In the gloom, he said, the whole scene had a "nightmarish quality," and he knew that any one of the massive chunks of ice or pitching logs could make kindling of the *Edrie* in an instant.

He decided he had to get out of Lituya Bay at once.

The risk was incalculable. By now the tide was at full ebb, and there was no way of knowing if the channel had been moved or perhaps even closed completely by the scouring of the massive wave. In any case, the outflow would be full of logs and ice charging seaward at twelve knots into the standing combers that sealed off the entrance during the peak of every ebb.

"I knew we were going to take a pounding as we went out," said Ulrich, "and hoped the trunk cabin and pilothouse would stand it. We might be swept clean and pounded under by the seas at the entrance, but it was a chance I had to take."

He tucked pillows and blankets around Sonny to cushion him from the shocks he knew were coming and told him to hang on for dear life. As he eased toward the entrance, he saw the light of another boat moving outside the bay and grabbed the radio. "For god's sake, don't come in here!" he yelled. "All hell's broken loose! Stay out!"

The voice that came back was that of Ulrich's friend George

Brockman, skipper of the *Theron*, who calmly asked Ulrich what he planned to do. In a brief exchange Brockman described for Ulrich what he could see of the entrance, then, in an act of remarkable courage, offered to station himself in line with the channel, in the path of the hurtling logs and ice-filled outflow, so that Ulrich could use the *Theron*'s masthead light as a beacon to steer by.

As soon as Brockman was in place, said Ulrich, "I braced myself and headed out." Steering madly to stay lined up on the *Theron*'s light, the *Edrie* swept headlong into the race, surrounded on all sides by tumbling debris. At the first comber the troller slammed into a wall of water that broke completely over the wheelhouse. A second comber did the same. The third and final wave broke so hard that the *Edrie* was completely submerged.

"But the stout little *Edrie* was equal to it," Ulrich later bragged with deserved pride. "She never faltered, and soon we had reached the comparative safety of the open sea."

"Comparative" safety was accurate: Boats coming to the rescue from up and down the coast began to encounter rafts of logs and debris while still miles away. In the middle of the heaving mess, in their tiny, half-swamped punt, the Swansons were feeling anything but safe. They did not know that the fleet's radio census had deduced that both the *Badger* and the *Sunmore* had been in Lituya Bay, or that the troller *Lumen*, with its owner, Julian Graham, and his seventeen-year-old son Kenneth on board, was already pushing slowly through the mass of logs outside of Lituya Bay looking for survivors. Upon learning that two other boats had been in the bay, Ulrich, too, decided to stay and join in the search, even though, as he later admitted, he was "badly shaken."

While the *Edrie* motored slowly to and fro and Ulrich peered into the darkness, the *Lumen* maneuvered into the mass of logs, sweeping a searchlight back and forth. For an hour and a half Graham and his son alternated searching with shutting down the engine and drifting, listening in the dark for cries for help. Hearing something like the mewling of a seagull, Graham turned the spotlight in the direction of the cry and instantly heard something that sounded more human. It did not take long for them to make out the *Badger*'s punt with the Swansons huddled in the bottom. Vivian was unconscious and Bill was in shock, but the Grahams managed to get them on board and head for a cove near Cape Spencer where a seaplane with a doctor on board could pick them up at first light and deliver them to the hospital in Juneau. At five thirty A.M., after the sun had been up long enough for the rescuers to be sure there were no more survivors, Ulrich gave up the search and began the long run home to Pelican.

The *Sunmore*, with Orville and Mickey Wagner on board, was never seen again. A search plane spotted an oil slick just outside Lituya Bay that marked the spot where they had gone down.

CHAPTER 10

THE 1958 EARTHQUAKE generated the largest mega-tsunami ever recorded on the planet. Before it was over, the Pacific Plate side of the Fairweather Fault ground at least twenty-one and a half feet north-westward against its North American counterpart and rose three and a half feet. The quake measured 8.3 on the moment magnitude scale,* four times as strong as the 1906 "Great" San Francisco earthquake, which is usually considered the benchmark of earthquake history in America. It also lasted over four minutes, compared to that infamously destructive California shaker's ninety seconds. Vivian Swanson's hair turned white before she was released from the hospital, and the only sign ever found of the three berry pickers left behind on Khantaak Island was a few paper plates drifting on the water. For days afterward the sea in Cross Sound and the Gulf of Alaska was littered with the carcasses of halibut, octopuses, and other bottom dwellers killed by the subsurface shocks. In Lituya Bay itself, all the vegetation was stripped away for a quarter of a mile or more inland; everything growing along both shores and on the spit was gone, leaving only knobs of bald bedrock veined with thin rivulets of silt. The spur above Gilbert Inlet was naked up to 1,720 feet. On the western side of the bay near the spit, where the *Sunmore* and the *Badger* took their final rides, the devastation reached nearly a mile inland. All in all, studies later showed, more than five square miles of land on both

---

* The moment magnitude scale has replaced the more commonly referred to but less accurate Richter scale, which suffered from "saturation" during quakes greater than approximately 7.3 on the Richter scale.

sides of Lituya Bay were inundated under water an average of 110 feet deep.

Beyond the lives of those spared, the single gift of the wave was the cottonwoods and their scent. As I slipped the kayak back into the water and climbed in, I thought of how over the five decades since the tsunami had occurred, life had once again proved to be indomitable, slowly reforesting the land in a process as dependable as the spinning of a finely geared machine. Whether in the wake of a tsunami or a receding glacier, the reforestation of newly scoured land is always the same. First come a few grasses and lichens, simple life-forms that can take hold and squeeze a living from the poor sediments left behind. As these grow, seed, die, rot, and grow again, they slowly manufacture a soil that is poor but sufficient for alders and willows to take root in. Alders thrive in a symbiotic relationship with tiny, soil-dwelling life-forms called actinobacteria, whose job is to convert atmospheric nitrogen into a form of nitrate nourishing to the trees. The deciduous alders' fallen leaves gradually build up and decompose into a nitrogen-rich compost that provides a suitable environment for cottonwoods.

Within twenty years or so after the Lituya Bay wave, these cottonwoods had already begun to grow tall enough to start shading out the alders and were adding their own bits of phosphorus and potassium to the recipe, which would in turn prepare the land for spruce trees to move in. By the time I arrived, fifty years after the wave, the scalped bedrock it had left behind was already covered in cottonwoods forty feet high, with a few spruce saplings scattered among them to show where a squirrel or bird had buried a cone or passed a seed through its digestive tract after feeding in the coniferous forest a quarter mile inland. In another fifty years the forest will be an even mix of spruce and cottonwood; give the process a century or two and the spruce needles building up around the base of the cottonwoods will eventually raise the acidity of the soil to a level beyond what the cottonwoods are comfortable with but ideal for hemlock and cedar. Within three or four hundred years—which is light-speed, geologically speaking—the cottonwoods will have completely disappeared, leaving the forest fully coniferous again. The sweet balm of Gilead that swirled around me as I paddled away will be a thing of the past—or it will be, I reminded myself, if Kah-Lituya allows it.

He probably won't. The geological and historical record shows that there have been four, or possibly five, great waves in Lituya Bay in the past three hundred years, and there are slabs of rock hanging on the walls at the back of the fjord that may be more tenuously attached than the one that created the 1958 wave. It is not possible to predict when Kah-Lituya will reawaken, but geologists agree that sooner or later the Fairweather Fault will inevitably lurch and release a slide, and the whole process will start over.

Paddling slowly, I stared up at the abrupt interface between cottonwoods and conifers that marked the apogee of the wave on the spur above Gilbert Inlet, nearly a third of a mile above sea level. I tried to play an actuarial game in my head, inputting the number of days I thought I might be in Lituya Bay into a calculation I had come across in one of Don Miller's geological studies that gave the odds of another great wave occurring on any given day at 9,000 to 1. But the mathematics of risk broke down when I remembered that Miller had made the prediction in 1960. Nearly 18,000 days had already passed. Lituya Bay was long overdue for another wave.

Thinking about it made me feel like someone was standing behind me with a cocked and loaded gun. The mountains sprang into sharp focus, with every knob, rock, vein, and granite scale in clear relief against the deep blue sky, and my hearing became acute; the fjord was so completely still that the silence became not just a lack of noise but a palpable thing, so that a faint hissing in my ears might have been the sound of deep currents humming through the skin of the kayak or the rush of my own blood. To paraphrase Samuel Johnson, it may concentrate the mind wonderfully for a man to know he is about to be hanged, but the juxtaposition of such sharp, clear beauty and the knowledge that Kah-Lituya might at any moment decide to devour me, my boat, the forests, and perhaps even a large chunk of the mountains was unnerving. I had planned to continue up the fjord into Gilbert Inlet to see the scar left by the massive '58 slide and perhaps even climb a short distance onto Lituya Glacier, but the kayak suddenly felt too small and delicately balanced for the landscape. I came about and paddled for the boat instead, telling myself that paddling was already irritating the pinched nerve in my neck and traveling another half-dozen miles might inflame it.

Back on the *Swift*, I ate some lunch and watched a raptor soar along the face of a timber-covered ridge sloping away from the mountain bordering Gilbert Inlet. For reasons I could not fathom, the chart gave the name of the ridge as Solomon's Railroad. The distance rendered the raptor little more than a speck that appeared and disappeared against the green of the forest, but I could tell by the flap-and-glide pattern of its drifting spirals that it was a northern goshawk. While I ate, the swallows put in another appearance, made a fluttering inspection of the scupper, then fled.

I wiped my plate and stowed it in a locker, then dug my pack and most of the gear I would need for the trek up the coast out of the hold. I was in no hurry to get started, but the sun was pleasant, and there were still a few preparations to be made. I checked the stove—a new high-tech lightweight ensemble designed to boil a quart of water in less than two minutes—again by lighting and relighting it several times using the unit's self-contained piezoelectric igniter. It worked flawlessly, but I double-checked anyway to make sure I had a bundle of wooden matches dipped in candle wax tucked into a waterproof film can; if dry tinder can be found, matches and wax will start a fire under almost any conditions, and I couldn't bring myself to completely trust a push-button gizmo.

Jon had lent me a small, ultralight one-person tent for the trip—my own weighed six pounds and was designed for expedition-level mountaineering—and I was wrapping silver tape* around the poles when the swallows showed up again. This time the male (I presumed) carried a thread of grass in his beak.

I stopped to watch his antics. The female was being coy, darting off a few yards, then returning to hover at the scupper, as if unsure of what she thought of the place. The male followed and lured her back; then she left again and he followed. I waited, but they did not return. An ache like a bruise had been lurking behind my sternum since the hummingbird had reminded me of Luisa that morning, and now there was something in the behavior of the swallows that unsettled me.

I stowed the tent in its bag, wrapped a few turns of silver tape around my hiking poles, and tried to sort more gear, but I could not concentrate. I kept misplacing things—the extra batteries for my headlamp disappeared, a Ziplock of tea bags wasn't where I'd left it, and finally the checklist itself was gone. I checked my pants pockets, the pack, under and around all the gear strewn about the deck. I even dumped the tent back out of its stuff sack to be sure it wasn't lost in the folds, but the carefully assembled list of items, divided into categories of "indispensable," "might come in handy," and "luxuries" through a process of marking out and relisting so protracted it had left the paper soft and creased along the folds, was gone.

I swept the gear off the deck and slammed the hold, then noticed my heart was pounding.

---

* Silver tape is considered indispensable by many outdoorsmen. Originally designed to seal the joints in metal air ducting, it is strong and highly adhesive and can be used to improvise repairs to leaky rafts, rubber boots, raincoats, and tents. I have also seen it used to provide first aid for heel blisters and to close open wounds, splint a broken canoe paddle, patch a torn sail, and close a tear in the fabric of a damaged airplane wing. For a backpacker, carrying a large roll is impractical, but a dozen or so turns around a set of tent poles or hiking poles means having some available without adding much weight to one's load.

I took a deep breath. This had been happening too often over the past year.

"Overwork," I said to myself. Misplacing things, forgetting things—my hands doing one thing while my mind was somewhere else had become commonplace.

When I broke ground for the house two years ago in early April, I had been boiling with energy, and life couldn't have been better. The sun had shone for weeks at a time, and my wife—then my fiancée—had come by the site regularly, sometimes with coffee or a treat she had baked. I would shut down whatever piece of equipment I was operating and take a break, resting my arm around her waist while she rubbed my neck and we talked about the landscaping she wanted to do or the layout of the kitchen.

Progress was rapid. I hired two helpers from a local construction company who knew the value of straight and level and wore leather tool bags that had grown shiny from years of hard use. Rod was a powerhouse, red-faced, lean, and strong; he worked at a dead run, throwing sheets of plywood around and driving iron stakes while I pounded holes in the bedrock with a hammer drill. Jason was younger, built low to the ground like a second-string fullback, and a casual observer might have thought he was moving slowly, but he could think in compound angles and was usually two steps ahead of me.

By the end of May, when the cement trucks came grumbling up the steep grade to the site and began pumping the footing molds full of concrete, the weather had turned warm, almost hot, so that as we worked to trowel the mixture smooth and get the plate bolts in place before the concrete hardened up, we were forced to strip down to T-shirts.

The terrain I was building on was tricky, with ribs of greenstone, deep hollows, and rock shelves that rose and dropped eight feet from the front of the house to the back. Rob went on to another job while Jason and I continued framing knee walls of rot-proof two-by-eights

atop the stepped concrete footing with the help of two fishermen left
short of money by a poor spring fishing season. By the middle of June,
after a long period spent working ten hours a day, six days a week, the
foundation was ready for the floor joists to be set in place. One corner
of Jason's mouth flicked up into a brief smile after a careful check with
a laser showed that our work had been true to within one sixteenth of
an inch across forty-two feet, measured corner to corner along the
diagonal of the growing house. He stepped back while I checked a second time, tapping the laser with a finger to test the bubble in its base,
and got the same result. Then we nodded at each other and agreed it
was "good enough."

Things rarely went that well again. Jason bent to pick up a board
a few days later, gasped, and turned white; something in his back had
given, a recurring injury of the sort that is common among Alaskans
who have spent years working construction, bent over the roller of a
longline boat in cold weather, stacking crab pots in heavy seas, or operating a skidder in a logging camp. He continued working, but between the pain pills and frequent doctor appointments the quiet pride
of getting a job done grew more elusive every day.

Juneau was in the middle of a building boom, and experienced
hands were hard to find. Carpenters, masons, plumbers, electricians—
anyone with a set of tools was booked months in advance. With the
date for our wedding fast approaching, either I found help to finish
the floor of the house or we faced last-minute changes to our plans for
the ceremony. I felt lucky to hire an acquaintance of my wife's, one of
her rock-climbing buddies who ran an ad hoc crew of younger men.
In the third week of July, two days before the wedding, the floor was
down, the back and south walls of the first floor were framed up, and I
was at the site until ten P.M., using a long-handled roller to spread a
coat of water-resistant sealant onto the plywood subfloor so it could
dry before the ceremony. From April to July had been one of the longest spells of uninterrupted good weather in Juneau's memory.

The day of the ceremony was dry but cloudy. A squad of friends helped ready a large tarp in case it rained. A trio with carpenter skills built a sloping ramp to the deck so a neighbor confined to a wheelchair by Lou Gehrig's disease could attend, then nailed gritty roofing material to its surface so the bride would not slip when she made her entrance. With no roof overhead, an unobstructed view of the mountains and the sea, and the borrowed chairs set out in curving rows, the freshly swept and cleared site had the feel of an open-air cathedral.

The ceremony went off without a hitch. Ed, with his thick white hair and beard neatly trimmed, looked proud as he gave the bride away; my brother stood beside me as my best man. As the morning progressed, the clouds got lower and thicker, but it did not rain, and at the moment of our vows the clouds parted and a shaft of sunlight lit the ridge, sparkled across the water, washed over the onlookers, and danced in the brown eyes of my bride. I had been told beforehand that it did not matter how the wedding was planned—what course the events took, who attended, or what kind of wine was served—because I would be oblivious to any part of it beyond the actual moment of binding, which proved true, because even now, as I try to record my feelings, it is all a blur, with the exception of the moment when I looked into the eyes of the woman I was marrying and saw them brimming with tears of joy. My heart, furled and stowed for much of my life, opened and lifted like a wind-filled sail.

It started raining the next day. A month later Hurricane Katrina rolled across the South, destroying tens of thousands of homes, and the prices of building materials started rising. The price of oil spiked and drove the cost of everything still higher. Every trip to the building-supply store or lumberyard brought a new shock, with increases of 10 percent, 14, 30, then 60 as the prices of the metal in nails and fasteners, roofing, the copper in wires, wood, paint, and anything that had to be shipped or had petroleum involved in its manufacture skyrocketed.

And still the rains fell. Through September and October a relent-less monsoon settled in over Juneau, pouring so steadily out of a leaden sky that I was forced to drill dozens of holes into the plywood subfloor to drain the water away in order to allow the framing crew to lay out the remaining walls. Professionals will tell you that inclement weather cuts production by a third or more; it is simply harder and slower to work fully clothed in foul-weather gear and to always be trying to keep power tools and materials dry enough to use. A tremendous amount of time can be spent just covering things with tarps and then uncovering them, and the weight of unending rain or snow bears heavily on morale.

Progress slowed to a crawl. The new crew proved problematic; things kept having to be redone. The assembly of timbers and beams supporting the second floor went into place, then had to be removed and reinstalled. A simple pony wall in the kitchen area was torn out and rebuilt three times.* With winter rushing toward me, no roof over-head, and no other hands available, I felt I had no choice but to keep the fumbling crew on, even as I watched day after day of effort and thousands of dollars wash down the drain.

But there were moments of splendor as well. On a rare sunny day my wife showed up unexpectedly and spent several hours helping sand and oil an immense stack of spruce planks that were to be our finished ceilings; on another she came by to help me clean, sweep, and cart away a truckload of sawdust and construction debris, and the sight of her covered in dust, with her silky black hair contained in a red bandanna, as she wrestled a large vacuum cleaner up a ladder to clean

---

* A pony wall is a short wall framed on top of a standard eight-foot wall, in this case as an addition built with "pockets" between sections of two-by-six framing into which the ends of the roof timbers and trusses were secured, so that the roof load would be carried by the fully framed wall underneath. Construction nomenclature varies from region to region—and sometimes from carpenter to carpenter—and pony walls, knee walls, and stub walls may be referred to interchangeably.

the timber roof trusses would have brought me to my knees had I not been simultaneously buoyed up by the near-unspeakable joy of believing we would be working together for the rest of our lives.

I went into the cabin of the *Swift*, poured a cup of water, and used it to wash down two aspirins. Then I went back on deck and sat in the sun again, sipping the water as I tried to lose myself in the silence of the bay and the knowledge that for now there was no rush to get moving. Dwelling on the frustrations of the building project had made me feel tense again, but the memory of those early, hopeful days with my wife tied a knot in my heart.

A lone gull drifted over the boat, cocking its head to stare down at me with one yellow eye before it tipped a wing and circled away. A second gull stroked by, and the first turned to follow. After it caught up, the pair flew side by side for a minute, then one or the other abruptly lifted and turned away. I took a last sip from the cup, then poured the rest over the side to hear it trickle into the salt water.

Shortly after our wedding my wife had gone away for more training and come home excited, and our dinner conversations had begun to revolve around her future plans. We volleyed back and forth the idea that with its view of the cove and quiet isolation, the small guest cabin I intended to build on a ledge below the main house would make an ideal place to work with future clients, until she called one day to say she had found a better space twenty-five miles away in downtown Juneau. After that an increasing number of late-night business appointments meant cooking and eating dinner by myself.

I took a deep breath and blew it out to push the thought away. The aspirin was kicking in, and I decided to get off the boat again; exploring Cenotaph Island might help clear my mind.

CHAPTER 11

Roughly half a mile across, steep, heavily wooded, and a little over three hundred feet high near the center, Cenotaph Island is an interesting place. Lituya Bay was formed by the advance and retreat of glaciers through a series of ice ages, the blue tongues of ice slipping down out of the mountains to gouge and pry at the bedrock until they had plowed a trench that in places was over five hundred feet deep. Yet somehow the stony mass that is now Cenotaph managed to stay in place, like an abrupt 800-foot-high peak in the middle of a narrow valley. When the glaciers retreated and the sea level rose, the valley flooded, creating the island that would supply La Pérouse's expedition, then myself, with a secure anchorage. For a while in the early part of the twentieth century it was also home to the only permanent white settler ever to take up residence along the entire 150 miles of coastline between Yakutat and Cape Spencer.

James Todd Huscroft first appeared in Alaska in 1915, when he worked as a miner in the town of Treadwell, on Douglas Island, across the Gastineau Channel from Juneau. All that remains of Treadwell today is a few stone foundations and a handful of stubbed-off pilings that mark where an extensive system of docks and wharves once stood, but at the time it was a booming place. Four industrial-scale gold mines and an array of thundering stamp mills that operated around the clock made it one of the largest communities in the territory. The mountains on the eastern side of the island were honeycombed with a web of mine shafts, and a complex of tunnels extended deep into the bedrock underlying the channel. On April 22, 1917, one of the shafts under the channel flooded and caved in, setting off a chain reaction that did not

98

stop until three of the four mines had collapsed. It was a miracle that the disaster occurred just as the work shifts were changing; the only casualty was a single mule, drowned at the bottom of a shaft during the initial flooding. Nevertheless, hundreds of miners and laborers were immediately thrown out of work. Shortly thereafter Huscroft packed a meager kit and headed for Lituya Bay.

Stout, bald as a melon, and shovel jawed, Huscroft was almost a caricature of strength. He was described by one visitor, who marveled at his ability to knock a thick log into pieces in a matter of minutes with a handsaw, as "a stocky, tremendously powerful man with a sad, kindly face [and] arms the size of a normal man's legs." Little is known of Huscroft's early years except that he was born in Ohio and that he claimed to have made and lost three fortunes, the last in a lumber business of some nature.

As I slipped back into the kayak and paddled away from the *Swift*, I started thinking about how my own life savings had evaporated under the pressure of rising construction costs. Working for wages as a hard-rock miner was certainly not a path to a fourth fortune, and I wondered if the rise and fall of Huscroft's finances, combined with a brush with death during the mine cave-in, had inspired a decision to spend the remainder of his life on a small island in a remote place of incomparable beauty. He was forty-five years old at the time.

In one of the few photographs of Huscroft I've found, taken in 1933 by the well-known mountaineer Bradford Washburn, he is older, in his early sixties, and stands foursquare and solid, suspendered in heavy pants, wearing a frayed shirt worn through at one elbow, and holding a pan of potatoes grown in a garden that met the bulk of his needs. In his other hand is a shovel, and there is something in the way he looks at the camera, with his head tilted a few degrees and his forehead faintly wrinkled, that is tentative, yet open and kind. The picture was taken on a sunny day, and Huscroft squints as he waits for Washburn to trip the shutter. But there is patience in the way he stands with the pan of potatoes resting on one hip and the handle of the shovel on the other; it seems to say that he could—and would—stand there all day if that was what the photographer wanted. Everything about the image makes me think James Huscroft was a softhearted man, and everything I've learned from other sources agrees with this impression.

"The man was obviously a hermit in the extreme," wrote the climber and writer Dave Bohn, who explored Lituya Bay in the 1960s, "but an extraordinary one, for all who met him were struck by his generosity and kindness."

"Jim Huscroft was the kindest man I have ever known," said Robert Bates, another climber who met Huscroft in 1932 when he went to Lituya Bay to reconnoiter an approach for an upcoming expedition to Mount Crillon. "[He] would give away anything he had and was always thinking of other people's problems."

Bates described in a letter to Bohn how Huscroft would walk down to the beach to meet anyone coming in by boat or seaplane and be waiting, watch in hand, to greet them with the words "I make it out to be 11:20; what do you make it?" After adjusting his watch, Huscroft always invited the guest up for some of his home-brewed beer or a meal. The one exception Bates noted to Huscroft's timely greeting came during a visit he made in 1933, at the height of the Great Depression, when Huscroft met him with a plaintive "Say it ain't so, Bob. Say it ain't so." When Bates asked what was wrong, Huscroft's reply was that he had heard that "the kids in New York City is eating out of garbage pails! I've been thinking about it all winter . . . There's all those salmon in the bay and goats in the hills, an' if I could just get some cans I could help some. Tain't right for kids to be eating that way, you know, an' I want to help 'em out. Been thinking about it all winter."

Huscroft made one trip to town a year, usually by hitching a ride on a passing boat headed for Juneau, where he would first buy a tub of salt mackerel and eat one or two, saving the rest to take home. Next on his list was enough snuff—or "snoose," as miners called it—to last a year. After checking off the rest of his shopping list, he would head up to the Elks Club, where the bartender had saved up an entire year's worth of newspapers for Huscroft to take back to Lituya Bay. Like a character in a Somerset Maugham story, Huscroft disciplined himself to read only one newspaper at a time, each one on the date coinciding with the one on the newspaper, from a year earlier. "It don't matter which year it is," he told Bates. "The news is all the same anyway. Only if I peeked ahead, it'd take away the fun." But he had been worrying about the New York urchins for nearly a year.

Forty years later, when I was a teenager just setting out to explore the sprawling beauty of Alaska, there were still a few of the "old-timers" scattered around the state, miners and trappers like Russian Mike at Nancy Lake, north of Anchorage; Tiger Olsen at Taku Harbor, down near Juneau, and Stan Price, who lived among a couple dozen tame grizzlies on Admiralty Island. These lone, aging men were inevitably tagged as hermits, but none seemed to fit the crotchety, socially inept mold of the true recluse, being to a man fond of company and generous to a fault. Almost all were deep thinkers and devourers of books. A few, like Tiger Olsen, had a monkish bent for the gnostic and meta-physical. None, however, had quite as notable a reputation for out-and-out kindness as Huscroft, whose greatest delight, according to Bates, was helping others. "Take it," he would say, no matter what the request. "I got lots more."

In fact, Huscroft had very little. Shortly after his arrival on Ceno-taph Island, he and a partner had tried their hand at fox farming, but a trapper working the area had asked to store his furs in Huscroft's cabin, and a wolf pelt infected with a lethal mange had spread the dis-ease to the foxes and wiped them out.* For years visitors were amused

---

* Fox farming was a common vocation among the inhabitants of Alaska's island archipela-goes in the years after World War I, when prices soared as women's fashions began to dictate the use of fur. The foxes were raised on small islands near salmon streams, which supplied a cheap source of food.

by Huscroft's two remaining foxes, pets he called Grandma, who would ride on his shoulder, and Tuffy, a blue fox who played constantly at his feet.

After the collapse of the fox-farming enterprise, he scraped along by salting away a few kegs of salmon to sell in Juneau, trapping a bit in the winter, or prospecting for gold. The latter never amounted to much, in spite of a persistent rumor that he had a "secret barrel" buried in a stream nearby that yielded nuggets on demand. Other than the bit of hard-earned cash needed for his annual supply of staples—flour, salt, sugar, tea, coffee, and, of course, snoose—Huscroft's mainstay was what Alaskans call subsistence and others call living off the land. Salmon, mountain goats, seals, sea lions, bears, and wild greens were all elements of his diet, and to this day the forelands around Lituya Bay are carpeted during the summer with wild strawberries whose flavor is so rich and intense that it renders the domestic version of that fruit pale and pulpy by comparison. Blueberry and huckleberry jam added a sweet touch to the thick, skillet-sized sourdough pancakes he enjoyed for breakfast 365 days a year.

But Huscroft's true wealth was in his garden, a patch of deep, rich soil that yielded a root cellar full of potatoes, carrots, cabbage, kale, and other crops that fed him year-round. Fertile soil is virtually non-existent in the glacier-scoured regions of the coast, but during the years Huscroft lived on Cenotaph Island, he patiently built his own, mulching skiffloads of laboriously gathered kelp into a mound of sand and silt and enriching it with a compost of salmon carcasses and clamshells. With twenty hours of daylight during the summer growing season, the garden, though small, was remarkably prolific. In the photograph the growth is lush to his knees.

I had made a photocopy of the picture before leaving Juneau, and I stuck it in my pocket before getting off the boat, thinking I might be able to use the outline of the hills behind Huscroft to decipher where his garden had been. Paddling north of the island, I passed the spot where La Pérouse had anchored, and at a stream where Huscroft had probably harvested salmon to feed his foxes, I stopped to watch a young grizzly dig at something behind a large drift log. The bear had its head down when I first spotted it—all I could see was the brown line of its back and the rise and fall of the hump between its shoulders as it dug—and I thought for a moment of maneuvering quietly toward shore in a way that would allow the current to drift me into a better viewing position, but no sooner had I dipped the paddle than the bear lifted its head, sniffed at the air, and bolted. Quick as a cat it was gone, disappearing into the sheltering woods with a light crackle of under-brush.

Ten minutes later I was pulling the kayak ashore on a shingled point on the west side of the island. Not wanting to outrage the pinched nerve in my neck again, I raised the rudder and locked it, then pulled the kayak up the beach by the bowline. It slid easily over the water-smoothed stones. Where the beach leveled out above the high tide mark into a carpet of dead grass, I pulled the picture of Huscroft from my pocket and looked around. There was nothing to indicate where his cabin or garden had once been, though I knew from old charts and hand-me-down accounts that I was in approximately the right loca-tion. When he'd first come to Lituya Bay, Huscroft had lived for a while in the remains of an Indian shelter on the southern shore near the entrance, then had built a small cabin on the northeastern side of Cenotaph. It had been a choice, I presumed, inspired by the spectacu-lar view toward the head of the bay and Mount Crillon. But it had not taken long to figure out that the west side of the island offered more protection from the winds that roared down off the glaciers in the winter. In his diary Huscroft had noted that during the twenty-eight days of February in 1934, the wind had howled from the head of the bay for twenty-six days in a row, then shifted and blown out of the north for the other two. Nor would he have had any exposure to what little precious sunlight made its way into the bay on rare clear days.

Within a year or two he had rebuilt on a sunny, level spot above the western point I was standing on.

I held the photo up to the horizon, then moved a bit and tried again. It was a simple matter to match a range of hills behind Huscroft to the contours of the shore and decide that here, or at least very close to where I was standing, was where he had once stamped his shovel into the ground and started to coax a living from the land. The smell of dry grass and new growth mingled with a faint musk of seaweed left high and dry by the tide, creating a faint, fecund scent like the ghost of a garden. It was easy to imagine him working contentedly, lost in the peace that comes with silence as he shoveled and stirred a rich compost of fish and kelp and his pet foxes played around his feet.

There is something in a garden that says *home* like nothing else, that stakes a piece of ground as one's own, as a source not of mere shelter but of sustenance. During the early stages of excavation prior to the start of building my own house, I had broken through a layer of duff and been ecstatic to discover a small pocket of soil as rich and dark as any Mississippi River bottomland. It had been deposited in a shallow declivity in the bedrock through the slow accretion of organic matter over the centuries since the end of the Little Ice Age, and discovering it was like finding gold. With buckets, a wheelbarrow, a shovel, and our hands, my wife and I scraped and gathered the precious muck into a stockpile that would barely have filled an average bathtub. It was a small start, we agreed, but a good one. We would add to it over the years by stirring in pails of compost and seaweed much as Huscroft had.

At my wife's urging, even before the first concrete was poured, I screwed a dozen cedar planks together to make a large garden box on a sunlit bench of land below the building site, then on my next trip into town picked up a load of manure and fertilizer. On a rare afternoon off work, she troweled peas, carrots, and several kinds of lettuce into the soil, then brought home a bag of flower bulbs to set out at the first sign of winter. I'd spent most of my life as a nomad, living on boats and in cabins, tents, and other temporary shelters, moving from season to season, first as a commercial fisherman and then in a variety of maritime and construction trades, before finally settling into guiding; I knew nothing of gardening. But the tangle of vines, leaves, and spidery carrot tops that shot up from the peat-black dirt that first summer looked permanent. I had given little thought over the past thirty years to settling down, but the act of putting down roots—literally—on a piece of ground as spectacular as the ridge, with its view of endless mountains and a free-flowing salmon stream nearby, had opened up a world of new dreams that made it easy to imagine how Huscroft, after having lived the life of an itinerant miner, must have felt as he watched rows of vegetables sprout from soil he had created with his own patient hands. I could imagine how at home he must have felt, how solidly *planted*.

And being a generous man, he wanted to share. Beginning in 1897, when Prince Luigi Amedeo, the duke of Abruzzi and the son of the king of Spain, summited 18,000-foot Mount Saint Elias after ten years of attempts on the mountain that had defeated, among others, expeditions from the U.S. Army, the U.S. Geological Survey, and the National Geographic Society, an enthusiasm for the unexplored coast began to burn among the world's mountaineers. It took more than a quarter of a century for the next expedition to probe into the "American Himalayas," but in 1926 two attempts were made to scale Mount Fairweather. The first approached from the east, through Glacier Bay, and failed. The second, led by a young research engineer named Allen Carpe, also failed, but Carpe became so enamored of Alaska's mountains that he returned in 1930, accompanied by a twenty-three-year-old Harvard-educated economist named Terris Moore. Set on approaching the mountain from the north via a long, circuitous route that began in the mining village of McCarthy, crossed over the Skolai Pass, and climbed up Russell Glacier, Carpe and Moore found themselves in a friendly but determined competition to be the first up Mount Fairweather with an expedition led by then-twenty-year-old Bradford Washburn, who would take the photograph of Huscroft I would use to identify his garden site. Washburn's team had already attempted the ascent from the coast near Cape Fairweather, but after encountering the hellish tangle of alder and devil's club that girdles the lower reaches of the mountains, they had turned back. On Huscroft's advice they then decided to start by climbing northwest along Lituya Glacier to Desolation Valley and up Fairweather Glacier, where they were stopped by a 400-foot wall of ice feet wedged between 2,000-foot cliffs. Carpe and Moore got no farther than Mount Bona, nearly 200 miles away, but in all of the comings and goings, Washburn became good friends with Huscroft. When Carpe and Moore returned in 1931 for Carpe's third attempt on Fairweather's summit, they, too, anchored in front of Cenotaph Island—probably in the same spot where I was anchored—to begin shuttling their equipment and supplies to a series of staging camps along the approach to the mountain. During the process they became friends with Huscroft as well. On June 8, 1931, after enduring sixty days of seemingly endless gales, torrential rains, and snowstorms, they became the first humans to reach the top of Mount Fairweather.

Standing in Huscroft's garden with the sun in my face, Washburn's photo in my hand, and silence ringing in my ears, I felt the hum of time wash over me. Seventy-five years earlier Carpe and Moore had stood where I stood, not long after clawing their way to the summit of Fairweather. Over the years I had lived in Ed's cabin, he had at times related stories to me of his experiences as an avid young climber. In the late 1940s, after Ed had taken part in the first ascent of Mount Hess, northeast of Denali in the Alaska Range, it had been Terris Moore who'd flown over the summit, as an objective observer, to confirm his accomplishment. Through my connection with Ed, and his with Moore, and Moore's with Carpe and Washburn, it felt like the distance between the hermit of Lituya Bay and me was no greater than the width of the garden.

After Washburn and Carpe spread word of Huscroft's hospitality, a thin but steady flow of mountaineers bent on exploring the uncharted region began to appear in Lituya Bay. Washburn came back in 1932, 1933, and 1934 at the head of ever-larger and more complex expeditions and would continue to climb in Alaska for decades. (In 1940 his wife, Barbara, became the first woman to summit a peak in the Fairweather Range by climbing Mount Bertha.) Tragically, Carpe was killed in 1932 during a climb on 20,300-foot Mount McKinley (now called Denali), but Moore stayed on in the territory and eventually became the president of the University of Alaska, and he and his cohorts frequently showed up at Huscroft's cabin. After Washburn described Huscroft and his garden in an article written for *National Geographic* magazine, the trickle of visitors to Lituya Bay became a small flood.

And Huscroft was ready for them. He had always welcomed the trappers, fishermen, prospectors, and other wanderers drawn by rumors of his hospitality and deep-dish berry pies, who sometimes dropped by in such numbers as to overflow his small cabin, and in 1930 he had started building a bunkhouse to accommodate them. The climbers quickly dubbed the twenty-six-by-sixteen-foot log structure the "Huscroft Hotel": it had eight bunks, a large woodstove with an oven, and hardwood alder floors. As I kicked through a thicket of dried thimbleberry stalks to peer into the gloom beneath the forest canopy, I marveled at the strength of the man and the sheer effort he had expended to fell and drag enough trees into the open to stack into the shape of a 400-square-foot shelter.

Huscroft was fifty-eight years old—six years older than me—and green logs are damned heavy. I had sawed and milled several truckloads of twenty-foot logs into material for my own house project, but I had had the help of a winch truck and a crusty ex-logger named

Monte Lewis. Monte lives in patched and faded overalls, with the smoke from a knockdown pipe clenched between his teeth rising up through the strands of an admirably neglected beard the way shreds of cloud twist through the treetops in the rainforest around Juneau, and he had a small sawmill set up on Douglas Island. Like most people who make their living in timber, Monte believes in hard work, which meant we laid off chopping, heaving, and sawing the heavy logs into planks and timbers only when the temperature fell to nine degrees below zero. When the water dripping from a copper tube plumbed into a five-gallon can to lubricate the whirling blade began to freeze into small pellets that flew from the roaring machine and stung our faces, he wedged his axe into a stump, pulled his pipe from his teeth, and declared it was time to "let 'er heal up," meaning we wouldn't go back to work until the temperature climbed back above zero.

Turning a man-high stack of logs into several thousand board feet of finished planks and timbers was some of the hardest work I have ever done, but in the end the sight of the wood stickered and stacked to dry at the building site was worth the weeks of frozen fingers and aching muscles. Huscroft's task of dragging, poling, and levering the logs for his "hotel" into place without machinery had undoubtedly been even more difficult. But as I stood back from the edge of the forest to imagine the two cabins snuggled side by side, with a pole-and-shake roof spanning the space between them to create a storage area for firewood and kegs of dried salmon, I knew the satisfaction he must have felt as he lifted each squared timber into place. And I marveled at the character of a man who would perform so much labor for people he did not know, who strained his back and blistered his hands for the benefit of those who only might—perhaps—someday come.

But he did and they came. For the next six years the bunkhouse was often full, and Huscroft's only surviving diary notes the arrival and departure of group after group of climbers, geologists, scientists, students, travelers, fishermen, and appreciative visitors. In winter he might not see another human being for months at a time, but during the summer the number of visitors swelled until it was a wonder he managed to feed them all with his garden. Somehow his patch of carefully nurtured ground always supplied enough produce to feed dozens of people, with enough left over to carry him through the winter. Or it did until Kah-Lituya changed everything.

CHAPTER 12

IN 1936, JIM Huscroft was sixty-four years old and starting to slow down. He tired more easily than he had when he first arrived in Lituya Bay, though he still thought nothing of strapping a heavy pack on his back and heading off to spend a few nights at one of the small shelters he had thrown up at various locations along the coast for his trapping and prospecting forays. In the spring of that year, he made his usual trip into Juneau, hitching a ride on the troller *Mine*. The *Mine* was owned by Nick Larsen, a friend of Huscroft's who had spent the winter trapping around Lituya Bay with a partner, Fritz Frederickson. Once in Juneau, Larsen and Frederickson set about selling their winter's catch, and Huscroft went off on his usual round of gathering up a year's worth of staples, picking up his newspapers at the Elks Club, and dropping by a few of the town's rough-and-tumble saloons. At some point during his rounds he made the acquaintance of a young man named Bernie Allen, who had heard enough stories about Huscroft and Lituya Bay to think he was interested in taking a stab at the hermit's lifestyle. Could he come along when Huscroft went back to Lituya Bay? he asked. Huscroft, of course, was agreeable.

By all accounts Huscroft and Allen got along well. The young man was personable, worked hard, and was excited by the adventure of living in such a remote and beautiful spot. It was starting to seem like Huscroft would have company for the winter when Allen was still there in October, even though the autumn had been a miserable one, with a series of gales drenching the coast with record rainfalls. October is by far the wettest month in Southeast Alaska, but a storm that began on October 20 and continued for the next six days dropped 150 percent of the period's normal rainfall.

Throughout the pounding storm, Larsen and Frederickson were stuck outside the bay aboard the *Mine*, rolling and heaving on the waves as they waited for the weather to abate enough to allow them to cross the bar. They were there to get ready for another trapping season, and at about four o'clock on the evening of the 26th, just before dusk, the combers finally laid down enough to let Larsen pilot the troller in.

They anchored not far from Huscroft's cabin. Frederickson later told a friend that they could see a light in the window, but the weather was still lousy, and after days of pitching and rolling on the ocean waves, they were too tired to row ashore. The rain was still hammering on the boat's cabin top when Larsen and Frederickson turned in.

The next morning Huscroft was up at daybreak, making his usual pancakes. Larsen and Frederickson were sitting in the fo'c'sle of the *Mine* having coffee. Allen was still in bed, in no hurry to get outside and face the soggy weather. There are a few conflicts in the various accounts of what happened next, but all agreed it started with a terrible noise that Allen later described to a reporter for the *Alaska Daily Press* as "the drone of a hundred airplanes at low altitude."

Huscroft yelled at Allen to get up. Larsen and Frederickson piled up the ladder into the wheelhouse to see what was going on. It was still gloomy outside, and no one could tell where the noise was coming from.

The roar just kept growing louder and louder. It continued for five minutes, then ten, then twenty. At six twenty A.M. an increasingly nervous Larsen started the *Mine*'s engine. Huscroft ran out of his cabin, expecting to feel the jolt of an earthquake; Allen tumbled out of his bunk in his long underwear.

Larsen suddenly barked, "Get the anchor up!" but didn't wait for Frederickson to follow the order before he gunned the engine and started steaming for deeper water. A thin white line had appeared in the gloom at the head of the bay, and he knew it could only be a huge wave, breaking as it rolled toward them.

Huscroft ran back into the cabin, shouting, "Get out, Bernie! Something's broke loose up there!," then ran outside again. He later described what he saw when he went back out to a U.S. Forest Service employee as "all the water in the bay rushing out toward the entrance in one big tidal wave."

The *Mine* had reached a spot in seventy feet of water a quarter of a mile northwest of Huscroft's cabin when the wave broke around Cenotaph Island. Frederickson later admitted he was "terrorized" when the wall of water struck the troller, throwing it aloft so fast he thought his feet were going to go through the cabin floor. Somehow Larsen managed to keep the boat under control as it hurtled skyward and plunged over the top, falling "at least fifty feet" down the back of the wave.

Huscroft and Allen bolted for high ground with the sound of frothing water and snapping timber right behind them. The *Mine* had barely righted itself when a second wave struck, then a third, and Huscroft stared, awestruck, as the surge of water rolled past the island and swept toward the mouth of the bay, then bounced back as it encountered the heavy ocean swells at the narrow entrance, sending an enormous "back wave" hurtling toward the island. Blocks of ice and tree trunks tumbled and rolled across its face.

Allen was already far up the hill, and Huscroft wasted no time plunging into the brush after him. The returning surge swept up the beach behind him, tearing away his dock and demolishing a shed in which he had stored fifty barrels of dried salmon; then it struck the cabins. The two men did not stop running until they were as high as they could go.

After the series of giant waves passed, the bay continued to heave and boil, but the roaring noise had stopped, and no more waves came out of the paling darkness. Huscroft and Allen stood shivering in the pouring rain at the top of the hill, listening to the sound of water sloshing back and forth below them. It wasn't until everything grew quiet that they could work up the courage to start slowly picking their way down again.

True to his nature, Huscroft barely gave the cabins a glance as he passed by on his way to the beach; his only thought was of his friends on the *Mine*, which he had seen enter the bay the previous evening. When he saw the battered troller picking its way through the floating debris toward the island, he shouted, "Thank God they made it!" and waved his arms to let Larsen and Frederickson know he and Allen were okay.

I folded the photocopied picture of Huscroft in his garden and slipped it into my breast pocket, then untied the bowline before sliding the kayak back down the beach into the water. Jim Huscroft, Bernie Allen, Nick Larsen, and Fritz Frederickson had all survived a tsunami that had washed 490 feet up the side of Crillon Inlet. Allen later told a newspaper reporter that he thought the wave had probably been caused by the collapse of an ice dam on Crillon Glacier, which had allowed a huge lake of trapped rainwater to flush into the bay. But a scale model of Lituya Bay built by geologist Don Miller at Stanford University disproved this theory. Nor had there been an earthquake, because neither Huscroft nor Allen reported any shaking. Other theories proposed a sudden surge forward by one of the glaciers, a landslide, and a meteor strike, but no evidence was ever found to support any of these. The only certainty was that it was a miracle Huscroft and his friends had survived.

For Huscroft, however, the miracle quickly turned into a disaster. After reassuring himself that Larsen and Frederickson were alive, he went with Allen to inspect the cabins, which were okay. There was mud up to the windows, and the floors were a sodden tangle of books, magazines, clothes, bedding, and supplies. But both were still structurally sound and sitting solidly on their foundations. And incredibly, the fire in the woodstove was still burning.

But Huscroft's heart must have dropped when he went to inspect the root cellar; it was flooded, and his entire supply of produce for the coming winter was spoiled. And his heart must have broken when he saw what the tsunami had done to his garden. There was nothing left of it; every last spoonful of the soil he had so carefully built up over the past twenty years had washed away.

Cenotaph Island got its name 150 years before the 1936 tsunami washed over the island. To this day no one knows what caused the wave. Bernie Allen got on the next passing boat and went back to Juneau, but Huscroft stayed, struggling through the winter on occasional handouts from passing boats and what little meat and fish he could catch. Those who knew him say that he never got over the loss of his garden, that the wave left in its place an old man in a state of slow decline who no longer showed any interest in carousing in the saloons during his annual trip into Juneau or having his cabin full of guests spinning yarns. By the spring of 1939 his health had deteriorated so badly that a passing friend, Ocey Nolde, insisted he come aboard Nolde's boat and go into Juneau to see a doctor. He was down to skin and bones but only reluctantly agreed, and Nolde said later that as they crossed the bar, Huscroft stood on the deck watching Lituya Bay fall away astern with tears in his eyes. Two days later he died, alone, in the fo'c'sle of Nolde's boat.

I lowered myself into the kayak and used the paddle to push away from shore. While I was thinking about Huscroft, the sun had fallen to a low angle in the northwestern sky, but the bay was still calm, and the warmth of its light on my face was comforting. The 1958 mega-tsunami that had sunk the *Badger* and drowned the crew of the *Sunmore* had also wiped out any remaining vestige of Huscroft's cabins, but as I listened to the buzzing call of a varied thrush in the forest that had sprung up where the cabins had once stood, I could easily understand his attachment to the island. La Pérouse had named the island Cenotaph for a stone tower he'd had erected there after twenty-one of his men had drowned when the longboats they'd been using to survey the inner shoreline of the bay had been caught in the outgoing tide and overcome by the combers at the entrance. But it seemed too peaceful and full of life for a place named for a monument to the dead and swept by tsunamis at regular intervals. As I paddled, a lone seal rose ahead of me, stared, and went down again; the explosive *chuff!* of a harbor porpoise breaking the surface for a quick breath only accentuated the silence.

The historic record never again mentions the stone pyramid La Pérouse had his men erect to commemorate the loss of their shipmates; if anything remained of it by the time Russian, British, and American fur hunters began to arrive a few years later, it, too, was undoubtedly eradicated by one of Kah-Lituya's tsunamis. But for some reason, although La Pérouse's name for the bay, Port des Français, did not survive into modern use, "Cenotaph" did. The only other names from La Pérouse's hand-drawn charts that stuck were La Chaussee, for the spit on the north side of the entrance, and le Paps, or the Paps, for a pair of neatly matched 500-foot hills that rise from the lowlands on the eastern side of the entrance. The outline of the two hills is said to have reminded the homesick French sailors of a woman's breasts.

The forest draped over the smoothly rounded hills was dark green under the blue vault of the sky. Every paddle stroke pulled me farther from land, out into the placid mirror of the bay. As my perspective of the hills changed, it became clear that the name had stuck for over two centuries because ever since La Pérouse had left the bay, the Paps had continued to remind sailors and fishermen of the women and girls they had left behind. There was something in the sweet, temperate air of the early spring day and the lush forest quilting the landscape that was distinctly feminine, and I found myself thinking of my own wife,

of how it was not so long ago that we would lie with our limbs en-
twined in a complex calligraphy of love, envisioning a future that extended out to grandchildren and laughing at how much fun it would
be (although we would need to be stern) when they scribbled with colored pens on the walls. Her two now-grown daughters were planning
families of their own, and when working on the house, I often imagined how we would soon be marking the growth of toddlers on a
doorjamb with a pencil and learning to love the inevitable *wabi-sabi*
beauty of the scratched floors, dented cabinets, and worn carpets that
are the proper work of rambunctious grandchildren.

Without realizing it, I had stopped paddling and started to drift
with my mind in a whirl of geology, home, and tsunamis. The map of
the lowlands around the Paps shows a thumbprint of topographic lines
dissected by lakes and forest corridors, and for reasons I cannot name,
this brought to mind a day early in our affair when I had traced one
finger slowly along the stretch marks on my wife's belly, as if examin-
ing a map of new terrain, and realized that everything in my life seemed
on course to change, forever and for the better. Since then, mysterious
pressures had begun building along a series of ever-drifting fault lines,
and a tectonic shift of some sort seemed unavoidable.

The thought brought on a grinding pang: What if the marriage
did not work out? What if our problems couldn't be resolved? Huscroft
had died old, alone, and depressed in the cramped fo'c'sle of Ocey Nolde's boat, which left me wondering if after twenty years in Lituya Bay
the smooth proportions of the Paps had continued to stir a memory of
someone from his past, and if it was this, along with a premonition
that he was leaving his home forever, that had brought tears to his eyes
as he and Nolde steamed out of the bay on their way to Juneau. Had
Huscroft been on the run from a failed romance when he'd come to
Lituya Bay? Had there been a connubial disaster of some sort in his
past that he had never shared with anyone?

If my own marriage failed, being divorced in my fifties would be different from being alone in my thirties or forties; I was caught in the onrush of time in a body going gray and sagging, and the odds of my entering into another relationship during the time I had left did not seem promising. And without the succor of the marriage, why bother with the house? With no family or lineage, it would be little more than a shell of a building, capable of sucking up endless amounts of work and money. I would have fractured my health and spent my life savings for nothing.

I put the rudder over and stroked hard to turn around. To my left lay the island, where every vestige of Huscroft's life had been obliterated; to my right a long ridge ran down from the mountains in a smooth curve that reminded me of the shape of my wife's back as she lay sleeping. As the preceding winter had progressed, I had seen more and more of her back, until it seemed as if I seldom saw her face at all. There was a burst of interest when it came time to choose paint for the walls, with repeated trips to the paint store from which she returned flush with excitement and bearing fistfuls of sample color chips, but after the paint was applied, her interest waned and plural pronouns disappeared from her vocabulary. It had been weeks, perhaps months, since I had heard her speak of "we" or "us."

It was late, almost nine o'clock, when I got back to the boat, and the stark details of the mountains were growing soft in the evening twilight. The swallows were still flitting in circles around the boat. As I came alongside, I could see a strand of grass in the scupper. They had started a nest; there were dabs of mud along the rim of the opening.

I climbed aboard and secured the kayak to a cleat, then wedged a small buoy into the scupper to plug it. There was no sense in letting the birds have false hope.

After a late supper I cracked the window over the galley sink a few inches and climbed into my sleeping bag. The water outside was still and dark enough to reflect the first stars. I tried to read for a while, but my mind kept leaping from image to image: my wife, Luisa in her sickbed, Huscroft, La Pérouse, and the tsunamis. I tried to relax, but my ears stayed cocked for a distant roar.

After departing Lituya Bay, La Pérouse had sailed south to California before crossing the Pacific to Macao. From there he continued on to Manila, the Sea of Japan, and the coast of Siberia, then set course for the South Pacific. When he left France, he was forty-three years old and healthy, but by the time he reached the Samoan Islands three years later, his hair and teeth were falling out, and he was muttering of dark "presentiments." At Tutuila a dozen of his men were killed in a fierce battle with the Natives. From there the expedition limped to Botany Bay, in Australia, where they stayed until March of 1788, before setting sail for Tonga.

They never made it to Tonga. After leaving Botany Bay, the expedition disappeared and was never heard from again. Buried under the pyramid of stones La Pérouse had erected on Cenotaph Island was a bottle containing a written account of the incident that had drowned twenty-one of his men in the combers at Lituya Bay's entrance. It began, "Reader, mingle your tears with our own."

As I burrowed deeper into my sleeping bag, a faint scent of cottonwood curled in through the open window. When I finally slept, it was with the sweet perfume of disaster in the air.

CHAPTER 13

I WAS UP early the next morning, boiling water for coffee and lighting a fire in the stove to drive the chill from the air. When I stumbled outside to relieve myself over the side, the deck was slick with frost, and a pale quarter moon was rising into the morning light behind Mount Crillon. While I waited for the water to boil, I tuned the ship's radio to the weather channel, then listened as a disembodied voice mumbled of swell heights and barometric pressures. The previous evening's thoughts of home and my stumbling marriage were still stewing in my brain, and I almost missed the phrase "winds light and variable," followed by "seas three feet or less." After the first cup of coffee I listened more carefully as monitoring stations up and down the coast reported lakelike conditions along two hundred miles of the gulf.

By eight o'clock I had eaten a batch of oatmeal from the pan and pulled the anchor and was motoring slowly past Cenotaph Island. I knew from the phase of the moon that the current pouring out of Lituya Bay at the change of the tide would be relatively minimal. So after a glimpse at the tide and current tables confirmed that the day's tide would be the smallest and weakest of the month, I convinced myself that I should take advantage of the unusually placid conditions and get a closer look at the coast south of the bay, in case I ever decided to hike from Lituya Bay back to Cape Spencer.* During the voyage north

---

* Quarter moons occur when the sun and the moon are at right angles to each other relative to the earth, and the gravitational pull of each cancels to some degree the pull on the sea of the other. This in turn creates weak, or "neap," tides. "Spring" tides, on the other hand, occur when the sun, the earth, and the moon are in alignment during new or full moons, and they are the largest and strongest of the lunar cycle.

the seas had been too rough to get close enough to the shore to see what the land was like.

The *Swift* slipped through the entrance with no more disturbance than if it had been entering a sheltered marina. The sea outside was so flat it was hard to believe that the smooth, silky water was the same unruly ocean that had thrown me about so violently only two days before, or that the clear blue sky had been so gray and threatening. On the horizon a large southbound vessel with the brightly varnished cap rails and cabin trim of a private yacht rolled slowly on a low, almost imperceptible swell easing in from the northwest.

I suppose it is a measure of my state of mind that I turned to port, nudged the throttle up to cruising speed, and had traveled several miles before I realized I wasn't looking at the shore or thinking about a future hike; I was running well offshore instead. It took a moment for the truth of what I was doing to rise up through the strata and substrata of my consciousness, but when it did, it was like having a swell loom up from the horizon: I was on autopilot, heading home, on a fixed course back to Cape Spencer and Juneau.

I started to throttle back, then began composing a list of reasons to keep going (there was so much work to do on the house; I didn't want to risk missing Luisa's memorial; I might never have weather this calm for the passage again; etc.). The stark white mass of La Pérouse Glacier was growing visible through the cabin window before I could allow myself to admit the real reason behind what I was doing: I missed my wife. I didn't want to end up old and alone like Jim Huscroft.

The needle of the compass swung back and forth, drifting first a few degrees to port, then to starboard as the *Swift* lifted over each passing swell. I wish I could say I composed a neat mental ledger with reasons for going home on one side and arguments for returning to Lituya Bay on the other, then reached a decision through some form of balanced reasoning. But rather than a neat toting of pros and cons, the process was in fact a messy one, a chaos of impulse and insecurity,

fears and emotions. Did I really want to go back to the stress of building and wondering where my wife was at night? And how would she
react if I reappeared before she expected me? I had been gone less than
a week; did she even miss me?

The compass quivered. I wavered but held the course. I had been
talking about the trip all winter, and for weeks anyone coming by the
house had been forced to step around piles of gear, freeze-dried food,
books, and maps in the dining area. The question of what I would say
to my friends if I abandoned the trek flitted through my head—a ludi-
crous consideration, of course, and one that can probably be attributed to the burden of the Y chromosome or free-floating testosterone.
Nonetheless, I was a bit reluctant to face the rough-edged ribbing that
would follow if I turned back before I had even started.

Then I thought of the dinner I had sat down to with my wife a
few nights before I had left. By then the gear for the trip was sorted
into a somewhat orderly stack in the middle of the dining room. A
bundle of nautical charts and topographic maps lay on the table. She
was stirring a pan of chicken adobo, a Filipino dish that is one of her
specialties, while she filled me in on the problems she was having with
a new associate. When the meal was almost ready, I started to clear the
charts from the table and thought to mention that I would be leaving
early on the morning of my departure.

"High tide's a little after six," I said. "If I leave by six thirty, I can
ride the ebb as far as Icy Strait."

"What?" she said, looking up from a clove of garlic she was chopping.

A taste like sour milk rose in my mouth as I remembered the
blank look on her face when I'd reminded her that I would be leaving
soon, and how she had asked, more distracted than curious, "Tell me
again where you're going? What is it you're doing?"

The compass swung from 150 degrees to 90, then 60, then 30,
before settling on the return course to Lituya Bay as I brought the

Swift around. With the puny tide and calm weather, I had no problem pushing through the current at the entrance. The adobo had been delicious, but it dulls the appetite to know you've disappeared from a loved one's radar.

Once inside Lituya Bay again, I unrolled a chart on the galley table and stared, trying to imagine the effects of winds and currents on various sections of the shoreline. Where I chose to leave the *Swift* at anchor while I was away was critical.

My choices were limited. Anchoring near Cenotaph Island was out, because Huscroft's records made it clear that the strongest winds blew through the bay from the northeast, and my biggest concern was dragging anchor. If I anchored on the east side of the island and the anchor lost its grip, the boat could be driven ashore and damaged. But if I anchored on the west side of the island and it broke free, the ebb might suck it out to sea through the combers at the entrance.

I traced a finger along the shore of Gilbert and Crillon inlets, as far from the entrance as possible, and considered for a moment an area of shallow water at the foot of North Crillon Glacier and another against the back wall of the fjord, then dismissed them; I would have to anchor so close to the near-vertical wall that the odds of a spring avalanche or rockfall hitting the boat or creating a wave were unacceptable.

Trying to decide was like planning a military campaign. Between storms, rocks, avalanches, currents, and the slim-but-still-possible odds of a tsunami, it was the equivalent of choosing a defensive position; I needed an avenue of retreat and a way to minimize the chance of casualties. I finally settled on an area along the northern shore where the steep walls of the bay's interior eased into the rounded hills and sloping ridges of the lowland; the softening terrain might mean that any wind blasting down from the head of the fjord would lose some velocity before reaching the *Swift*'s position. For nearly a half mile in both directions, the water ranged from thirty feet deep to a hundred instead of the two hundred to five hundred feet prevalent throughout the rest of the fjord. This meant that with plenty of line out, if the anchor did lose its grip, there was a chance it might grab again before the boat was driven into deep water and out the entrance.

The anchor rattled over the bow as I payed out sixty feet of chain, then a hundred feet of line, and put the engine in reverse. When the anchor bit into the seabed, the line grew tight and the engine slowed. I payed out another fifty feet of scope,* then opened the hatch and wrestled a second, heavier anchor that I usually reserve for riding out storms onto the deck. The second anchor went over the side, and by maneuvering carefully with the engine, I managed to drop it a couple hundred feet from the first anchor, at an angle perpendicular to the shore, so that the *Swift* rode at the yoke of a Y that would allow it to swing with changes in the wind direction and current. Then I put the engine in reverse and backed down hard, pulling first toward the head of the bay, then toward the entrance, then toward shore, revving the engine to simulate a pulling force I estimated to be the equivalent of a fifty-knot gust hurling itself against the cabin.

The anchor lines grew bar taut, but the anchors held. As a final measure I retrieved a length of hose meant to serve as a spare in case of a problem with the engine's cooling system; cutting it in half and splitting each piece lengthwise along one side with a hunting knife, I slipped a piece of the stiff hose over each anchor line at the point where it went over the side, then secured it in place with multiple lashings of twine.

---

* Scope is the ratio of anchor line to the depth of water beneath a vessel. Because the effectiveness of an anchor increases as the angle of the line to the seabed decreases, a larger ratio is preferred. For example, a 7-1 scope, or 350 feet of line out for a boat anchored in 50 feet of water, will hold much better in a strong wind than a smaller scope of, say, 2-1, or 100 feet of line used in the same depth. Anchors pulled at a low angle to the seabed tend to dig in, whereas strain more perpendicular to the seabed may cause an anchor to "break out," or come loose. "Paying out more scope" means putting out more line so the angle decreases.

If a storm rolled in and the *Swift* had to ride out a prolonged period of pitching in choppy waves, the improvised chafing gear might prevent the anchor lines from rubbing through and parting.

The surface of the bay was rippled by no more than a suggestion of wind, and the spring air was so warm that despite the patchy snow dotting the beach, I had started to sweat under my coat from wrestling with the anchors, so I shut down the engine, peeled down to my shirt, and leaned on the gunwale as I tried to imagine what other dangers might threaten the *Swift* while I left it unattended. In spite of the three glaciers at the head of the bay—Lituya Glacier, North Crillon Glacier, and Cascade Glacier—icebergs were no problem; twenty years earlier, when I had first sailed to Lituya Bay, there had been icebergs dotting the water, but in the interim all three glaciers had gone dormant. Lituya and North Crillon had slid to a halt in the late 1980s. Cascade had receded up the eastern wall of the fjord to hang like a shrunken thumb several hundred yards from the water. And if Kah-Lituya decided to kick the Fairweather Fault into motion or topple a mountain and set loose a tsunami, there was nothing I could do about it.

I went into the cabin for my hiking boots and removed the laces. Then I found a bottle of waterproofing oil in a drawer and started applying it to the leather, pushing back a feeling as I did so that there was always something waiting to rush out of the darkness—an avalanche, a tsunami, a gunshot, a cancer—by concentrating on rubbing the pungent fluid in with a circular motion. Wet feet was something I could prevent.

CHAPTER 14

THE LOADED BACKPACK went over the side into the gray inflatable skiff with a thump. Rain gear, extra clothing, a stove, food, a camera, a lightweight fishing rod, binoculars, a large hunting knife and a small saw—with everything I might need to stay dry and reasonably well fed stuffed into the pack, it had the weight and heft of a large sack of potatoes. A side pocket held the luxury of a paperback novel to help pass the time if extreme weather confined me to my tent. I could save weight by ripping out pages for fire starter after I read them. In the same pocket was a plastic hip flask of scotch.

The next thing to go into the skiff was a small inflatable kayak, carefully deflated, rolled, and lashed. Once onshore I planned to strap it to the outside of the pack along with a disassembled kayak paddle and a thin sleeping pad. The pump for the kayak was an ingenious contraption, a cone of lightweight fabric, open on one end with a plastic nozzle at the other, that allowed the user to capture a gulp of air by twisting the open end to form a bladder, then squeezing it to force the air into a valve on the kayak. Though slower and more cumbersome than a foot pump, it was a well-designed, ultralight alternative.

Then came a vinyl "river bag" containing an emergency blanket made of Mylar and heat-reflective foil, a pack of rescue flares, a jar of wooden matches, two fat candles, a light sleeping bag, and a spare handheld marine radio. A one-pound chocolate bar sealed in a plastic sandwich bag went in on top of enough canned food to last several days. Before lowering the bag into the skiff, I looped the *Swift*'s longest mooring line through the handle.

The outboard started on the first pull, sputtered and died, then started again after I flipped off the choke. I let it idle while I climbed back on board and sat at the galley table writing a note explaining that the boat was unattended because I was hiking to Dry Bay; if a passing fisherman or cruiser grew curious enough to investigate the empty boat, they might easily interpret my absence as a sign of something gone amiss. I did not want to instigate a search for a mysteriously missing person, so I signed the note, dated it, then thought to add the telephone number of a friend back in Juneau to contact if I had not returned within two weeks. I left the finished note on the table, using a spare bag of rice as a paperweight.

It took an hour or so to skiff down the bay to a bight north of the entrance, move the backpack, inflatable kayak, and river bag ashore, motor back to the anchored *Swift*, wrestle the skiff into the davits, lift it out of the water, and launch the sea kayak, but the shuttle was necessary because the pack and river bag were too cumbersome to fit into the gear compartment of the slender kayak, and I did not want to risk leaving the inflatable skiff on the beach. Bears are curious creatures, given to exploring new things with their mouths, and while a grizzly coming across the hard-shell kayak might knock it around a bit, I had heard enough stories of inflatable skiffs being torn to shreds to think damage to the kayak would be preferable. I might be able to improvise a patch of some sort for any holes punched in the molded-polyethylene kayak by ursine canines, but returning to a skiff in tatters would mean being marooned.

Once the skiff was secure, I took a last look around the cabin, checked the anchor lines, and slipped into the kayak.

The *Swift* grew small quickly as I paddled away, its dull gray hull a perfect camouflage against the granite background. From a half mile off, it disappeared into the towering landscape, and I felt a pang at the thought of returning to find that the tide or a storm had taken it. It had been my home for more than a decade and the mainstay of my guiding business for twenty years. A hundred thousand miles of salt water had passed under its keel, and I had shared innumerable unforgettable experiences with clients and friends on its decks.

Twenty years, I thought, the phrase prompting a quick calculation in my head: I was fifty-two years old, the boat twenty, and by dividing my age into the boat's, then multiplying the result by a hundred, I pulled "38 percent" from the air.

It was an irritating habit I had fallen into lately, this breaking down of the phases of my life into percentiles and fractions (for example, I had lived in Alaska forty years, or 75 percent; been at sea on the *Swift* or other boats more than half; been friends with Luisa 40 percent; etc.). It was as if I felt that by constantly measuring and calculating, I could somehow affect the amount of time I had left, which, using the biblical allotment of threescore and ten, minus my fifty-plus, was perhaps fifteen or twenty years. With three quarters of my life gone, ever smaller bits, like the two or three years it might take to finish the house (8 to 12 percent of the time remaining) or the time I had spent with my wife (to date, 4 percent of the possible total), were of growing importance.

A flock of sea ducks clustered over an area of shallows close to shore rose whistling in alarm at the approach of the kayak, peeling one after another from the surface of the water into the air as a long line of wildly flapping wings. To the west an armada of slow-moving clouds sailed as stately as Spanish galleons across an infinity of blue that stretched from heaven to horizon. Behind me the mass of the Fairweather Range bulked in endless files of peaks and ridges, fading into an eternity beyond my ability to comprehend. In the span of that world, with only the thin shell of the kayak under me and so much light and space all around, a human life seemed nothing more than the tiniest bubble rising briefly to the surface of creation. Every paddle stroke pulled me closer to the entrance, from where the sound of the surf striking the outer shore came across the dead-still waters of the bay as a metronomic whump like the muffled beating of the ocean's heart. We are candles, I remember thinking, and the wind is rising.

I turned ashore near the navigation aid marking the inshore channel, levered the rudder out of the water and backstroked to slip the kayak sideways to the beach, then braced the paddle across the cockpit to steady the boat as I stepped out. The pack, inflatable kayak, and vinyl bag were still where I had left them, leaning against the base of the navigation aid.

Shouldering the river bag, I pushed into the forest until I located an easy-to-climb tree and then began working my way as high as I could go into the branches. It took a couple of tries to toss the loosely coiled mooring line over a branch with one hand while clinging to the bag and the trunk of the tree with the other, and an awkward, one-handed, hoist-and-grab process to lift the bag higher. But once it was aloft and the line was lashed to a lower branch, I felt better, knowing that if I came back to find the *Swift* lost, there would be the added insurance of the Mylar blanket, sleeping bag, food, and candles—enough to get by on until I could flag down a passing boat. Climbing down from my perch, though, with the sharp young spruce needles scratching my face and my hands sticky with sap, I began to chide myself for the folly of thinking I needed the river bag and its minimalist camp ingredients cached near the beach to provide an extra touch of security. I already had enough in my backpack to support myself for an extended period and the *Swift*, with all its creature comforts and supplies, awaiting my return. In a place as unpredictable as the glacier coast, security is an illusory concept at best, and the river bag suddenly seemed an absurdly redundant precaution. After returning to the beach, I hoisted the kayak to my shoulder, carried it up the beach until I came to the trees, and lowered it to the ground to slide it deeper into the forest by the bow, laughing as I did so at the further absurdity of needing four boats—the *Swift*, the skiff, the kayak, and the small inflatable waiting to be lashed to my backpack—to go for a walk.

After lifting the kayak across a downed log, I flipped it upside down so it would not fill with rain. Back out on the beach it took a bit of experimenting to devise a way to lash the bundled inflatable kayak, the paddle, a life jacket, the sleeping pad, and a hundred-foot coil of rope to my pack, but I finally settled on rolling the disassembled paddle and the coil of line up inside the deflated kayak, then wrapping the thin, closed-cell foam pad around the lot and cinching the resulting bundle across the top of the pack. The life jacket clipped easily to a loop on the rear of the pack. It would swing as I walked but be handy for use as a padded seat when I felt like resting. Hoisting the loaded pack to one knee, I slid one arm through a shoulder strap and tried to stand upright, groping behind me for the remaining strap with the other hand.

Two seconds later I was flat on the ground, with one leg folded under me on the slick cobblestones, my arms pinned in a tangle of hip belts and straps. Lying there stunned, I wondered how a backpack could have learned judo; the top-heavy load had thrown me as easily as a black belt drops a stumbling tyro.

Never mind that I knew there probably wasn't another person within fifty miles; my first impulse, before taking inventory to see if I was hurt, was to scramble to my knees and look around to see if anyone was watching. I felt relieved that the only witness to the pratfall was a black oystercatcher—a spindle-legged bird not known for its grace that would be perfectly camouflaged among the dark stones of an Alaskan beach were it not for an enormous orange bill and the nervous habit of giving away its position with a series of high-pitched shrieks, which is what it did when I stood up and grasped the pack straps to try again. The oystercatcher burst from its hiding place between two boulders and flew away.

Moving carefully, I shouldered the pack, tightened the hip belt, and shrugged to settle the weight before I started walking. I had not gone a hundred feet before I knew it was too much. The load was

reasonably comfortable for the moment, but during the course of working on the house over the last year, I had come to recognize the
straining sensation I could feel in the tendons and ligaments of my
knees as the harbinger of an ache that would gradually grow and
spread into the rest of my joints throughout the day. It was sixty miles
to Dry Bay, and it suddenly seemed very far away.

Half an hour later I had emptied the pack, spread its contents
across the ground, and eliminated everything I could possibly do without. The fire-starter novel, the scotch, the fishing rod, the binoculars,
and the camera—everything that was not essential went into a plastic
bag and was stored in the bow of the kayak. I dithered over leaving the
life jacket behind but finally decided I would risk the river crossings
without it in order to rid myself of its minor weight. The rivers were
small and their waters protected, I argued. If I ran into high water
somewhere along the way, I could simply wait until it went down again.

The abandoned gear probably weighed five pounds, maybe less,
but shedding it made the pack feel, if not physically, at least psycho-
logically lighter. I had enough food to last between a week and ten
days, even with the increase in appetite that comes with living and
sleeping outdoors. If I ate well the first few days, the load would decrease rapidly, and I could spend more time gathering wild edibles.

Forming a plan has a way of making you think you know what
you're doing, and it was with a patina of confidence that I began probing the fringe of the forest for an opening I had been told was there,
the remains of a trail cut north from Lituya Bay by a gang of gold
miners in the early 1930s. The miners had intended to use a Ford
Model T to prospect the coast in comfort and had set out to build a
proper road, with logs corduroyed across the boggy spots and rocks
pitched into the deeper holes, but what I found was a swath of small-
diameter second-growth trees packed shoulder to shoulder with just
enough space left between them to serve as a path. In places where
brush or young saplings had sprung up, I was forced to angle side-

ways to keep the paddle lashed across the top of my pack from snag-
ging in the branches.

According to old mining records, the prospectors had gone bank-
rupt so quickly that their equipment, tents, and even caches of food
had been abandoned to the elements, but I was not more than a few
yards into the forest before I realized that in one respect the ambitious
road project had been a success: Judging from the amount of scat and
the number of platter-sized tracks pressed into the soft ground beneath the trees, the narrow, brush-encroached "road" had become a
bear highway. In the first hundred yards I stepped over a dozen clumps
of partially digested grass that ranged in color from the pale olive of
last autumn's leavings to the dark green of samples so fresh and wet-
looking that the only thing to suggest they had not been deposited in
the last few minutes was a lack of steam rising into the cool air. The
tracks were so thick in one area that I could distinguish the claw marks
of three different animals—two medium-sized grizzlies and one big-
footed bruiser—overlapping in a single divot of sand. Patches of wispy
brown hair clinging to the trunk of a young spruce tree beside the
trail showed where bears had used the rough bark as a signpost, rubbing the scent of their backs and bellies against it to leave notice of
their passing.

I plucked a tuft and sniffed it, catching a trace of something dry
and musky, like a hint of old dog bed, then stopped to think about the
trail ahead. There was something comforting about the narrow green
corridor after the overwhelming mass of the mountains, a confinement
that seemed to bring the world down to a manageable size, but even as
overgrown as it was, the trail still offered an energy-saving path of
least resistance to bears roaming through the mad tangle of alder,
devil's club, and berry bushes. If I stayed on it, the odds of an encounter were fairly high.

I felt for the bear spray in its holster on the hip belt of the pack
and decided to keep going. The only alternative was to go back to the

beach, cross the spit, and head north along the shore, and I knew that for a mile or more north of Lituya Bay the beach was a relentless jumble of boulders and cobbles piled one on top of the other, a moraine of rubble bulldozed into place by the advance of Lituya Glacier during the Ice Age. As the glacier gouged the fjord out of the bedrock, much of the stone it ripped loose was shoved out of the fjord and spilled north along the edge of the ocean, where it has been lying in a heap ever since, slowly being polished by the surf into smooth, ankle-busting boulders that vary in size from cannonball to small car. The only person I had talked to who had walked that part of the coast in the last ten years had called it "boulder hell" and said he would never do it again. The trail was said to outflank the worst of it.

Shoving my way through a cluster of head-high spruce saplings, I lifted one arm to protect my eyes from the needles, then froze at the sound of movement ahead. Leaves rustled, then went silent, then rustled again. Listening carefully, I thought I could hear a ragged, uneven panting.

I put one hand on the bear-spray holster and loosened the flap. My heart rate kicked up a notch as I stood frozen, ears straining to define the source of the sound; the hairs on the back of my neck struggled to sense the micro-movement of air that indicates something is very close and in motion.

Then it was behind me. And all around.

A flicker of movement through the trees to my left caught my eye, and I let out my breath; they were alive with small bodies, fluttering from branch to branch and alighting on the ground to kick through the detritus at the bottom of the trees. It was a flock of migrating thrushes. The "breathing" I heard was the muffled start-and-stop flutter of their wings.

A varied thrush with a bright orange stripe over its eyes flicked past a few feet away, followed by a flurry of hermit thrushes and robins. Farther along I could hear the faint *whit!* of a Swainson's thrush.

Everywhere I looked, birds were moving through the forest in groups of two, three, five, or a dozen.

It did not last long. The pulse of birds passed in a few minutes, and the forest grew quiet again. The great migrations of birds that flow up the coast from wintering grounds as far away as California, Mexico, Panama, and Argentina are the first line in the poem of spring in Alaska, and it was reassuring to know that in spite of the recent brutal winter, the clock of the world was still ticking. Their brief presence had enlivened the day with their passing.

I was in a reverie, thinking of how the next tick of the seasonal clock would be the wild explosion of green that hurls Alaska's mountains and forests headlong out of the cold grays and blues of winter into an almost lascivious state of lushness within the space of a few days. In the more fecund parts of the great arc of forest that sweeps a thousand miles from Ketchikan in the south to Kodiak Island on the other side of the gulf, halfway to the Bering Sea, twenty hours of daylight combine with copious amounts of rain to photosynthesize hundreds of tons of new growth per acre. Thickets of spindly, dry stalks and spare, leafless shrubs become almost impenetrable overnight, interlaced with hip-high ferns, head-high devil's club, and knee-tangling grasses. Skunk cabbage can grow four feet tall in three weeks.

Hard on the heels of the mad, loud tick of unruly green would come the musical tock of the wildflowers: first the yellow marsh marigolds and buttercups, then pale red columbines and purple shooting stars, followed by chocolate Kamchatka lilies and swaths of blue irises and forget-me-nots. Hedges of loganberry would soon be putting out perfectly white blossoms so fast it would be like watching popcorn cook off. By the solstice every meadow, riverbank, and opening in the forest would be a palette of colors as dazzling as the boldest van Gogh or Monet.

Then would come the salmon, their bellies swollen with the promise of another generation, muscling their way up the rivers to spawn. And when the salmon arrive, the real party starts, with bears, wolves, eagles, killer whales, sea lions, and otters scrambling to get at the silver hordes. The thrushes, I knew, were just the first pulse in an approaching storm of life in many forms, all hurrying to feed, grow, and procreate before the rushing hands of the clock swept summer aside and slid autumn, then winter, into its place. There is always so much to do, it seems, and so little time.

I was five minutes down the trail, still chewing on the bittersweet notion of brevity, when a loud *huff!* jarred me from my reverie. I jerked to a halt, heart leaping at the sight of a broad furry bottom disappearing around a tree just ahead; while I had been woolgathering, I had almost walked into a brown bear coming the other way. And judging from the surprised snort and the speed of its departure, I imagined that the bear, too, may have been lost in contemplation as it strolled toward the beach. Startled into flight by the sudden appearance of a tall, shambling creature coming its way, it had spun around and started to run before I'd seen it.

The encounter was over before I fully realized it had started, but a full dose of adrenaline was already burning through my veins, and I stood, heart racing, with my eyes fixed on the spot where the bear had disappeared, waiting for it to return. It took me a second to notice that the bear spray was already in my hand, that my autonomic response had been to draw it and I was holding it, arm extended, with the safety clip off. I thought to check the direction of the wind (I did not want the caustic spray blowing in my face if the bear came rushing back and I was forced to use it), but there was none. The forest was silent, the trees so still that the panting of my own breath sounded violent.

For two minutes, five, ten—I really can't say how long—I stood quietly, listening intently for some sign that the bear might be coming back. I stared down the trail, waiting for a branch to move.

There was nothing. No rustling in the underbrush, no squirrels chattering in alarm.

After my breathing settled, I lowered the spray, replaced the safety clip, and leaned on my hiking poles. A raven somewhere down the trail let out a shriek, then another, which I took to mean that it had seen the bear and the bear was still moving, putting as much room between itself and the odd creature on the trail as possible.

I told myself to relax but kept the spray in my hand, thinking about what to do next. The forest no longer seemed a comforting embrace, but more like a maze, or a spook house with too many dark corners. Still, if my information was correct, another half hour on the trail would take me beyond the worst of the bouldered beach. The topographic maps of the area showed a series of muskegs dotted with small ponds north of Lituya Bay, and with a bit of luck, I thought, the trail might open up and the visibility improve, making it less risky to continue.

I had almost made up my mind to keep going when a stick or branch cracked somewhere beyond a band of spruce trees to my right. I jerked upright, then bent low to try to peer under the spreading branches. Another snap, and the muffled sound of something walking, branches sliding along furred flanks, a shoulder pressing into a patch of old berry stalks with a sound like rustling paper.

The Tlingit call the grizzly Elder Brother or Old Man with Claws out of respect for the power of an animal they consider an emissary from the spirit world, and twenty years earlier I had listened as a Tlingit elder addressed an immense brown bear, bulldozing its way through a nearby tangle of underbrush toward us, as Grandfather; he went on to explain to it that we were sorry to have disturbed it, meant it no harm, and would be grateful if it would allow us to go on our way unmolested. At the sound of the elder's steady voice the lumbering brown bear stopped, peered at us through a patch of leafy alder, and began easing away. Afterward I decided it would be foolhardy to try to improve on an interspecies communication technique developed by a people who have been doing it for hundreds of years, and I have since

used the same etiquette on several occasions when an encounter threatened to escalate, always with good results.

So I shouted, "Hey!," not wanting to surprise whatever was coming if it stepped out onto the trail too close to me. I was almost certain
it was not the bear that had fled a few minutes earlier, but another one,
or perhaps a moose. I thumbed the safety off the spray and started
backing up the trail, my senses keyed to any motion, sound, or smell,
while trying to speak in a calm but firm voice. "I'm here. No sur-
prises," then "I don't want any trouble."

The forest fell silent. I waited, thumb on the trigger of the spray.
More silence.

Whatever it was seemed to have frozen at the sound of my voice
and was probably doing just as I was doing, standing without moving,
listening, sniffing the air, waiting.

A hundred things snap through one's head at such moments. In a
microsecond I had thought to check the wind direction again (still
calm); told myself it could be a moose (though for some reason I felt
certain it was a second bear); looked for a tree to climb (I have been
treed by a belligerent moose before); steeled myself not to run if it was
a bear and for some reason it charged (which it almost certainly would
not do, there now being no reason for it to feel surprised or threatened; in any case, because the majority of charges are bluffs, the safest
thing to do is stand one's ground); and last, felt a kick of regret at having decided not to carry a gun, even though Joel had offered to lend
me a .44 Magnum handgun when I'd mentioned I was not planning to
carry a rifle (owing to complications with carrying a weapon in a
national park, the bulk and inconvenience, etc.). I pushed the regret
away with the thought that even if I had brought a weapon, I would
have left it behind with the stuff I had cached in the kayak to save
weight.

I shuffled through all of these thoughts and several similar ones
in the space of a breath, before time took on a peculiarly elastic qual-

ity, passing slowly yet fully, with each of my senses fully tuned to one moment, then the next and the next, with each heartbeat and breath parsed from the one before it and the possibility of the one to come after by the necessity of inventorying what I could hear, see, or smell now, with no more distraction by what I could have done, or should have done, or would do next if any one of a dozen different scenarios developed in the following moment. In short, I stopped thinking and started simply sensing.

An empty mind does not miss much, and details stood out clearly—the complex colors of the mosses patterning the ground beside the trail; the cool smell of old snow drifting out from the shadows beneath the trees, mingling with the earthy compost of last year's dank and rotting grasses; a distant, faint piping so high-pitched as to be nearly inaudible that I knew to be the call of a greater yellowlegs, a sandpiper known for its habit of circling endlessly above whatever patch of marshy ground or shore it has claimed as its own, while emitting a staccato cry so relentlessly irritating that it has been known to drive humans, dogs, deer, and other birds out of the neighborhood. The yellowlegs was probably orbiting above one of the ponds I had noted on the topographic map, and the faint quality of the call gave me a measure of its distance, and thus the probable distance to open ground—information that my subconscious used to convince me that the best course of action would be retreat. I was no more than three or four hundred yards into the forest—a quarter of a mile at the most— and I had already had two run-ins. Over the next mile or so, before the trail curved back toward the beach, how many more grizzlies would I meet? Two? Three? Maybe more? Perhaps none, but there was no way to know, and after two encounters in less than half an hour, I decided to take my chances with the boulders.

I hunched my shoulders to ease the weight of the pack, tightened the hip belt, and started slowly back down the trail, glancing behind me every few steps. A jay whistled somewhere in the distance, but it was the calm *too-weet* of one jay talking to another and not the *ca-ca-ca* of an alarm call.

The forest fell quiet again. I called out, "Hey, I'm leaving," then remembered my manners and added, "Sorry to bother you." After decades of living and working in proximity to every species of Alaska's wildlife, from humpbacks to hummingbirds, I seldom hesitate to speak to an animal as if speaking to an equal, though the practice has on occasion brought an askance look from a client or a bit of amused ribbing. I usually reply by asking if they have ever spoken to a pet, or if when traveling in a foreign country where they do not understand the language, they give up speaking and resort to grunts and hand waving. It did not feel strange to try to make peace with the bear (or moose, or whatever was out there) with a liberal application of courtesy; what felt odd was a clear impression that I was suddenly talking to myself. Whether the animal was out-waiting me or had cat-footed away without making a sound, there was no sense of another presence, no tension in the air. I felt alone. The forest felt like an empty house.

So I holstered the spray and kept walking.

CHAPTER 15

BOULDER HELL. IT was a good description. It seems like it took hours of stepping carefully from stone to stone, with the metal tips of my hiking poles clicking against the smooth, hard surface of each boulder as I braced and balanced, leaned and reached, and swung myself across the up-and-down obstacle course, feeling carefully for the stone that would roll or shift beneath my foot before I committed my weight. A fine mist drifted across the beach from the booming surf, and gulls chanted above the sound of the waves. It is a defining characteristic of the mammal class that all of its members have a total of 206 bones, which in humans includes 26 in each foot, or 52 in both, for a quarter of all the bones in an adult's body. Then there are 3 bones in each knee—the patella, the tibia, and the femur, the last of which also knobs into the fused ilium, ischium, and pubis of the pelvis at the hip joint, from where the twenty-nine vertebrae of the spine ladder up to the shoulders (clavicle, scapula, and humerus) and the skull, which I began to think I must have been out of when I decided to trade the slight inconvenience of going toe-to-toe with a few grizzlies for the start-and-stop mixture of mincing steps and heavy leaps required to work my way across the boulder field. No two steps were alike, no course across the jumble preferable to any other, and before the boulders finally petered into gravel and the gravel into sand, I could feel the effect of the combined weight of my 180 pounds and the 50 or so pounds of the pack and kayak in every one of those 206 bones. It could not possibly have taken as long or been as far across the moraine as I remember it, but when I finally walked out on the other side onto level ground, it was a huge relief.

I unbuckled the hip belt, let the pack slide off my aching shoulders, and sat on a drift log to look around. While crossing the boulder field, all I could look at was my feet. Now a long run of beach stretched away before me between a dark forest and the sea. A stiff wind cut through my clothes, and a flock of gulls drifted sideways overhead in the breeze. In the distance the blue-green hump of Cape Fairweather pushed into the sea.

A dozen western sandpipers fluttered to a stop at the edge of the surf and took off again. High overhead, a thin, wavering line of dots broke apart, coalescing again as I watched and reshaping itself into a lopsided V. A rusty, musical trumpeting, barely discernible above the thump of the surf, identified it as a flock of cranes.

Half a million sandhill cranes migrate to Alaska from wintering grounds in Texas and Mexico every year, flowing north up the middle of the continent to spread across the Arctic and into Siberia. The ones overhead were probably part of a small breakaway population of some 25,000 to 30,000 that travels the Pacific Flyway every spring to reach nesting grounds in Bristol Bay, a thousand miles west of Juneau. It seemed late in the year for the cranes to be migrating—they often reach their destination by mid-April—but the unusually long and lingering winter may have delayed them. All along the coast of Alaska, from the Canadian border in the south to the Arctic, dozens of species and millions of birds were probably running late for their appointments with procreation.

The V formation stretched and re-formed as it drifted inland, finally disappearing out of sight beyond the tops of the trees. I knew it was going to take more than a late winter and a hungry spring to stop the cranes; the fossil record indicates that they have been around for at least ten million years, making them one of the oldest living animals in the world, and during that time they have been through several ice ages, immense volcanic eruptions that darkened the sky for months, and assorted other environmental calamities beyond imagining. They flew above Alaska when it was still the home of saber-toothed tigers and woolly mammoths, watched the camels and rhinoceros-like creatures that once populated the Great Plains die off, and witnessed the steady hand of evolution create great herds of bison. For the last 150 years they have spiraled aloft in the thermals over North America as the bison's prairie has been swept under by a tsunami of cornfields and asphalt parking lots.

The honking rattle of the cranes' calls grew thin and faded as the flock moved away. The tide was falling, exposing a swath of muddy beach studded with broken rocks, and I watched as a cluster of sandpipers swooped in from nowhere to settle down along the foaming edge of the surf, where they darted back and forth, needling tiny worms from the sand. A quarter of a mile or so offshore a whale rose, surging to the surface like a submarine. Its back was black and shining in the gray-green waves. It spouted, took a single deep breath with a *paaah!* like a distant cannon shot, and dove again before the wind could tear the spume of its spout away.

The whale was too far away and its appearance too brief for me to be sure what species it was, but humpbacks are ubiquitous in Southeast Alaska. Several thousand migrate north every spring from wintering grounds off Hawaii and Mexico. Over twenty thousand gray whales also make the 8,000-mile journey up the West Coast from calving grounds off Mexico's Baja peninsula to the Arctic. The bulk of them have passed through Southeast Alaska by April, however, so although it was possibly a gray, I thought it more likely to be something else—perhaps a sperm whale, a minke, a fin, or a sei. Others, like the gigantic blue whale and the North Pacific right whale, have been driven so close to the verge of extinction, owing to the rampant slaughter that lasted until an international ban on whaling was put in place in 1986, that seeing one would be like finding a brontosaurus. A right whale calf spotted in 2002 in the Bering Sea was the first documented sighting of a North Pacific right whale calf in over a hundred years.

Birds, whales, herring, salmon—I slipped to the ground to sit with my back to the log, dug into a pocket of the backpack for a bag of raisins, nuts, and chocolate chips, and watched the sandpipers flutter into the air and speed off toward Cape Spencer while I tried to envision the hundreds of species converging on Alaska from all over the globe. Even monarch butterflies are not exempt from the annual nervous compulsion that animal behaviorists call zugunruhe, the irresistible urge to cast themselves into the sky above their winter home in California and blow two thousand miles north to Alaska. Experiments have shown that the increasing sunlight of long spring days can penetrate the skulls of even caged domestic birds to reset some internal clock, which in turn sets off a storm of endocrine-induced, cage-beating restlessness and hyperphagia, or gluttony, meant to lay on a supply of energy-rich fat for the trials of migration.

As I sat there alternately consuming handfuls of my own energy-rich food and swigs of water from a plastic bottle, I imagined tying a different-colored thread to each species swarming toward Alaska and watching the sky over my head and the sea at my side turn into an arabesque of every color in the spectrum, a tapestry woven over the globe from the Arctic Circle to Patagonia. The arctic tern migrates 24,000 miles a year between Antarctica and Alaska, but has the advantage of being able to land and take off from the surface of the water when it needs a rest; the blue ribbon for pure, stouthearted endurance has to be awarded to a relatively short-legged, plump-bodied wading bird called a bar-tailed godwit. One female fitted with a radio tag by scientists on New Zealand's South Island was subsequently tracked by satellite as it flew 7,145 nonstop miles across the entire Pacific.

"It was the equivalent of a human running 43 miles an hour for more than seven days," said Rob Schuckard, the New Zealand ornithologist who headed the study. The godwit lost half its body weight during the trip, prompting Schuckard to call the long-billed bird an "outstanding organism."

Godwits, like many birds—the common mallard among them—are able to perform phenomenal feats of endurance by "sleeping" on the wing, shutting down first one side of their brain, then the other as they fly.

Most members of the avian nation have developed senses and abilities that are almost beyond my capacity to comprehend, the most miraculous of which come into play during migration. Tiny bits of magnetite in their heads sing to them of the earth's magnetic field; all of those chicks about to be born in the Arctic and the marshlands of Alaska's interior ("colts," in the case of the sandhill cranes, an archaic term that reflects the newly hatched cranes' ability to spring from the shell into almost instant mobility on gangly legs)* would spend the first nights of their lives memorizing the stars, instinctively supplying themselves with an infallible map of the constellations for their upcoming journeys. But most incredibly, birds, it seems, are able to hear in "infrasound," frequencies so far below anything the human ear can pick up that their existence has been proved only in recent decades. Pigeons, for example, react to sounds as low as 0.05 hertz, while humans can hear only down to 20 hertz. This means we can hear things that vibrate as slowly as twenty times per second—far lower than the lowest note on a bass fiddle—but birds can hear things that move only a bit more often than once per *minute*—and the only thing that moves that slow is the planet.

The minute, achingly slow movements of tectonic plates, volcanoes, and "microseisms," generated by ocean waves a thousand miles away radiating from steep-sided mountains and valley walls, all help

---

* All cranes are precocial, meaning they are able to walk and feed themselves soon after hatching. Superprecocial species such as the mound-building megapodes of Australasia hatch fully feathered and able to fly.

create an acoustic map of worldwide sonic patterns and landmarks that allows birds to remain oriented while navigating across thousands of miles, through fog, storms, and the dark.

"Birds flying over the Rockies can hear the surf of both the Atlantic and Pacific," claimed Susan Sharbaugh, a senior scientist at the Alaska Bird Observatory, during a lecture at the University of Alaska, although "hear" might not be an accurate description of the ability. A blind person's ability to sense the size of a room or the distance to a wall might be a better metaphor for the birds' experience, except their "room" is the entire planet.

I finished the last of the water and slipped the empty bottle into its holder on the hip belt as I thought about how much larger and more powerful the things we do not know or understand are than the things we do. Another cluster of western sandpipers twittered to a halt in the same spot where the earlier gang had stopped to feed, then immediately bolted, leapfrogging up the coast in a nervous land-and-leave sequence that brought them back to earth, then into the air every hundred yards or so until they disappeared in the distance. Smoke from the surf smeared the horizon, blurring the outline of Cape Fairweather just fifteen miles away, but in my mind's eye I could imagine the view the cranes and high-flying raptors must have as they work their way north, with the largest selection of 16,000-foot peaks in North America pressing in on one side and the sea, with its line of white surf shuttling back and forth, down below.

The ice fields, peaks, and fjords of Glacier Bay National Park cover 3.2 million acres and butt up against the even larger Wrangell–St. Elias National Park and Preserve, which, at 13.2 million acres, is the largest park in North America; it extends north all the way to the village of Slana on the Copper River, 400 miles away. In 1992, when Glacier Bay and Wrangell–St. Elias national parks were joined with Canada's Kluane and Alsek-Tatshenshini provincial parks to form a transborder UNESCO World Heritage Site, it became the largest

chunk of protected wilderness in the world, a sprawling jigsaw of glaciers, powerful rivers, eye-bulging peaks, and untracked forest that
encompasses more than 24 million acres. And that is just the beginning of the world spreading out below the migrating flocks. If I wanted
to—and had the gumption to cross several ice fields, glaciers, and
fjords and pick my way through the jumbled Fairweather Range—I
could keep going after I got to Dry Bay, walk north until I passed
Yakutat, then circle around 18,000-foot Mount Saint Elias and head
up the Copper River until I came out at Slana. And if I had any boot
leather left, I could head due north across the edge of the Clearwater
Mountains into the Yukon–Charley Rivers country, cross the Yukon
Flats at the Arctic Circle, and wander up the Sheenjek River until I
reached its headwaters in the Arctic National Wildlife Refuge. From
there I could step across a divide through the Davidson Mountains,
drop into the Kongakut River drainage, and follow that north to the
Beaufort Sea, a thousand miles from where I was sitting. Along the entire distance I would cross only a single road, somewhere near the tiny
settlement of Tanacross.

Envisioning the immense, untrammeled distance before me, I
wondered if this was how the pioneers of the 1800s felt when they
stood at the edge of the known world with a vast, sparsely peopled continent unrolling in front of them, in the grip of a mitochondria-deep
human zugunruhe that has wrestled with our desire for the security
and comfort of a home since the first *Australopithecus* wandered across
the burning plains of Ethiopia, holding out to us, it seems, an eternal
promise that there might be something better, more thrilling or enriching, on the other side of the horizon, on the next continent, in a
different town, at a new job, or with another person. If only we just
keep moving . . .

It was thrilling to think of being able to travel from that bouldered lip of my own known world all the way to the Beaufort Sea (and
from there, if the ice was thick and stable enough and it were humanly

possible, across the top of the world for another 4,500 miles until I staggered ashore in Norway's Svalbard islands) without encountering a single man-made impediment. But the trade-off for this sense of wonder was that I had never felt so small or so alone. I have never been a particularly bold or brave man, and the mental image of all that distance and space pierced me with a trembling loneliness that even the presence of another person could not have allayed.

I stood up, brushing the sand off my hands, and shouldered the pack, determined to shake off the feeling. What I was doing was not difficult by Alaskan standards. People dash off on footraces through a hundred miles of wilderness carrying nothing but a sleeping pad and a few pounds of granola, run dogsleds 1,100 miles through the frigid heart of winter, make solo ascents of virtually unclimbable spires, and think nothing of paddling homebuilt kayaks through the Aleutian Islands.

As I looked to make sure I was leaving nothing behind, the thought came to me that so far the trip had been a metaphor for life, from leaving the womb of the boat, with its ready supply of nourishment and comfort and the amniotic pull of the sea, to crawling and scrambling infant-wise on all fours across the rocks. Now it was time to walk upright and find my way. Grimacing at the trite analogy, I reminded myself that while the birds, fish, and whales might need all manner of astounding navigational abilities, all I had to do was keep the Pacific Ocean to my left and North America to my right, and I could not possibly get lost.

CHAPTER 16

I UNSCREWED THE cap of the water bottle and bent to fill it from a creek that should not have been there. Either my navigation was off or the map was inaccurate, but in an area as dynamic as the coast of Southeast Alaska, where glaciers can crawl several miles in a few years and whole mountains fall down, misplacing a small watercourse was no big deal. The aerial survey the map was based on had been done forty-five years ago, and almost nothing was the same, so the odds of the map or my navigation being wrong were fifty-fifty either way. It was not much of a river at the moment anyway, just a sheet of water that barely reached my ankles. The flock of teal and pintail ducks that had fled at my approach would have had to squat to get their butts wet. This creek and one I had crossed earlier were both so low that I was starting to wonder if I was carrying the kayak for no reason.

I took a swig from the bottle, capped it, and put it away, then decided to walk upstream a bit. La Pérouse had written of a Tlingit fishing camp, on one of the creeks within a few hours' walk of Lituya Bay, that had an intricate weir designed to make harvesting salmon easier, but a couple hundred yards upstream there was still nothing to indicate I was in the right place.

The odds, of course, were against it. In the two centuries since La Pérouse sailed off to oblivion, some areas along the coast have risen eight to ten feet above sea level through a process called isostatic rebound. During the Ice Age, when ice fields the size of inland seas blanketed the Fairweather Range to a depth of several thousand feet, the sheer weight of the ice compressed the earth, bedrock and all, like a brick placed on top of a sponge. When the ice started melting, the

earth began decompressing, as if it were taking a deep breath and giving a sigh of relief. In Glacier Bay the rate of rebound has been measured at over half an inch a year—too slow to watch without delicate
instruments, but the geologic equivalent of a mountain range doing
calisthenics. As the land rises, the old shoreline moves farther inland,
which meant that the location of a two-hundred-year-old waterfront
campsite might now be deep inside the trees. If there were any trace of
an ancient fishing camp, it would take a better-trained eye than mine
to see it.

It was low tide, and the trickle of water curved downstream between waist-high cutbanks that were a sure sign the stream ran deep
and swift during periods of heavy rains and when the snow in the alpine was melting rapidly. For now, the frosty nights were keeping the
snow in place. I poked farther upstream, stepping from stone to stone
along the nearly dry creek bed, then climbed up the cutbank, hoisting
myself over the top onto one knee and stabbing the hiking poles into
the ground to pull myself upright. The ground was soft and peppered
with sharp spires of new grass. Gray and black coils of goose droppings
lay scattered among the new growth where a flock had stopped to rest
and feed. Bears, too, had been at the grass—both black and grizzly,
judging from the tracks; grizzlies leave spade-sized indentations
tipped with long claw marks, and black bears have a rear track that
looks more like a small, misshapen human foot, with the points of the
claws closer to the pad.

I snapped off a blade of grass and rolled it between my fingers for
a minute while I watched upstream for movement, feeling for the
bumpy, triangular cross section that identified it as a sedge before putting it in my mouth. I chewed for a minute, then spit it out. It wasn't
bad; it was just grass—a bit fibrous for my taste, but obviously attractive to the geese and bears. Everything along the creek bank had been
cropped close to the ground, leaving ragged tufts and patches that
made the thin new growth look like it had been trimmed with shears.

Seeing no movement upstream, I walked farther in, angling away from the tree line until a line of fresh tracks on a muddy bar caught my eye—a wolf, I thought at first, but getting closer, I saw that they were too small and struck in a non-canine gait pattern. A faint line of web between two toes told me it was a river otter, traveling with the queer hunching lope of a Mustelidae, or member of the weasel clan. The tracks disappeared at the edge of a thick bed of last year's grass but were aimed at a low opening into the forest. Bending low to keep the pack from hanging up on a branch, I used one hiking pole to push a stalk of spiny devil's club aside and stepped through.

Beyond the fringe the forest opened up and I felt a flutter of trepidation, the stories of the *kushtaka* flickering through my mind the way the otter-men are said to flit back and forth between the spirit world and the shadows of the forest. The forest here was different from the woods closer to Lituya Bay; beyond the reach of the tsunamis, the trees were older, bigger, with deeper spaces between them and darker greens. The stillness beneath the canopy seemed to absorb light the way the quilt of moss creeping up the tree trunks absorbed the sigh of the wind and gave it back as silence. The green maze of rough-barked pillars crisscrossed with windfalls and thickets of brush made the thought of a soul-snatching shape-shifter luring me off into the netherworld seem not so far-fetched; after a few minutes of walking beneath the light-filtering canopy, I found it difficult to stay aligned with the sun, to distinguish north from south or east from west. It was only a few hundred yards to the beach, but it felt like I was in the middle of a thousand square miles of forest that all looked the same. Were it not for a slight slope of the land that would lead me back to the creek, it would have been easy to take a few missteps in any direction and begin to drift in aimless spirals until I disappeared.

A tingle went up my back at the thought of the number of people who over time must have wandered, growing thin and ragged, deeper and deeper into the dark forests and alder thickets on the trail of the *kushtaka* and never come out again. North of Yakutat lies a forest made up of trees growing at fun-house angles, each leaning in a different direction than its neighbors. The entire forest is growing atop the Bering Glacier, rooted in debris and soil collected on top of the ice as it crawls so slowly through the mountains that an entire oddball ecosystem has had time to develop. The helter-skelter attitudes of the trees are the result of the slow heaving and melting of their platform as it flows forward, its arboreal covering tilting and waving like the spines of a sea urchin crawling across the ocean floor. A hiker taking a single careless step on the mossy floor of the ice-cored forest could disappear into a yawning crevasse forever.

In "Mont Blanc" the poet Percy Bysshe Shelley wrote of how the glaciers of the Alps "creep . . . like snakes that watch their prey from their afar mountains," and his wife Mary Shelley's classic *Frankenstein* ends with the monster disappearing into the ice of the Arctic like a traveler dropping into a sinkhole on the Bering Glacier. The coast, I thought, with its icy serpents, moving forests, drifting watercourses, and population of angry, earth-heaving gods like Kah-Lituya, is itself a *kushtaka*, always changing shape, shifting back and forth between life-giving and deadly.

I went back the way I had come, worked my way through a crackling fringe of dead stalks at the edge of the forest, and walked back to the beach. An eagle sitting in a tree overhead spread its wings and dropped into the air at the commotion, flapped hard to gain speed, then rose, banked, and coasted out of sight up the creek. It did not seem possible for the small trickle of water fanning out into the surf to support a run of salmon pushing in from the sea, but a single violent storm could change everything. At the end of September a weather trough called the Aleutian Low drifts into the Gulf of Alaska and begins spinning off a series of low-pressure systems that make the gulf one of the most storm-pounded regions in the world. During winter the gulf averages a storm every five days, some with winds strong

enough to generate waves more than a hundred feet high. Standing on
the beach with the breeze in my face, I found it terrible and thrilling to
envision what it would be like to be on the exposed coast with such
swells charging in from the west, rising even higher as they encountered the ocean bottom a mile or more out, then beginning to lean
forward and break. Every wave would be like having a train wreck at
your feet, a thunderous avalanche that would shake the ground, squeeze
the breath from your chest, and drive an elemental fear in under your
ribs to take its place.

And it could go on for days. Twenty-five years earlier I had been
working on a tugboat towing bargeloads of logs across the gulf from a
logging camp on Afognak Island to a sawmill on the Kenai Peninsula
when one such storm had roared in from the southwest. For three days
the anemometer mounted atop the *Gale Wind*'s wheelhouse bounced
back and forth between 80 knots and 100, with higher gusts pegging
the needle at 110. The skipper used every one of the screaming engine's
twenty-nine hundred horsepower to bring the 90-foot tug and 210-foot
barge into the tenuous shelter of a slender cove, where we shortened
up the tow and circled endlessly to keep from being driven ashore.
Lashing the tug alongside the barge to increase maneuverability
meant crawling on hands and knees below the steel bulwarks for
protection from four-inch hawsers that parted with reports like
artillery fire. If the swede wire—a compound nylon-and-braided-
steel cable with a breaking strength of well over a hundred thousand
pounds—snapped, it would cut a man in two. On the first day I was
frightened, on the second terrified and praying, and by the third, before the needle of the anemometer started easing a knot, then two
knots or so every half hour to signal that the storm cell was passing, I
had drifted into a calm acceptance that an "end" of some sort was inevitable.

Steel, horsepower, and the skill of the captain brought the *Gale
Wind* through, but for the remainder of the journey, after we pulled

out of the sheltering cove into the rolling post-storm swells of the gulf to continue on to our destination, there was something about the color of the light on the heaving gray-green waters and the taste of food as I sat at the galley table listening to the rumble of the engine and the rattle of crockery in the cupboards that was somehow unreal. Everything seemed too sharp and too clear to be true.

A storm like that, with its megatons of explosive energy, could rearrange everything I was looking at, push surge after surge of raging water up the creek, bulldoze it open and dig pools sufficiently deep for salmon to spawn in, or shove enough sand, rocks, and debris into its mouth to force it off in another direction. Boulders the size of an SUV could be knocked around or disappear entirely, buried under mounds of sand hurled up from the deep. If I ever came this way again, even the boulder hell could be gone or completely reconfigured.

I sat on a stone to rest a minute, leaning back to let the rock take the weight of the pack, and thought about how things come and go, rise and disappear, seem solid but are in fact transient. Nestled in the brown grass beyond the reach of the surf was a white plastic bleach bottle and a slat from a packing crate marked with faded Asian writing—bits of jetsam dropped over the sides of fishing boats out on the gulf or cast off from lands on the far end of ocean-spanning currents. In their salt-worn state they had the look of artifacts from an extinct civilization. The notion that the earth itself could be constantly changing shape seemed to lift the lid off the world and fiddle with its inner workings. If the ground we walk on is fluid, what is there that can be fully trusted?

During the storm on the *Gale Wind* I had, of course, considered the possibility of death and given some thought to the friends and family I would leave behind. But I have almost died several times—by wandering into a field studded with leftover land mines in Southeast Asia, by being blown out of a raft by a wild hammer of water during a Class V white-water run, and through assorted misadventures aboard

other boats on various oceans, among other things. The big question
at such times always seems to be whether anyone truly loves us or will
miss us when we are gone. Of course, no one "almost" dies—either
you do or you don't; if not, it's just a dicey situation you got out of. And
over the years I have known enough people who went down with boats
or small planes or were killed in logging accidents or other forms of
industrial mayhem to understand that in the larger picture, death often leads to no more than a few column inches of newsprint or a
round of glasses being hoisted to someone's memory in a bar. Things
return to business as usual fairly quickly.

I leaned forward to lift myself from the rock, then sat back again
to consider camping where I was for the night, telling myself I was
tired from the long hump across the boulder field and the few miles I
had covered, then realized that the appeal of stopping had more to do
with proving to myself that after laboring nonstop on the house for so
many months, I finally had no appointments to keep, no commitments
to fulfill, no work to get done. I could do as I pleased. I could take a
nap or just sit and watch the tide rise and fall. I could scribble in the
sand with a stick or keep walking. It is a Newtonian basic that a body
at rest tends to stay at rest, but just knowing that I was free to let my
mind and body wander in such circuitous directions instead of checking chores off a list gave me the energy to get moving. So I pushed to
my feet and started walking. A few miles to the north lay a creek that
had been the scene of one of the strangest tragedies ever to occur in
Alaska. I had been working on a novel and a screenplay based on the
event for several years, and I wanted to see where it had happened.

CHAPTER 17

IT STARTED WITH a paragraph at the end of a story on the front page of the May 12, 1900, issue of the *Alaskan* newspaper, headlined SLOOP LOST. According to the article, a month earlier, on April 15, at the tail end of the terrible winter of 1899–1900, the schooner *Dora B.* had been in tow behind the steamship *Excelsior* outside Lituya Bay when the towline parted. The seas were heavy, and after determining the *Dora B.* to be a "staunch and completely seaworthy vessel," the *Excelsior*'s captain decided not to attempt to recover the tow, because doing so in such boisterous weather would be dangerous. Instead the crew of the *Excelsior* stood by and watched as the four men aboard the *Dora B.* hauled in the broken towline, raised a sail, and shaped a course for Lituya Bay. It was late in the evening, and the *Dora B.* was never seen again.

"The supposition is," continued the article, "that she was driven ashore and broke up. The body of a man supposed to be one of the four men on board was found on the beach at Yakutat but no clue was obtained as to his identity."

Lituya Bay had claimed another four lives, and that was that. But the final paragraph of the four-inch article reported in an almost off-hand manner that the *Excelsior*, after entering Lituya Bay during its search for the missing vessel, had returned to Juneau to report that there had been a "lynching" there.

"Two men were murdered last fall," read the yellowed clipping from the files of the Alaska State Historical Library. "And it being impossible to communicate with the authorities, and fearing to set the murderer at large . . . the Lituyans thought it proper to take the law into their own hands." The result, concluded the article, was the "ele-vation" of the criminal.

It was not a great piece of journalism, even by the standards of the time, and it suffered at the hands of a writer who apparently did not know the difference between a sloop and a schooner, each being a very different rig, and both descriptions being applied to the lost ves-sel in the space of three lines. He also got the number of murder vic-tims wrong; only one was killed and another wounded. Nonetheless, a bit more digging quickly uncovered a strange and horrific story that had leaked out to the rest of the world to be distilled through various filters of yellow journalism, until it appeared in William Randolph Hearst's *San Francisco Examiner* a year later as a lurid account of north-ern justice under a headline that screamed, WOMAN HANGS A MAN . . . AND THE LAW UPHOLDS HER! Whether the *Examiner* found it more disquieting that murder had been done or that a female had done the hanging is debatable, but the *Examiner*'s standard of journalism is not; Hearst's reporter got the hanged man's name wrong. Tagged as Michael Dennin, the killer was actually named Martin Severts. When Jack London wrote up the story for *McClure's Magazine* six years later, he apparently cribbed from the breathless *Examiner* piece, because he, too, called the killer Dennin. London then went a step farther and, for reasons I could never discover, called the woman involved Edith Whit-tlesay, although her name was Hannah Butler.

It took three hours of easy walking to get to where Justice Creek ran as clear as air over gray and green stones. The sun was hanging low in the west, and there is little that feels better at the end of a day than shedding a heavy pack. I had seen two more bears, looking up once just in time to spot a line of brown fur hobbyhorsing away be-hind a stand of tall dead grass a hundred yards away, as a young brown bear loped off at what looked like an easy pace but carried the animal quickly into the trees; the second was a darker animal grazing on a distant point that apparently picked up my scent, fleeing well before I got close enough to make out any details. Every time I left the beach to poke into the trees, there was a well-worn trail just inside the brush line, packed as wide as a grocery cart by years of heavy feet.

As I had expected, the late spring had pushed a large percentage of the bears coming out of hibernation along the Fairweather Range down onto the narrow strip of snow-free coast in search of food. Four was not an unusual number of bears to see in a day of walking in Alaska—the most I have seen is twenty-four, and there are places in the state where fifty or sixty are possible. But it was comforting to catalog the four I had encountered—five including the one I had spotted while kayaking to Huscroft's island—and to note that all had run at my approach. Along the way, small knots of shorebirds passed at regular intervals. A great blue heron unfolded at my approach to the creek and threw itself into the air with an ungainly flap and a squawk.

After rummaging through the pack, I carried the stove, the utensils, the bag of freeze-dried food, and the water bottle a hundred yards away to avoid having the smell of food permeate the ground where I planned to sleep. While I set up the stove and sorted out a package of spaghetti for dinner, I thought about Hannah Butler and the other people involved in the story. Hannah Butler was an Englishwoman who first came to North America in 1898 to work as a handmaiden to a Victorian Lady on a grand tour of the continent. While they were passing through Chicago, she met and eloped with Hans Nelson, a miner bound for the goldfields of Alaska. After arriving in Skagway, the newlyweds fell into a partnership with three men: Fragnalia Stefano (known as Harkey), a popular teamster from Juneau named Sam Christianson (or Dutchy), and Martin Severts, with whom they traveled to Lituya Bay after hearing rumors of a vein of fine placer gold there. Stormy weather often cuts into the low bluffs along the beach, exposing a layer of dense sands that contain minute flakes of the precious metal, which can then be laboriously extracted by flushing lighter material away with water pumped over the ribbed surface of a sluice box. North of Lituya Bay the auriferous layer is also heavy with garnets, which give it a reddish tint the miners referred to as "ruby." It was the ruby sands that brought Hannah Butler-Nelson and her cohorts to Justice Creek, where they built a rude cabin.

It was hardscrabble mining in an exceedingly remote and rugged place, with little chance of a big strike that would make them rich. After months of hard labor the five had only around eight hundred dollars' worth of fine gold dust to show for their efforts. By autumn, with winter approaching, they were discussing leaving and had started watching for a passing ship to flag down. Then on October 6, as the five were sitting down to dinner, Severts got up, walked outside, came back inside carrying a gun, and started shooting, killing Harkey immediately and firing a round into Christianson's neck, wounding him. Hans sat frozen until Hannah leaped up and threw herself at Severts, at which point he, too, hurled himself into the fray. One newspaper account said that Hannah managed to throw a towel or cloth around Severts's neck and choke him into unconsciousness while her husband pummeled him.

Reports of what happened next are mixed, but all agree that the Nelsons tied Severts in a bunk and began guarding him around the clock to prevent him from escaping, hoping all the while that a passing ship could be flagged down. But the days grew shorter, winter rolled in, and rescue never arrived. As winter deepened, it became increasingly difficult for the Nelsons to take turns keeping watch over their prisoner, nurse the injured Dutchy, and gather enough food and firewood to warm and feed themselves. They all began to slowly freeze and starve. Severts, suffering from his prolonged confinement and bondage, began to beg to be killed, but Hannah could not reconcile her Victorian belief in a civilized system of law and order with the urgent need to dispatch him. Although Severts wished to die, she apparently preferred to die herself rather than give in to the tempting practicality of a summary execution and "mob justice."

The solution was elegant, though bizarre. At Severts's request, the surviving miners—including the prisoner—held an election incorporating Lituya Bay as a community. Then they elected Hannah as the community's judge and Hans as a prosecutor. Hannah made careful handwritten notes of all the proceedings, as well as a transcript of the trial that followed. Two Indians were summoned from a nearby encampment to act as witnesses as Severts signed a confession stating that he had intended to kill them all for the gold, then return to Juneau and blame the murders on the Indians. At the conclusion of the trial Judge Nelson pronounced him guilty, and, as newspaper accounts later related it, the convicted prisoner was then taken to a nearby tree and "elevated."

It is not clear whether the *Excelsior*, after discovering the marooned prospectors, brought them back to Juneau or continued with its search for the missing *Dora B.* and arranged for another vessel to evacuate them, but in any case the records indicate that immediately after being rescued, Hannah contacted the authorities and turned over the transcript of the trial. After reviewing her notes, a federal judge presiding over the territory ruled Severts's death a judicial execution and declared Hannah Nelson a "plucky little woman."

The stove roared, the water boiled, and I tore open the package of freeze-dried spaghetti and poured in the water as the directions stated. Perhaps the savings in weight was worth it, but I missed the comfort of preparing food, the chopping, slicing, mixing, and spicing that is as much a part of the pleasure of cooking as the actual consumption. All I had to do was wait ten minutes for the crunchy stuff to absorb the boiling water, and I was assured enough carbohydrates to keep my body fueled, but the efficiency, rather than being a virtue, seemed a deficiency, in that it sped up the process and eliminated the slowing down and concentration that can distance one from a day's events and be as nourishing as the food.

While I waited, I watched gulls drift back and forth over the white line of the surf, glancing over my shoulder now and then to make sure the smell of cooking had not drawn any bears, and thought about the hanging. As late as 1971 there was a handwritten note in the Alaska State Historical Library in Juneau verifying Hannah's account of the event. The note has since disappeared.

That did not bother me; history muddles things, dropping facts and stirring the truth in all directions, as the various versions and twists I had come across during my research of the incident show. The question that lingered was what effect such a traumatic experience had had on Hannah and Hans.

Hannah Butler had come of age in the staid, emotionally strait-jacketed environment of Victorian England, and for her to have met and eloped with a common workingman like Hans indicated an explosion of love so strong that she was willing to abandon, perhaps forever, whatever connections she had to her class, culture, and family. For a British woman of the late 1800s, this was tantamount to a permanent self-exile.

I opened the package and stirred the spaghetti with a fork. The smell of tomato sauce rose out of the bag on a wisp of steam. Behind the hanging there seemed to be a larger story, one of a romance so overpowering that a young woman was willing to throw herself head-long into a world rife with unknowns in the company of a virtual stranger. Could there really be such an instant and impregnable connection between two people that it could withstand the stress and terror of seeing murder done, of freezing and starving, and the fear of being murdered should the killer escape? Leaving aside the utter horror of having to put a noose around Severts's neck and dig graves for the dead, the strain of sharing a small, cramped cabin through the deprived months of a terrible winter might have been enough to make even the smallest tics of one's companion gnaw and chew until they became unforgivable irritations. Hannah and Hans had been rescued, but I had wondered for years after learning of the tragedy if their marriage had survived.

I twirled a forkful of spaghetti and blew on it until it was cool enough to put in my mouth. It was not bad, but I was probably hungry enough to eat one of my socks if it was drenched in tomato sauce, and sitting there alone on a rock in the middle of that vast solitude eating a one-dish meal out of a foil bag sent a bubble of yearning through me for the days when my wife and I had shopped for, planned, and prepared meals together, shuttling back and forth between my cabin and her apartment as we had tried to out-please each other during our courtship.

Like Hans's and Hannah's, our convergence had seemed wildly romantic, a magnetic drawing-together over decades of time and distance that in the space of a few days had boiled over into something that seemed to have the capacity to become permanent. I was at the harbor, heading out to put out some crab pots. She had a small halibut that needed filleting. I had a sharp knife, and she thought a boat ride sounded fun. There was dinner together that night and the next, and on the third night she reminded me that we had met twenty years earlier, on a late-summer day in a soaking rain. The coffee shop I frequented was packed with tourists trying to get out of the storm. I offered to share my table with an attractive woman accompanied by a little girl who kept her nose in a book while I tried to make conversation with her mother. Both seemed nervous about making small talk with a bearded stranger, so I knocked back my coffee and said goodbye.

"I always remembered you," she told me the next morning, leaning back against a bolster of pillows as she reached out to take the coffee I had brought back to bed to share with her. "You were so nice. I always wondered who you were." That we had come together two decades later seemed to hint at some great order in the universe, a map of such scale that our entanglement was inevitable.

I walked to the edge of the ocean and waited for a wave to push a surge of foam up the beach, stepping back in time to avoid wetting my boots and bending to rinse the empty meal bag in the slurry of water. Then I stood and watched the waves roll ashore as I wondered what had gone wrong. What once had seemed part of a larger design now seemed a shadow play, full of disorder, or a Kabuki where little was revealed. The lump of freeze-dried food in my belly grew heavy as I thought of how coffee in bed every morning had quickly become a custom until suddenly one day it was not; we were always too busy to linger. She was contracting with two offices and running her own business. I was always in a hurry to be at work on the house by seven A.M.

A flicker of disquiet as ephemeral yet disturbing as a strand of spiderweb floating across one's eye moved through me when I remembered the number of times I had dropped by an office where she had said she would be working on a given day, only to be told that she was not on the schedule, or I had called and been told she was somewhere else or with a client. Things had become so hectic I could not keep track.

I swung the washed bag at arm's length to dry it as I walked back to the grassy bench beside the creek where I had left the pack, then put it back in the small bag holding the rest of the food and picked up the coil of line to go find a tree from which to hang the bag. It took a few minutes to locate a tall spruce with a suitably high but accessible branch and three tries to toss the line over it. With the bag pulled aloft and the end of the line tied to a second tree, my food supply was secure from bears. It was late, and long shadows were reaching out from the trees. By the time I got the tent unpacked, rolled out, staked down, and sprung into shape with the flexible poles, the sun was going down and everything inside the edge of the forest was slipping into darkness.

I was pulling the sleeping bag out of its stuff sack when I heard something that sounded like someone running a stick back and forth across the keys of a badly tuned xylophone. Someone else was keeping time with an asthmatic bicycle horn.

The eerie, discordant music floated down the creek. It was that strange moment when the sun has fallen far enough below the horizon for its rays to strike the upper atmosphere at the proper angle to be reflected back to earth and briefly beat back the oncoming darkness. The light flared, painting the forest a deep green and the water of the creek a color somewhere between rose and gold, then faded as I stared toward the sound. The odd song fell silent, then started up again. I began easing upstream, pausing every few yards to listen.

All the color was gone from the world by the time I spotted the cranes a hundred yards from camp. Everything but the sky was in shadow, and the gray birds were nearly indistinguishable against the forest background. Bobbing and weaving, the tall, gangly pair danced, stepping this way and that with wings extended, then pausing to throw back their heads and cry out with their long, pointed beaks thrust toward the sky. The air was cold, and in the near dark, with the creek chuckling to itself as it turned from silver to black under a sky dotted with a single pale star, the rusty yodeling sounded like the musical instruments of an ancient civilization being played to celebrate a migration that has continued without interruption for millions of years.

I stood and watched until a last call echoed back and forth. The cranes fell silent and became still. I eased away, feeling my way back to the tent across the uneven ground with my feet. There was still enough light for me to cover my pack and gear with a light tarp and worm into the sleeping bag without using my headlamp. I remembered reading somewhere that cranes mate for life and that ornithologists, with a scientific aversion to any phrasing that might imply emotion or affection, theorize that the complex, synchronized duet of the "unison call" strengthens "pair bonding."

I curled into the sleeping bag and stuffed a coat under my head for a pillow, thinking that I would go up the creek in the morning and look around for any remnants of the cabin used by Hans and Hannah Nelson. Their marriage, it turned out, had endured their ordeal; ten years after first learning of the tragedy, I had come across a thin pamphlet of the sort history enthusiasts put together in small towns, this one describing Atlin, a mining community of around four hundred souls located just across the border in northern British Columbia. The section detailing Atlin's gold rush history mentioned a Mr. and Mrs. Hans Nelson moving to town several years after the hanging to operate a dry goods store.

I was drifting off to sleep when a faint warbling floated in over the sound of the surf, followed by a low-pitched moan. I rose up on one elbow to listen, but for a long minute there was nothing else. Then again came the higher tone, followed by the lower note, and silence. A third exchange was more extended, drawing out into a series of alto and baritone yodels I recognized as the howling of a wolf pack, calling back and forth as they roamed.

I unzipped the door of the tent and rolled over onto my belly, propping my chin on my fists, to listen, but I heard nothing more. Wolves, too, mate for life, and this pair seemed to have said what they needed to say and moved on.

After a few minutes I zipped the door closed and nestled down into my sleeping bag. The beauty of spring is that it allows us to hope. Maybe when I got home, everything would be okay.

CHAPTER 18

I SLEPT LIKE a milk-drunk baby and was jerked half awake by a roar. Part of my brain was shouting, "Bear!" and telling me to grab the pepper spray while another piece was shouting, "Don't!" at the hand scrambling to unzip the tent flap. The sound was gone before I could do either.

I froze, stupefied and groggy, wondering if I had dreamed it. I was just starting to breathe again when the noise started over, this time coming with a rush that sounded like the beat of a helicopter wing or something huge and panting running past the tent—and again it was over before I had time to fully panic. Mystified, I fumbled with the zipper, threw back the tent flap, and crawled out on my hands and knees just in time to see a trumpeter swan skim down the creek and flap hard as it rose up the bank, passing a few feet overhead. The noise was the sound of seven-foot wings slicing the air. The bird was so close I could see every detail of its feathers and feel the pulsing beat of the wings. As surprised by my sudden appearance as I was by the swan's, it banked hard to avoid me, flapped once or twice to right itself, and sped off in pursuit of its companions.

The sun was up, but the tent was still in the shadow of the trees and covered with a thin layer of frost, so I crawled back inside and looked at my watch; I had slept only four hours, but the rush of being snatched so abruptly awake prevented me from going back to sleep. I realized that although I had seen swans every spring for decades, it had always been from a distance, and I had never once considered what they might sound like in flight or thought about the power required to push North America's heaviest bird through the air. (Imagine placing a forty-pound sack of flour on top of a large fan, then try to imagine how hard the fan would have to blow to lift the bag off the ground. The aerodynamics are different, but the tremendous thrust required would have accounted for the roar I had heard.) Then I wondered what it must be like for the swans themselves to fly with such a sound in their ears, what other birds hear when a flock of forty or fifty swans goes by, and whether it is a relief to the swans when they settle to the ground and silence returns. Is it like shutting off a jackhammer or a noisy power tool? I really had no idea. Then I wondered what else I was missing, what more must be right before my eyes every day that I do not see.

It was too much to think about before having morning coffee, so I crawled out of the tent and hurried into my clothes, blowing on my hands to warm them as I retrieved the food bag from its tree and set up the stove. While I waited for the water to boil, I dug the handheld radio out of the pack, switched on the power, and rotated the dial to the weather channel. The broadcast was so faint I had to hold the radio to my ear to interpret the scratchy voice fading in and out against a background of static. While I listened, the upper limb of the morning sun rose above the trees, lit up the surf, and spread a slow carpet of light up the beach. The day was clear, but a pale haze blurred the western sky. The weather forecast called for southwest winds to twenty knots with rain.

After the water boiled, I carried a mug of coffee down to the sun and sat on a log to drink it. I was stiff from sleeping on the ground and mildly sore all over. I fired up the stove again for a second cup, but realized I missed the smell of coffee burping out of a pot onto the embers of a fire. Then I began to wonder if this, too, was a sign of middle age, a warning that I was in danger of becoming stuck in some bygone "good old days" when everything was somehow better, or at least more tolerable, if for no other reason than that using my body hard and sleeping on something other than a soft mattress did not lead to pain.

The haze in the western sky turned gray and began crawling north in the time it took to boil water and prepare another freeze-dried meal—scrambled eggs this time, with flakes of something red and chewy that might have been peppers and others that could have been ham—and while I ate, I decided not to look for the Nelsons' cabin. Ornithologists studying the crane population in Southeast Alaska recently decided there may be a very small population that nests somewhere in the archipelago, and although no nests have been found, I did not want to disturb the dancers I had seen if they were such a pair. Plus, the thought of walking on Severts's bones or those of his victim while poking around looking for the remains of a hut that had probably been absorbed by the rainforest long ago seemed macabre.

By the time I finished eating, the frost on the tent had melted into a layer of tiny drops, so I picked it up and shook it before carrying it fully assembled down into the sun to dry while I packed. In truth, I thought, I should be grateful that the "good old days" of canvas tents and wool long johns were past, because the high-tech raincoat and rainpants I had in my pack and the synthetic clothes I was wearing were going to get me through the wind and rain that was coming in relative comfort.

The rain came an hour after I started walking, first as a fine mist that settled on my face and hands like cobwebs, then as steady pelting drops that gathered on the bill of my hat and hung there until they grew fat enough to fall. Hard on the heels of the rain came the wind. Knots of shorebirds fluttered past in groups of five to a dozen, skittering north on their way to the mudflats at the mouth of the Alsek River. From there they would fly on to the immense, rich delta of the Copper River, up on the eastern edge of Prince William Sound, to feed and fatten in groups of as many as a quarter of a million per square mile. After a series of gusts that flapped the sleeves of my raincoat and lashed at the tops of the trees, the wind settled into a stiff but steady breeze.

A mile later I was growing chilled from the wind, and rain was starting to soak down my collar, so I pushed into the timber until I came to a game trail running parallel to the beach and then kept walking out of the wind and beyond the roar of the surf. The loudest sound was my own breathing. A branch breaking underfoot sounded like a rifle shot. Only by listening carefully could I make out the hiss of rain trickling through the canopy. The mossy trail was largely silent beneath my boots.

At the base of a tree larger than the rest I unbuckled the pack and let it slide to the ground, unstrapped the bundled kayak, and pulled the tarp from the pack, followed by the stove and a pot. Behind the tree the ground was scabbed with patches of dirty snow, so I scooped off the top layer to clean it of twigs and needles, then filled the pot and put it on the stove to heat while I lashed the tarp to a branch for a lean-to. When I pulled the lines taut, the patter of rain on the tarp drummed a light tattoo.

Heedless of the damp moss, I stretched out under the tarp in my rain gear and blew on the tea to cool it, then leaned back and drank it. After the cup was empty, with the warmth of the tea in my veins, I put my hat over my face and took a nap.

I do not know how long I dozed—perhaps ten minutes, perhaps an hour—but it was long enough for the chill to creep back in, and I woke up hugging myself, although even then I continued to lie there for a minute to revel in the fact that I had no schedule to keep. At that moment I was as free as it is possible to be in the modern world. Loosed from even the normal constraints of day and night by the length of daylight at that latitude, all I had to do at that moment—or the next or the next—was whatever I wanted. Time itself was unmoored—or was until I started to shiver; I could continue to revel in my freedom or I could be warm, so I shook the rain off the tarp, folded it, packed it, shouldered my load, and started moving.

The trail ran between corridors of trees with trunks like weight lifters' thighs, grew faint, passed under branches so low I had to stoop to get by, then grew wide and distinct again beyond the next copse of trees. In places it appeared as a row of staggered holes, where for years every passing grizzly had stepped precisely into the track of every other bear that had ever preceded it, regardless of size or length of stride, until the ground had been worn into a dotted line of depressions. Why grizzlies walk so faithfully in the steps of their ancestors in some places but not in others is a mystery. No other animal I am familiar with does anything similar.

By afternoon the wind was easing, and I veered toward the beach, pushing through a chest-high stand of last year's wild parsnip. The brittle stems crackled like a brushfire, frightening a dozen sparrows into the air. Offshore, beneath a clearing sky, the sea was green, rising and falling back on itself.

After the quiet of the forest trail, coming back out into the open was like walking into a crowded party. Black-headed Bonaparte's gulls dove at the waves, chattering in angry voices; a pair of eagles drifted in a lazy helix overhead; within a mile I crossed the tracks of a mink and a bear. At a point bisected by a rib of black rock a flock of sandpipers and dunlins sped by, followed by a few turnstones and a plover.

The mind has a way of linking random moments so quickly that at times life becomes a tapestry of memories and reminders that can overrule reality; something as commonplace as a single note of song or a smell can snatch us up from where we are and drop us down somewhere else, which is what the sight of the plover did for me, by whisking me off the cold, rain-washed beach in Alaska and onto a strand of sun-warmed beach in Hawaii, where I had last seen a plover.

In the Hawaiian language the name of the delicately patterned, gold-tinged shorebird is *kolea*, a somewhat derogatory term for "one who takes and leaves," after the bird's habit of arriving hungry in the fall and leaving as soon as it grows fat. *Pluvialis fulva*, the Pacific golden plover, spends the winter flitting along tropical beaches and chasing bugs across golf courses, until March, when the males begin exchanging their winter plumage for a wild ensemble of sweeping black and white curves that flow from their heads down their breasts and shoulders, giving them an appearance as formal and dramatic as that of the protagonist in an Italian opera. In April males and females alike leave the beaches to gather in grassy meadows 9,000 feet up on the shoulder of Mauna Kea volcano, where they wait until it is time to launch en masse, spiraling higher and higher above the island on the thermals rising from the volcano until they reach the jet stream at 20,000 feet and shoot north for Alaska. Three days and 2,500 nonstop miles later the survivors of the grueling marathon flutter to a landing among glaciers and grizzlies.

The plover I saw in Hawaii had not started to change plumage yet. It was February, and my wife and I had boarded a jet four days earlier to head south along the plover's track in reverse. We had ten days to rest and, I hoped, enjoy each other's company. Before our departure I had worked so late one night laying a fine, buckwheat-colored wool carpet in the upstairs bedroom that after unbuckling my tool belt and lying down on the floor to rest my back a minute, I had fallen asleep and not woken up for two hours. She did not come home until ten P.M.

Standing there with the weight of the pack on my back and a light sprinkle of rain in my face, watching the plover needle among the rocks, I remembered the plover in Hawaii darting back and forth along the edge of the gentle blue surf surging ashore on the beach where we were lying. The sand was warm, and when I leaned over to kiss her, she smelled like tanning oil. For four days we had hiked, napped, snorkeled, gone to bed early, and slept in. On Valentine's Day, there was a table for two at a posh restaurant, complete with candlelight, a rose, and fresh tuna.

"I've had enough," she said that night as we crawled into bed. "I'm ready to go home." Stunned, I said something angry to cover my hurt and surprise. We were halfway through the vacation.

"I've got responsibilities" was her only answer. "I'd rather not be here."

The plover shot into the air and sped away. Once in the Arctic it would stand guard while its mate laid four eggs in a down-lined depression, then incubate them while she fed ceaselessly to build up enough fat for the southward migration.

I realized my shoulders were aching. Maybe I had not tried hard enough in Hawaii. Maybe I could have done something differently. In the end, she had not returned to Alaska, but the rest of our days on the island had been tense and unenjoyable.

I watched the plover disappear in the distance, wondering if I should turn around and head home again. Maybe we could fix things up, talk our problems over before the damage became irreparable. Then I remembered how she had not seemed to care that I was leaving on the trek or even known where I was going; how she no longer spoke of "we" or "us"; how she had stopped asking how my day had been and how noncommittal she had become when I asked about hers.

The wind grew colder. I looked down the beach toward Lituya, then north to Cape Fairweather. It was gray and raining in both directions. I shifted the pack on my shoulders, tightened the hip belt to take the weight, and started up the beach after the plover.

CHAPTER 19

I<small>T WAS HIGH</small> tide, and the surf was surging into the slough three miles south of Cape Fairweather. I had seen four more bears since leaving the forest and going back to the beach, including two balls of fur that had followed their mother out into the open a quarter of a mile behind me, then an immense creature with a waddle like a football player's who had eased out of sight when he had seen me. I wondered if the sow and two cubs had stood in the brush watching me go by, or if it was simply a matter of luck and timing that had brought them to the beach so soon after I had passed. I had hiked inland up the slough for a half mile or so, thinking I might find a shallow spot to cross, but the banks were steep and undercut in places by rushing water. After finding several sets of grizzly tracks in the mud and a deeply worn trail along the bank, I had grown leery of the thick brush and turned around.

The Tlingit name for the area around the slough is Dzix'Ayi, meaning "steep waterfall," but there was nothing in sight that fit that description. This did not surprise me; Fairweather Glacier has been shrinking for years, the slough has expanded, and in places brush and trees had sprung up so thick in the wake of the receding glacier that the growth seemed literally impenetrable. Steep Waterfall was an ancient name, and it was entirely possible that when the Tlingit had first settled the coast during the tail end of the Ice Age, the glacier had been enormous, reaching all the way to tidewater as a wall of ice veined with cataracts of meltwater hundreds of feet high.

Walking up the slough, I had come across a low, shattered stump that I thought indicated how tremendously and often the cape had changed. Larger in diameter than any living trees in the area, the gray, knee-high trunk poking up from the mud was a remnant of an ancient forest, buried until recently under the glacier. Thousands of years ago, at the start of the Ice Age, torrents of sand and gravel washing down the sides of the glacier had inundated the base of the trees ahead of the surging ice. Then the glacier had slid forward on top of the gravel, shearing off the trees as it had progressed. The remaining interstadial* stumps had been preserved in an oxygen-free environment beneath millions of tons of ice until the glacier had receded.

Neither fossilized nor petrified, the stump was indistinguishable from contemporary driftwood except for a peculiarly smooth, almost waxy feel to its surface and some delamination between its growth rings. Interstadial wood discovered along the banks of a river draining from a glacier near Juneau has been carbon-dated at 2,500 years old. An interstadial "forest" in Glacier Bay dates back approximately 7,000 years, and a root wad found on the southern shore of Lituya Bay was dated at 9,000. When I scuffed a wrist-sized root free of sand and mud with the toe of my boot and tapped it, it felt solid, even though it might have been a sapling when humans were just starting to develop agriculture.

With the tide high, the slough was too deep and wide to cross without inflating the kayak, and it was late, so I dropped back down to the mouth and set up camp. After putting up the tent, I went to work gathering driftwood for a fire and using a small saw to cut a spindly log into arm-sized chunks. The "saw"—a thin flexible finely toothed wire with a steel ring at each end—was slow but patiently effective when pulled back and forth like a shoe-shine rag across the silver surface. The dry wood in the center would make starting a fire after a day of pounding rain easier.

---

* *Interstadial* refers to warm periods between episodes of glaciation, during which the climate warmed up enough to allow lush forests to grow.

I had been carrying the saw for over thirty years, long enough for the oil of my fingers to have burnished the steel rings, and using it gave me time to think about the interstadial wood, about the aeons that had passed since the tree had sprouted, grown, been covered over with ice, preserved, and uncovered—and about how its decay was inevitable now that it had been exposed to the atmosphere. Rot would set in, and after it had survived intact for thousands of years, the minerals and nutrients locked in the ancient cells of the stump would be set loose to be absorbed by the roots of the grasses, sedges, alders, and spruce saplings rimming the slough, rejoining the cycle of living growth and decay.

The vast expanse of time involved made a human life seem so short and fleeting that after carrying the sectioned log back to camp, I dug into the pack for the Buddhist prayer flag Luisa had given me, spread it on a large drift log beside the tent, and weighed it down with a stone. While I split the dry heart out of a piece of firewood with a knife, kindled it into a pile of splinters and shavings, and touched a match to it, I thought about going back up the slough in the morning to cut a section from the interstadial stump's root. Perhaps a piece large enough to slice into a drawer front for the tokonoma cabinet I planned to build using the mesquite wood salvaged from my family's ancestral ranch and the three-hundred-year-old hemlock I had cut down while putting in the foundation of the house. Then I decided against it. The stump was bound to decay, or might even be washed away by a spring flood or covered with mud, but cutting into it would feel like a violation of some sort, like plucking a stalactite from an unexplored cave for a keepsake.

I built up the fire, cribbing a half-dozen logs across each other, and sat back to watch the blaze. When it was burning well, I set up the stove, boiled a quart of water, and whipped up an instant dinner of something Italian-sounding that the bag described as a delicious medley of chicken, mushrooms, and carrots but that might have been more honestly labeled as a compost of chewy flesh, fungus, and roots.

I put another log on the fire, poked it, and sat back to watch the evening fold into dusk. The prayer flag flapped in the breeze. The logs of the fire dropped like an animal settling into its nest amid a spray of sparks. Somewhere in the tangle of trees and brush behind me a great horned owl boomed, and its mate answered.* A few minutes later the male called again, this time much closer, and I stoked up the fire a bit, thinking I might see the shine of its eyes in the night if it was close enough.

The owl's renowned ability to see in the dark is a result, in part, of the tapetum lucidum, a membrane at the rear of its eye that gathers and reflects light back to the retina, where it strikes sensory cells five times as dense and numerous as a human's. Most nocturnal birds and animals have a tapetum lucidum—deer, wolves, whip-poor-wills, lemurs—and it is this that causes their eyes to shine in the beam of a headlight or campfire. But owls, like most birds, have other advantages as well; unlike humans, they have no blood vessels in their retinas, which reduces scatter and refraction and allows them to make more efficient use of low light. A more dramatic difference is the way birds' eyes *use* that light, as well as how their eyes are structured; differences that create for birds a way of perceiving the world that is beyond our limited ability to imagine. The nature of light and the colors it creates at varying wavelengths is the issue.

Color is not, as we perceive it, an intrinsic property of the object being observed, but a function of the mechanism interpreting it—that is, the eye upon which light of various wavelengths falls and the neurological system of the brain that decodes the information. Every retina—human or animal—contains rods and cones, which are the photoreceptors that translate light into nervous impulses, which are then telegraphed to the brain. Rods provide black and white vision in dim light, and cones turn bright light into color. Humans have three types of cones—red, green, and blue—which absorb most effectively at

---

* The male great horned owl calls five times, a female eight.

those points in the spectrum. As any second-grade art student knows, all colors in our human world are some mixture of these three. We are blessed in this respect, because most other mammals, with the exception of a few old-world primates, have only two types of cones, providing them with color-limited vision that can perhaps best be emulated by turning down the red adjustment in a color television.

Birds, however, have at least four types of cones. Some may have five. Tests have also proved that most, if not all, birds can see ultraviolet light, which occurs at the far end of the spectrum, at a wavelength beyond our ability to perceive. And although the ability to perceive ultraviolet light increases the *range* of light in which a bird can see, it is throwing the fourth or fifth type of cone into the equation that lifts the bird's world into a place beyond our imagining, by creating a qualitative change in the very nature of color and vision that cannot be translated into human experience. Birds literally see in another dimension, where there are colors and hues we cannot envision. We have no fourth button on our television to allow us a reference point from which to emulate the effect.

I did not hear the male again, but the female kept calling. It was late, deep dusk, but still light enough for the rods in my own retinas to be working. Gray and black, black on dark green, the surf a line of pale white in the gloom. In spite of the growing night, with their ultraviolet vision the owls could see the urine marks and small droppings of their rodent prey glowing like chips of bone or pearls under a black light, as well as things in that other dimension for which I had no concept.

I waited until the fire burned down, edging closer as it grew smaller and the night grew colder, until it was time to cover the last embers with sand and slide into my sleeping bag. Zipping up the tent door pitched my world into darkness, leaving me with only my hearing. And that, too, faded as sleep overcame me.

* * *

In the smallest hour of the night the boom of the surf woke me. It was rising, growing higher as I slept. When I opened the tent to look out, a crescent of waxing moon hung low over the horizon. A single bright star—Venus, I thought—dangled beneath its lower limb like a pendant from a diadem. Even at that hour there was still so much light in the sky that only the brightest stars could be seen, peppering the heavens with incomplete constellations. Lying there, I remembered once realizing as a child that the stars are still present during the day, just not visible to us because of the light from the sun, and being struck nearly dumb by the thought, much as I was when I read in one of my schoolbooks about how the bold hues of autumn leaves are, in reality, present throughout summer. The colors are simply hidden beneath the green of chlorophyll, which bleeds away as the days grow shorter, leaving the ever-present yellow of carotenoids and red of anthocyanins visible.

The moon was the color of a new dime, and the blue and white twinkle of Venus was breathtaking. I wondered what the flocks of plovers heading north at 20,000 feet were seeing, what array of colors and patterns they saw in the stars, or how the seas breaking far beneath them appeared in ultraviolet light. What else were they privy to, I thought, that I could not imagine, speeding through the dark heavens in their unimaginable planes of light, listening to the ultrasonic groans of the earth's tectonic plates heaving below them?

Wondering about this started me thinking of all the other things we do not know or simply cannot comprehend. From there I drifted into wondering what I was missing in my marriage, what I was unaware of that could explain the inexplicable slide from harmony to dissent, from heat to distance; sorting through memories, I tried to think of what I might have done wrong. I have a tongue as sharp as a fishhook when hurt or angry, and I wondered if I had gone too far at some point, said something too piercing—or had I not said enough? Men show love through action—in my case, by building a home, digging up a plugged septic system at an apartment building she owned in the middle of the night, working up to my ankles in human waste in an attempt to placate unhappy neighbors, or taking a day off to go into town to do her laundry when she was too busy to do it herself. But women seem to need other things, small words and gestures that men are at times oblivious to.

A series of waves higher and more violent than the rest rolled ashore, rising into a crescendo that roared and hissed up the beach. I wondered for a moment if the growing surge might reach the tent, then slid into worrying about what I would do if the marriage ended. I squirmed on the thin sleeping pad, trying to get comfortable. The ground was hard and my back ached. I felt too old to start over again.

I refolded the coat I was using for a pillow and tried to settle down. The moon drifting above the violent, hammering waves was beautiful in its serenity, and I tried for a moment to calculate how many more times in my life I would have an opportunity to see such a thing. Twelve waxing moons a year for twenty years (at best) equaled 240 moons; divided in half—or more likely, thirds—for overcast weather, that meant perhaps 80; dividing that by my chances of ever being on a beach again at just such a moment, with powerful surf rolling ashore as the moon was going down, drove the odds into the single digits. The irritating math of mortality collapsed altogether when I considered that I knew almost nothing about the transit of the moon or Venus, how often one intersected the other, or if such a thing would even happen again in my lifetime. When I looked out of the tent again, they were already drifting apart, hurtling through the emptiness of space at different speeds.

CHAPTER 20

Hard shit here."

That is the only note I scribbled on the topographic map I had been using to log campsites, thoughts, and observations during the trek, the only description I penned of the day spent slogging across Cape Fairweather. Why I sketched in a crude arrow pointing at the particular spot on the north side of the cape where I finally descended back to level ground on the far side of the five-mile-wide, five-hundred-foot-high mound of rubble, muskegs, alder thickets, ponds, rushing streams, and small, postglacial trees huddled as close together as the crowd at an outdoor spectacle escapes me. Perhaps I blocked it from my memory as something particularly difficult, because the entire traverse now resides in that single notation as an experience that bordered on dreadful.

The surf that morning was big, a storm of collapsing buildings that charged in one after another to fall thundering against the shore. The tide was rising, and the surge of the waves pushing into the slough formed a series of Vs that raced through the channel and ricocheted back and forth until their energy had dissipated.

By the time I was packed and ready to go, a weather front was moving in, with gray clouds sagging down and the first sprinkles of rain peppering the slough. After I moved inland a short distance to calmer water, it took longer to unbundle the inflatable kayak and pump it up than it did to make the crossing. The kayak was small—a shade over five feet long and three feet wide, with just enough room between the tubes to stuff the loaded pack in and squirrel myself down into the remaining space with my legs draped over my cargo. Even calling the elongated doughnut a kayak was stretching the term, but it was enough for the relatively placid crossing.

The slough was the color of pooled steel, and the south wind building behind the oncoming rain helped push me across. A flock of ducks scattered at my approach. Farther up the slough I could see something white that I thought must be a swan. After decades of emphasizing to my guiding clients the necessity of wearing a life jacket whenever we were on the water, I felt naked to be paddling without one. The roar of the surf made me feel vulnerable, although I calculated that the current pushing into the slough was probably nudging me inland, away from the mouth.

A couple of miles ahead the blunt snout of the cape came and went between curtains of rain. During the Ice Age, Fairweather Glacier plowed up a plateau of rubble as high as a fifty-story building. When a series of violent earthquakes tore through the region in 1898 and 1899, the jumbled moraine sheared off, leaving a steep face littered along its base with enormous boulders. Over the years pounding surf has ground the boulders into fantastic shapes.*

I had been warned that there was no easy way to cross Cape Fairweather. Ten years earlier a group of four friends had made the traverse, and when I asked one of them what the best course was, he curled his lip at the memory. Hank Lentfer is big, rawboned, and powerful, and his voice rumbled when he said, "The only way to do it is just do it. You just have to go," meaning it was going to be a head-down, keep-moving endurance test. It was tempting to think that, approaching from the south, I could make my way around the cape by hopping from boulder to boulder along a narrow strand of beach exposed at

---

* An 1893 topographic map of the Cape Fairweather region shows a straight coastline projecting nearly three miles farther out to sea than its present position, including a mile-long lake in an area that is now part of the continental shelf. This was not a case of careless cartography. The 1898 and 1899 earthquakes were so violent that some areas of the coast rose and fell more than fifty feet, altering the shoreline dramatically.

low tide, then climbing up to side-hill across the face as the water rose, but I had been warned by a second member of Lentfer's group that this was a sucker's bet. Richard Steele worked as a wilderness ranger in Glacier Bay National Park for years and has probably spent as much time on the outer coast as anyone alive today, and he made it clear that trying to cross the face along the tide line could result in being trapped by rising surf. He laughed as he described how he had once narrowly escaped just that predicament, but then looked at me with a hard eye to make sure I understood he was not joking.

The rain had settled into a steady downpour by the time I started climbing, following a faint segment of game trail that started up at the verge of a steep, eroded cliff overhung by undercut trees, then quickly petered out in a warren of wind-twisted spruce and brush. Pushing on, I came to other faint paths now and then that seemed to wander from narrow opening to narrow opening, but the problem with game trails is that even a large bear is only four or five feet high at the shoulder, and I am a shade over six, probably closer to seven with the bundled kayak on my pack. Every step seemed to mean pushing through a barricade of eye-poking branches and limbs that grabbed at the paddle strapped across the pack, snagged my coat and hat, and reached out to scratch my face with sharp needles. Because the terrain was so uniformly uneven, with no consistent pattern of ups or downs and no prominent features to funnel game in any particular direction, any animals crossing the cape probably had to do just as I was doing: following the path of least resistance where possible, then pushing through the tight spots as I encountered them.

Climbing higher, I began to encounter crusts of knee-deep snow. Skirting a pond like a sump where the first pale green tendrils of buckbean and marsh marigold were starting to show required "postholing" across a field of rotting snow. At each step a skim of ice crumbled into the tops of my boots. The first few times, I stopped to finger the kernels of ice from around my ankles, but I quickly gave up and

cursed myself for not having brought gaiters. The melting snow gradually wicked through my socks until my feet were soaked.

The terrain rose, dropped, was cut by up-and-down gullies lined
with thick, grasping brush. Climbing in the downpour, in loose-fitting
rain gear that clutched and bound at every step, was exhausting. My
feet were cold, but I was soon wet with sweat under the rain gear. At
first I was concerned about coming face-to-face with a bear, but I put
the thought out of my mind; between my cursing, grunting, crackling
through the brush, crunching through the drifts of snow, and stumbling, I figured every living thing on the cape could hear me coming
for miles. Stopping to break out the stove and melt a pan of snow to
replenish my water bottle, I thought that I must—*must*—have wandered
somehow into the toughest possible route for the crossing. There simply had to be an easier route I had not found.

By late afternoon I still had not found it, but the slope of the terrain started to ease, then to drop again. Veering to seaward, I started
to probe for a way down, making a false start down a too-steep gully,
then climbing down a crumbling ridge of stone that required grabbing
at roots and branches to keep from falling. When I finally stumbled
out onto the beach north of the cape, I was so beat, sodden, and be-
draggled that it was all I could do to slide the pack from my back and
dig out a pair of dry socks. It was still raining, but I had been out of
water for several hours, and I recognized the dull throb in my head as
a sign of dehydration.

Puzzling over the map, I was not sure where I was, but according
to the chart, there was a stream somewhere ahead, so after resting a
while, I grunted back into the pack and started walking.

Flocks of shorebirds flew by at regular intervals, tumbling on the wind
like blowing leaves. The stove hissed as it boiled a pan of water from
the small creek, which I had come to after walking a mile or so. I put

the pan aside to cool while I set up the tent in a copse of trees to escape the wind and stretched the tarp over the tent to shelter it. I was wet and cold but too tired to gather wood and start a fire. I barely remembered to rope the food bag up a tree before I crawled into the sleeping bag and passed out.

I rose to consciousness only once during the night, just long enough to understand that it was the drumming of heavy rain that had woken me. I could hear wind in the trees and the tarp over the tent flapping, but the surf was diminishing, which meant the gale was passing. Burrowing deeper into the sleeping bag, I was immediately gone again.

I woke thickheaded and sore, with my calves cramping. The wind had stopped, but it was still raining. I inchwormed out of the tent, crawled into my clothes, and looked around. The sea was gray-green, the sky streaked with black. The light was dull, and I was lethargic, moving slowly as I placed a small stone on one edge of the tarp to sag it into a funnel, balanced the water bottle under it to catch the trickle of rain, then waited until it was half full before I drank it.

The insides of my boots were still wet from the snow, and my sweater felt damp under my raincoat. It took several cups of hot tea, an aspirin, and a double breakfast to get moving. During the slog across Cape Fairweather I felt as though the pack had gained twenty pounds, so before stowing the food bag in it, I rummaged through the remaining freeze-dried meals, sacks of nuts, chocolate, and plastic bags of dried fruit and sorted out enough for three days, consolidating it into a plastic bag, which I then lashed to a branch as high as I could climb in a nearby tree. I planned to retrieve the cache on my way south, reasoning that there was no point in carrying it all the way to Dry Bay only to turn around and carry it back again. I might be cutting my

food supply close if it took longer than I thought it would to reach Dry
Bay and return, but three days of food should be enough for the final
leg from Cape Fairweather back to Lituya Bay and the *Swift*.

Walking on, I felt beat down and stiff. There was a steady ache in
my back and hips. I thought about stopping for a day to rest at a beach
tucked behind a small hook of land sticking out into the sea, where the
ground was crusted with a layer of an unusual soft purple color that I
took to be the ruby sands sought by the early prospectors, but I was
concerned that the rain might make the next river north impassable.
When Lentfer and Steele had traversed the coast a decade earlier, they
had flipped a raft during the crossing, dumping one of the four people
in their party and nearly losing some vital gear.

My worries were unfounded. The Tlingit called the small, silty
river that flows into the gulf a mile north of that small hook of land
Yáxwch'i héen, which translates literally as Sea Otter Creek (*yáxwch'*
for "sea otter" and *héen* for "creek"), making it one of the few geographic
features in Southeast Alaska to retain its true name. And true to its
name, a lone otter kept pace with me as I approached, eyeing me curi-
ously from just outside the surf.

Yáxwch'i héen bore no resemblance to the frothing current I had
envisioned after hearing Lentfer and Steele's stories. It was low tide,
and by bracing carefully with my hiking poles, I managed to pick my
way across in shallow water near the mouth, where the creek fanned
out before flowing into the diminishing surf. My feet were still wet
from the snow on Cape Fairweather, so I didn't care when it rose to
my knees and sloshed into my boots.

I had been walking for only a couple of hours, but I decided to
make camp, build a fire, and dry out. I knew, too, that going on when
I was already tired might be imprudent. Fatigue leads to poor judgment, and poor judgment leads to accidents. In such a remote location
a careless slip could have serious consequences.

In the time it took to set up the tent, secure the food in a tree, gather firewood, and get a blaze going, the rain slowed to a drizzle and stopped. While I made and drank a cup of coffee, a bright crack appeared in the clouds. By the time the fire had burned down, the beach was bathed in sunlight.

I pulled off my rain gear and stripped out of my damp clothes. The chilly air made the dry shirt and pants I hurried to dig out of the pack feel even warmer. Scuffing a hole in the ground beside a drift log on the bank of the river, I lined it with my raincoat, scooped it half full of water, brought a quart of water to a boil on the stove and mixed it in, then sat on the log to soak my aching feet, after stripping the laces from my boots and propping them open-tongued by the fire to dry.

It felt great. I sat back and let the sun wash over me, reheating the footbath once or twice and turning my boots to help them dry while I considered my options. I was not quite halfway to Dry Bay and was tempted to turn around, but the thought of going back across the cape was uninviting. A day of rest in the improving weather would certainly make it easier to go on to Dry Bay—and from there, covering another thirty miles to the dead end of an old logging road that would eventually lead to Yakutat was an option, provided I could resupply with food from the salmon fishermen on the Alsek River. But it was hard to think of walking another eighty miles while I was still tired. Before leaving Juneau, I had investigated the possibility of chartering a floatplane to pick me up in Dry Bay for a flight back to Lituya Bay, but the recent explosive increase in the price of fuel had driven the cost up to seven hundred dollars, which was enough to pay for a bundle of lumber, a dishwasher, or any of a hundred other things the house was still waiting for.

I used my damp shirt to wipe my feet, then pulled the raincoat from the hole and spread both on the log to dry while I continued pondering. Turning the possibilities this way and that, I considered the pros and cons, but could arrive at no conclusion.

A flash of white far out at sea caught my eye, and, looking closely,

I made out a ship, rolling on a southbound course, flags of spray flying over its bow as it shouldered into the swells. I thought I could see the gantry of a dragger, or a research vessel of some kind, but it was too far offshore to tell.

I watched the ship until it disappeared over the horizon, then ate a handful of nuts and dried fruit before pulling the prayer flag from its pocket and tying it to a branch. The wind had swung to the north, and the flag lifted and fell in the breeze. Many Buddhists believe that every flap of a prayer flag sends a prayer toward heaven, and I still remember that moment, with the flag fluttering in the wind and the sun throwing my shadow at my feet, as one of the most pleasant I had had in months. The chuckle of Sea Otter Creek sounded almost friendly. It was hard to believe it had once engulfed a 600-ton ship and swallowed it.

CHAPTER 21

It was blowing a gale on December 11, 1938, and there is no place in the world darker than the Gulf of Alaska at midnight in the middle of a winter gale. There is no horizon, no stars, nothing level in the world—just the deck under your feet, rising and falling in so many directions at once that the only thing any sensible man can do is climb into his bunk and hang on. All you can do is keep an eye glued to the compass that glows with a subdued red light, meant to keep your vision adjusted to the darkness so that when you scan the black world outside the wheelhouse windows, you might—just might—be able to distinguish the slight difference in the depth of the nothingness you are staring into that means you are about to run your ship straight into land. That pale, creamy line in the darkness could be surf breaking over a reef, or a flicker of light might be another ship appearing and disappearing in the swells, on a course that will bring you into collision. Steve Johnson, third mate of the 160-foot converted whaler the *Patterson*, did not have any of the satellite navigation equipment, radar, or sophisticated depth-sounding equipment of the trawler I had watched beat its way over the horizon—all the *Patterson* had was a compass mounted in a binnacle and an ancient tube radio.

The *Patterson* was three days out of Kodiak with a deck load of gasoline in steel drums. The weather was "stinking," blowing snow mixed with rain and seas that just kept building. The captain, Henri Bune, had been sailing in Alaskan waters for over two decades, first on square-rigged ships, then on steam- and diesel-powered vessels. He had chased whales, run freight for the salmon canneries, and pushed into the ice of the Bering Sea and the Arctic to trade for ivory. His second-in-command, a Swede named Gustaf Swanson, had also earned his master's ticket in Alaskan waters, and both thought the prudent thing to do after departing Kodiak was to set a course for Cape Saint Elias, at the entrance to Prince William Sound, where a lighthouse could guide them into shelter if necessary or, if the weather moderated, confirm their position so a new course could be set for Cape Spencer, three hundred miles to the south. What neither seems to have considered was the effect the pile of fuel drums on the deck was having on the compass. The steel barrels were throwing it off.

They never spotted the light at Cape Saint Elias. The wind backed from the southeast into the northeast, the temperature dropped, and blowing snow obscured everything. When the time Bune had calculated it should take to reach Cape Saint Elias had lapsed, he ordered a dead reckoning course for Cape Spencer.* Although no one on board knew it, the *Patterson* was lost.

The first indication that anything was wrong was a hard thump somewhere forward, at ten minutes to midnight, just as the second mate came into the wheelhouse to relieve Johnson of his watch. A second blow struck as Captain Bune ran to the bridge.

Bune telegraphed the engine room for full speed in reverse, then sent an order to the radio shack to send an SOS. No sooner had the radio operator complied than a third hammering jolt was felt, this one so violent that it disabled the radio.

Some of the sixteen crewmen aboard panicked, but others kept their heads. Someone—the records do not indicate who—fought his way forward to check the damage and sent word back to Bune that what he had first thought was snow-covered mountains looming in the dark off the bow was actually monstrous surf pounding a sandy

---

* Dead reckoning is navigation based on time, speed, and direction from a "fix," or known location. Piloting is navigating by visible landmarks, and celestial navigation uses the sun, moon, and stars. All three have generally been supplanted by electronics and satellite systems. The *Patterson*'s last sure fix was Kodiak.

shore. Hearing this, Bune made a remarkable counterintuitive decision that confirmed his seamanship and probably saved several lives: He sent an order to the engine room for full speed ahead, calculating in an instant that the *Patterson* was hard aground and had no chance of backing off; the only thing to do was to try to drive the ship as far up the beach as possible, so that when the tide dropped, if the hull remained intact, his crew would have some chance of getting off.

The ship slewed in the waves and ground forward. When the *Patterson*'s 325-horsepower engine had driven the ship as far up the beach as it would go, he ordered the lifeboats rigged and a store of survival supplies assembled.

The waves were tremendous, breaking over the stern and shoving the ship sideways to the beach. A photograph taken at daybreak from a seaplane responding to the SOS shows the *Patterson* lost in a surge of stark white foam with the dark curl of an incoming wave hanging over the hull like a fist drawn back to hammer it. The masts lean at a crazy angle, and the ship's bottom is exposed. From the bow of the ship dangles a "Jacob's ladder" of ropes and planks. After one crew member was washed overboard and a second man was lost after he insisted on going over the side to try to rescue him, the crew of the *Patterson* rigged an ingenious system known as a breeches buoy to escape to shore. Launching a lifeboat during a lull in the waves, four men managed to row ashore, drag the heavy lifeboat up the beach, then use it as an anchoring point for a line from the ship's bow. The supplies were lowered on a second line shackled to the breeches buoy line. Then the remainder of the crew went over the side down the wildly swinging Jacob's ladder and used the lines to pull themselves through the surf.

The photographer's name is not on the photo, but it was probably taken by an affable, stocky young man from Idaho named Shell Simmons. A picture of Simmons shows the quintessential Alaskan bush pilot, wearing a fur-collared leather flight jacket, with an intelligent face, a devil-may-care grin, and wrinkles of good humor around his eyes. Daring, innovative, and apparently fearless, Simmons started his flying career with a damaged Stinson monoplane he bought for one dollar. A few years later he upgraded to a boxy Lockheed Vega, a work-horse known for its carrying capacity and heavy-weather abilities. He had already earned a reputation for hair-raising rescues around Alaska when word came that the Coast Guard in Ketchikan had received the *Patterson*'s broken SOS indicating it was aground somewhere between Cape Fairweather and Yakutat. Simmons climbed aboard at first light, took off into the gale, and felt his way through the blowing snow and fog to the outer coast. The Coast Guard was in the process of assembling a crew and dispatching the cutter *Haida* from Ketchikan, but it was hours away, and it was Simmons who found the *Patterson* and radioed the cutter with its location. There were, he reported "about a dozen" survivors on the beach at Sea Otter Creek. (There were actually eighteen, plus the ship's cat, which had been sent down the breeches buoy line in a basket.) It was low tide, and there was not enough water in the creek for Simmons to land. Nor would there be high water during daylight hours for at least a week.

With visibility dropping and the severity of the squalls increasing, it was two o'clock in the afternoon before Simmons found the *Patterson*. He had no choice but to head back to Juneau. When the *Haida* arrived at the scene just before dark, its crew found the surf so heavy that a violent cross sea was breaking two miles offshore. There was no way to reach the men on the beach.

Thus began an ordeal that was to last until Christmas Eve. For a solid week the survivors huddled in a makeshift camp as the storm continued. Simmons made several air drops of supplies to the stranded men, taking off at first light into conditions no sane person would fly in to probe his way out to the coast through fog and squalls and making it back to Juneau just before dark, while the *Haida* and a second cutter, the *Morris*, which had been diverted from a voyage from Seattle to Seward to help, wallowed and pounded in the waves. Many of the crewmen on both vessels were completely disabled by violent seasickness.

After a week a desperate plan was devised to help the castaways walk out to Lituya Bay, where they could be picked up by seaplanes and the *Haida*, whose commander thought he might be able to get his surfboats through the breakers at the entrance. A third vessel, the *Cyan*, was also standing by. A critical link in the plan was to somehow get a guide to the stranded men, someone who knew the coast and could escort them south to meet the rescue party. A complicating factor was that many of the shipwrecked men were in their sixties and a few were in their seventies. The world was nearly a decade into the Great Depression, and no one could stop working just because he was getting old. More important, they were sailors, not hikers or outdoorsmen, and more accustomed to short walks on a rolling deck than to forcing their way across twenty-five miles of glaciers and flooding rivers in wind-driven snow and rain.

At a meeting in Juneau the first problem was solved when it was decided that a trapper named Nels Ludwigson, who had spent a couple of seasons running a trapline near Cape Fairweather, was the most likely man to get the *Patterson*'s crew out. The only trouble was that no one knew where he was. When they finally found him, he was in jail, serving a ten-day sentence for getting drunk and trying to break up a bar in downtown Juneau. A cooperative judge quickly suspended Ludwigson's sentence, but there was nothing to be done about the survivors' ages or physical conditions; they would just have to do the best they could, march or die.

Simmons hustled Ludwigson aboard the Lockheed early the next morning along with several boxes of food and jerry cans of extra fuel Simmons planned to cache on the beach in Lituya Bay.

After dropping off the fuel, they headed north up the coast, with the plane slamming through pockets of violent turbulence. A terrified

Ludwigson tried to cover up his fear with nonstop complaints and cursing.

Once over the castaways' camp, Simmons steered the Lockheed in a tight circle and dumped the boxes of supplies out the door, then flew as low as he dared to inspect the creek for a landing. It was too turbid to see any obstructions.

He was about to give up when he spotted a series of mountainous waves about to break across the mouth of the creek. Realizing that as the combers broke, they would hurl a flood of frothing water up the creek, he immediately banked the Lockheed into a plunging dive and landed on the brief upsurge of water.

It was an insane thing to do, but it worked. Simmons gunned the engine to drive the plane to the bank, quickly threw open the door, pitched a white-faced Ludwigson out, and shouted at the sailors that he had room to take the two worst cases of hypothermia. Third Mate Steve Johnson and Chief Engineer McDowell were helped aboard. Johnson had pneumonia, and McDowell's feet were nearly frozen.

Taking off was as bad as landing. Simmons had to taxi the Lockheed downstream into the mouth of the creek, then turn around to take off against the current. On the way downstream he hit a sunken log, and a huge sea broke just as he reached the mouth, smothering the Lockheed in a slurry of foam and sand. While he was turning the plane around, another wave roared in, flooding the creek, and he gunned it. The heavily loaded plane lifted off the water at the last second, passing so low over the sailors' camp that the canvas tents shook in its prop wash.

Only a lunatic would have had the temerity or sheer courage to do what he had done, but Simmons returned to Juneau a hero. He tried to shrug it off but later admitted to a reporter that if there had been another pound on board, "we'd never have gotten out of there."

As soon as he received word that Ludwigson was on the beach, the commander of the *Haida* ordered his cutter to head for Lituya Bay, where it was joined by the *Cyan*. Both managed to get surfboats manned by crews of volunteers through the wild breakers at the entrance. Within hours a shore party was headed north to meet Ludwigson and his castaways.

There were things in the report later released by the Coast Guard that puzzled me, including references to the northbound guardsmen's being forced to crawl across a mile-wide logjam over deep, swiftly running water; a dangerous crossing of a watercourse dubbed "Twelve Mile River"; and the rescue party's finally meeting up with Ludwigson and his charges at a large waterfall—none of which described any features I had seen, unless Twelve Mile River was the Fairweather slough during a strong ebb tide and they had skirted Cape Fairweather at sea level atop driftwood piled up by the pounding surf. Perhaps whatever geological structure had once formed a waterfall was wiped out by the terrible earthquake in 1958. In any case, what is clear is that the conditions were desperate. The temperature fell to zero with blowing snow. After the first night only four of the presumably fit young guardsmen were able to go on. These were the party's leader, Ensign Rollins; a gunner's mate named Brown; and two volunteer citizens from Juneau, Anthony Thomas and Howard Hayes. The rest were too weak to continue and had to turn back for Lituya Bay.

Meanwhile, Ludwigson was heading south with sixteen aged, exhausted men and a cat. Rollins and the others had to build a log raft to cross one river, almost losing a man when he lost his footing and was swept downstream. By the time the two parties made contact, some of the *Patterson*'s sailors could barely crawl. But in such weather, stopping was not an option, so they headed out in single file, with two of the rescuers taking point and Ludwigson and two others coming behind to help the slowest castaways. At one river some of the men were afraid to attempt the crossing, and Rollins was forced to spend nearly half an hour in waist-high cold water, coaxing them across one by one.

Sitting on the log in the sunshine in dry clothes, I found it hard to imagine how men in their sixties and seventies, after more than a week of being shipwrecked on the beach, had been capable of making a forced march over terrain that I had just taken three days to cover and that, for all my camping gear, hiking poles, hot food, and dry clothes, had left me feeling bruised and tired. All I could think was that perhaps no one quit because each man knew that if he stopped or lay down, anyone who stayed to help him would die too. A man on his own may give up, but the same man will keep going if others are depending on him.

Seventy years later Sea Otter Creek held no hint of the disaster. All of the survivors, including the cat, had made it out by Christmas, but every last trace of the ship was gone. Six hundred tons of steel had evaporated, including a cast-iron engine the size of a tanker truck. The following summer searchers found a skull and a pair of boots with feet and leg bones still in them, but it was impossible to be certain the remains were those of either of the two drowned crewmen; two brothers from Juneau had disappeared while prospecting in the same area the previous September. The decomposed body parts could have been from any of the four missing men.

My boots were dry when I slipped them on, so I wandered upriver to look around. There was a windrow of driftwood and man-made detritus, tossed off fishing boats and passing cruise ships, scattered along the verge of the woods. Some of it was at least twenty feet above sea level, which gave testament to the height and power of winter storm waves, but none of it could have come from the *Patterson*. There is not much in the record regarding what became of Ludwigson, Rollins, or the others who made such heroic efforts to get the survivors out, but Simmons went on to see his small air company grow until it was absorbed by a major airline.* The hangar he flew out of has been converted into a waterfront bar where I would probably meet friends for a drink after I returned from the trek. All but a few old-timers have forgotten the *Patterson*, but Shell Simmons's name will be around for a while; the road that runs in front of Juneau's airport is named after him.

The north wind picked up while I was poking through the trees, whispering in the branches, and I went back to the creek mouth for my coat to cut the chill. The sky had gone clear and icy blue. I decided that if the seniors on the *Patterson* could keep walking and crawling through a day and a night and all the next day, I could keep going too. Another thirty miles and I would have completed the circumnavigation of Mount Fairweather.

---

* Jim Huscroft also strapped on a pair of snowshoes and set out with a packload of grub and blankets when he first heard of the wreck, but had to turn back when his arthritic old legs failed him.

I woke up cold the next morning. Unzipping the tent revealed a world white with frost, and the air was sharp. As I hurried into my clothes, hopping from foot to foot to pull on my socks and work my feet into my boots, a shower of tiny crystals slid off the tent to the ground. When I went to retrieve the food bag, something large had walked beneath the tree. Judging from the trail, it had almost certainly been a bear; the frost had been knocked from the grass in a swath as wide as my shoulders. Before lowering the bag, I followed the trail just long enough to read how the animal had turned and walked up the bank of the creek, going upstream far enough to cross and enter the forest out of sight of the tent. I decided not to follow any farther; the bear had clearly wandered down the beach until it had sensed my presence, perhaps smelling the ashes of the fire or spotting the tent, then diverted up the river to go around me. I could not tell if it had passed within minutes or hours, but it had made an effort to avoid me, and I would afford it the same courtesy.

It was early, around four o'clock, but I had slept long enough to feel rested except for the usual kinks and knots that come with being middle-aged and sleeping on the ground. The stove hissed in the frigid air, and steam rose off the first cup of tea, then a second as I huddled on a log with the sleeping bag over my shoulders. Watching the sky go from white to blue and a snowbank under the trees go from blue to white, I wondered what magic of light and color could cause such opposite effects simultaneously. The growing daylight poured over the mountains, setting fire to the horizon, then sweeping in from the sea, greening the waves and whitening their tops as it came. When it reached me, it threw my shadow across the beach in an instant. There was a growing warmth, then a glitter of sun peeking through a gap in the trees that immediately grew too bright to look at.

The fog seemed to come out of nowhere. One minute the world was a thousand miles wide; then the horizon grew vague, and tendrils of vapor began to rise off the river. Before I finished the second cup of tea and slung the remains to the ground, there was only the tent, the log I was sitting on, and the sound of the ocean. The trees were shapes behind a gray veil, the sun a pale pearl in the sky.

I dawdled over breakfast, waiting for the fog to lift, but it appeared to be growing thicker, so after an hour or so I shook the moisture off the tent, folded it and stowed it, strapped the kayak to the top of the pack, and started walking.

Moving through the fog was a combination of peaceful and disorienting, and I kept stopping to listen, not knowing if I was hearing something moving in the forest or only imagining things. I thought I heard women crying. There were voices ahead and laughter. The sound of footsteps. Something growling.

I finally managed to scare myself silly by imagining that I was about to walk into a bear or tumble into some blind hazard, so I moved down to the sand at the edge of the surf, where I could look over my shoulder and see my own tracks following me. When I looked again, a wave had erased them; it felt like I was walking into oblivion.

I walked for hours, moving slowly, seeing nothing but waves, an occasional drift log, or the vague shape of a boulder. The sun was past the meridian when a light breeze out of the north began to push at the fog and stir it. The wind picked up, subsided, then picked up again, peeling the fog away layer by layer until suddenly there was blue sky overhead. Within minutes I was walking through a world of green trees and blue waves again.

The wind kept increasing. Soon there were whitecaps cutting across the waves. Where there had been the chill of the fog, there was now the knife of the wind, and I had to zip up my coat to dull it. A few minutes later I stopped to get out a hat and gloves. By the time I was moving again, it was blowing twenty knots.

I was surprised to find the next creek running deep and strong. I could tell from the smooth power of the channel at the mouth that it was not going to be possible to wade through this one as easily as I had all the others, so I probed upstream until I found a wide spot where the stream broke into channels, took off my pants, stuffed them in the pack to keep them dry, and started moving slowly out into the current, reaching ahead with first one, then the other hiking pole to brace myself. The first two channels were shallow, but before I was halfway across the third one, the water had risen to my calves, then my knees, then my thighs.

I was careful to be sure I had both poles set firmly on the bottom before making a move. It was slow going, and the current heaving against my legs was getting stronger with every step. There was a moment of near panic when a rock moved under one foot and I teetered, stabbing furiously with the poles to regain my balance. The strength of moving water is always greater than one remembers, and every time I have had to ford a swift river, I have been surprised by the rapidity with which the power of the current grows, each additional inch of depth seeming to square the force trying to knock my feet out from under me. What at first might seem manageable becomes suddenly and startlingly on the verge of taking control, like the slow, easy coils of an anaconda becoming a muscular squeeze. It is standard procedure when crossing a river to leave the hip belt of your pack unfastened so it is easier to get out of if you slip and it takes you under, and by the time I reached the middle of the creek, the current was whipping the loose belt around my waist. After only a few minutes in the cold water my calves began to cramp. My steps were reduced to careful, minuscule gropings, and I had to move with my knees slightly bent, angling downstream, creeping crabwise across the slick rocks.

Finally there was a step that did not take me deeper, then another and another until the water began to drop. My feet were numb when I at last scrambled out on the other side, and I told myself that at the next stream I would turn back and inflate the kayak as soon as the water reached my knees.

I found an opening out of the wind in the trees and used a shirt to dry my legs before putting on my long underwear, socks, and pants. Then I spread the shirt on a tree limb to dry while I boiled water for tea and lunched on dried fruit and chocolate. The burn of cold water on my skin became a pleasant sensation when the blood returned to my legs. With a second pan of water boiled and cooled to refill the water bottle, I was ready to start moving again.

Walking back out into the wind was like reentering the current. It was blowing hard enough to flutter the sleeves of my coat, the kind of stiff wind old-time sailors called "half a gale." In the stronger gusts I had to duck my face into my shoulder to shield my eyes from blowing sand. I tried moving into the forest again, but the only trail I found petered out in heavy brush, started again, then faded and curved inland. I worked my way back into the open, where every step was as much work as if I were walking uphill.

A couple of hours later I stopped for a break after crossing a small watercourse that barely wet my ankles, ducking upstream far enough to get behind a screen of trees. According to the map, the rivulet drained from a large lake at the foot of Grand Plateau Glacier. Perversely, after the deep and threatening crossing of the previous creek, the shallow water worried me.

Where the glacier emerges from the Fairweather Range, it is five miles wide across its face; the lake, which has a surface area of several square miles, is drained by a few small streams that drift and meander through the ridges and hills of the lowlands, and a single large, powerful outflow that drops through a slalom course of boulders. The larger outlet lay three or four miles ahead of me. Like everything else on the map, though, the positions of the glacier, the lake, and the streams that drain it were at best approximations, and two weeks before leaving Juneau, I had walked over to the cabin of a neighbor who had once lived in Yakutat, thinking he might be able to recommend a bush pilot who could advise me on current conditions. After chatting for a while, Dean reached for the phone and called a friend who he thought might have flown the coast recently.

Dean cradled the phone against one shoulder and leaned on the kitchen counter, drumming a piece of paper with a pen as he outlined my plan to his friend. There was a snort of tinny laughter followed by an indecipherable burst of words from the receiver, and Dean grinned at me as he agreed, "Yeah, he's a crazy fucker." Then there was a brief discussion of a group who had tried to hike the coast the previous summer and the two bush planes that had been wrecked when they'd had to be rescued.

"How about the lake?" Dean asked after scribbling "he says you'll never make it!" on the piece of paper and sliding it across the counter to me. "Is it open yet?" Given the severity of the preceding winter, I was concerned that even by mid-May the lake might still be covered with rotting ice. If it was, I would have no way to cross it.

After a few more jokes about life insurance and psychiatry, Dean hung up and explained that there was open water on the lake just east of the mouth of the main drainage. "He said it's breaking up. The opening is small, but who knows? Maybe it will have melted off by the time you get there."

I leaned back against a tree and listened to the wind, wondering if the low water in the creek meant that the stiff northerly had shoved the softening ice into its outlet and clogged it. The main drainage from the lake flows through a braided warren of islets, car-sized boulders, and rocks in a rush so potentially violent that when I called a park ranger stationed in Dry Bay for advice on the trek, he warned emphatically that it would be foolish to try to cross it. At the mouth the cascade spreads out before flowing into the sea, but the bottom of the river is studded with files of boulders and shattered rock that make stepping into a crack or a hole and being trapped by the force of the current a dangerous possibility. Even a knee-high current can hold someone under if it is flowing fast enough. If the outlet was clogged with ice, the only way to keep going would be to work my way inland until I came to open water through brush so thick it might make Cape Fairweather look like groomed parkland. Another option would be to push inland until I reached the glacier and try to cross it, but doing that alone, with no ice axe or crampons, seemed a dubious proposition.

Reminding myself that it was also possible that it had been so cold the night before that there was no snowmelt or runoff to fill the creek, I gave a mental shrug and decided there was no point in worrying about it until I got to the outlet and learned the facts.

I was on my feet again, about to put on my pack, when a shape in the grass caught my eye. There was a slender curve, then an eye and a beak. Toeing the matted residue of last year's summer rye aside, I bent down and tugged a piece of driftwood the length and diameter of a child's toy bow and arrow free. A small knot near one end formed the eye, and the stubbed remains of a secondary root or branch formed the beak. Time, sun, and however many miles of tumbling in the surf and sand it had taken to bring the stick to the creek, then push it high onto the bank and quilt it beneath last year's grass had also worn and rubbed the knot and root down until they had taken on an uncanny resemblance to a traditional Tlingit carving of a raven.

According to the art historian Norman Feder, Tlingit art was "perhaps the most complex and developed in North America," rich with highly stylized carvings that decorated everything from spoons and bowls to totem poles and immense wall-sized carvings, all ripe with themes meant to convey the connections between humans, animals, and the Tlingit cosmology, in which Raven was a primary character. It was Raven, in the form of Yéil, who had made the world.

The wood was damp from lying beneath the grass, which accentuated the swirls of the growth rings that formed the eye. Eyes in the shape of circles and ovals are often the central motif of Tlingit art, perhaps because they are the means by which a sentient being looks out at the world and, conversely, the portal through which the world may look back into the consciousness of that being. The stubbed root made a perfect beak, as blunt and chiseled as the tool with which Raven was said to have pried open the clamshell from which humans emerged, then the wooden box in which his grandfather kept daylight captive, bringing light to the world.

Prankster, savior, creator, and troublemaker—it seemed fitting to find this limber switch with the whimsical herald at one end hidden in the grass near Grand Plateau Glacier. Once I crossed the lake at the foot of the glacier, I would be within striking distance of Gus'eix̱, the village site where the first Tlingit to settle in the Dry Bay area had built a clan house of planks split from enormous trees. The Lukaax̱ádi, as they called themselves, knew Gus'eix̱ was a fine place to build their house. Not long after Raven had brought daylight to the world, he had spotted a large canoe floating out on the sea near Gus'eix̱; carving a long cane in the shape of an octopus tentacle, he had used it to pull the canoe ashore. The canoe—or "ark," as some versions of the story refer to it—held every kind of fish in the sea. A house attached to the bow contained all the birds. When Raven opened the door, he gave birds to the world. It is said that Raven's tracks can still be seen in the sand near Dry Bay at the place where he dragged the canoe ashore.*

I hefted the stick in one hand, then ran my fingers along its surface, feeling the smoothness of years of sun and salt, as fine as anything a woodworker could hope to replicate with sandpaper or a blade;

* Raven's ark is not the only Tlingit story with an Old Testament flavor. Mount Fairweather's real name is k̲ées' Kanadaa, which translates as "high tide all around," and ancient stories tell of a time when the people and animals had to take refuge there to escape a terrible flood.

the last thing I needed was more weight to carry, but there was something in the texture of the wood, the delicate curve of the shaft, and the way the eye-knot seemed to stare out at the world that made me want to carry it home and keep it.

I hesitated, started to toss it down, then thought better of it and pushed the small end of the stick into the ground, thinking that if I was not going to carry it away, I could at least leave it standing upright so it could look out to sea, from where Raven had brought fish and birds to the world. Then I put on my pack and walked away.

I was only a few steps away when I went back and got it.

The prayer flag stuttered in the wind, which had eased a bit but still blew with enough force to remind me that there was nothing but a thin line of beach and four thousand miles of open ocean between me and Japan. Lashed to the Raven stick for a tiny mast and braced upright in a cluster of rocks, the flag fluttered and popped while I wrestled with the tent, which kept trying to blow away every time I relaxed my grip to reach for a stake. The unhemmed edges of the flag were starting to unravel, but I figured that if, as the Buddhists say, every flap was a prayer, supplications for Luisa's soul were streaming heavenward at a devoted acolyte's pace, so I let it fly.

I was still a mile or more from the main outlet of the lake, but the beach had gone from easy walking to a thick jumble of boulders, an obstacle course I was too tired to negotiate, so after a hundred yards of scrambling, I had turned around and gone back to make camp for the night on level sand. The wind was throwing itself against a steep ridge skirting the beach, creating an updraft in which a dozen ravens tumbled and soared like flakes of ash rising above a fire. They were the first sign of life I had seen all day, so I hunkered in the lee of a massive drift log to watch their aerial antics while I cooked and ate first one bag, then another from my diminishing stock of freeze-dried food. It was clear from the way they rose and dropped on the updraft, first rocketing skyward, then falling in barrel rolls and various sweeping maneuvers, that their behavior was play, undertaken for the sheer enjoyment of using the wind to show what they could do, much as a gang of skateboarders will take turns showing off daring moves. The wind was too loud to hear their calls, but I had no doubt that if I could have, and had been fluent in raven-speak, I would have heard a whooping, back-and-forth cacophony of good-natured insults and praise, with perhaps a few catcalls directed at the pathetic earthbound biped down below, who for some reason was trying to hide from the glorious wind behind a log.

They were still there, weaving their complex diagrams in the wind, when I crawled into the shuddering tent and zipped myself into the sleeping bag.

CHAPTER 23

I DREAMED OF Luisa. Nothing symbolic or deeply meaningful; she was just there, wearing a floppy blue beret that hung to one shoulder. In the manner of dreams, the image was already fading by the time I was awake, and maybe it was just the flapping of the prayer flag that had insinuated thoughts of her into my sleep, but the dream did serve to remind me how she had always had a way with hats and the ability, or perhaps the grace and self-possession, to bring a spirited sense of fashion to odd bits of clothing that on others would have appeared simply outlandish.

I was still thinking about her while I stirred up some instant oatmeal, drank a cup of hot chocolate, and prepared for the trail. The first time we had met she'd been wearing red rubber boots, a gray wool coat with frazzled cuffs, and a warm smile, in spite of the frigid downpour that was sweeping along the shores of Admiralty Island, where we and a half dozen others had gathered for a long week of bear watching and photography one early May. The smell of the hot chocolate reminded me of the first night of that trip, when we had gathered around a tiny sheet metal wood-burning stove in an old-fashioned canvas tent to warm ourselves with mugs of cocoa dosed with peppermint-flavored schnapps, which is a dreadful drink unless one is cold and wet enough.

The memory ached like a sore tooth. I probed at it a bit longer with more memories of that week—a sunny hike through an open meadow, a burst of laughter at the absurdity of trying to bring pasta to boil over a smoky fire in heavy rain, and the odd, surprisingly comfortable feeling of knowing that one is among kindred spirits.

Then I willed myself to put such thoughts away. The dull ache in my back brought on by sleeping on the ground was pain enough without adding the sharp flavor of loss. Besides, the thought of having to hump my way across a mile or more of another boulder hell to the main outlet of the lake, then fight my way upstream was making me grumpy. That first week of bear watching with Luisa and Joel had become a spring ritual that lasted several years, during which we explored a large portion of Admiralty Island, but now I just wanted to *not* scramble and drag myself across another boulder field and *not* push myself through a mile of brush while hoping to avoid any close-quarters encounters with bears . . . and it was thinking about bears that presented me with a possible solution.

Given that no bear traveling the beach would want to walk across the jumbled moraine of boulders and sharp-edged rocks any more than I did, it was likely that over the centuries they had established another route. And finding it was simple. After packing up my gear, all I had to do was walk a few hundred yards back down the beach, turn around, and start walking north again, trying to put myself in the mind-set of a bear that had been avoiding the rough patch throughout its life. At the point where the beach began to go from sand to rock, I veered toward the forest, probing into likely openings along the base of the steep ridge behind the beach. On the third or fourth try I pushed aside a low branch and stepped onto a game trail as distinct and clear as a path through a city park. The first thing I saw was a pile of fresh bear droppings. The second thing I saw was another pile, but the trail looked easy, so I went on.

An hour later I was standing on the shore of the lake. The water was milky turquoise, the color of the sky reflecting off the lake's burden of silt, granite ground so fine and weightless by the movement of the glacier that it hung suspended in the water column and turned it opaque. There was still ice on the lake, but it was half a mile away. Beyond the ice the view was stunning. Grand Plateau Glacier lay draped over the mountains like a wedding veil. Immense, glaring-white peaks pushed up into a hard blue sky.

Grand Plateau Glacier crawls out of a staggering warren of 3,000- to 9,000-foot mountains that run generally parallel to the coast north of Mount Fairweather, riven in all directions by a web of ice fields and glaciers that spans the area between Alaska, British Columbia, and the Yukon. Before the partitioning of the region into the territories of modern nations—and more recently into a cluster of national and provincial parks—the Tlingit knew and used the network of glaciers as travel corridors, moving back and forth between the coast and the interior, where they traded with the Champagne and Aishihik First Nations and the Athabaskan Tutchone. In 1999 three sheep hunters— Mike Roche, Warren Ward, and Bill Hanlon, all from Nelson, B.C.— were eight hours above their base camp, high in the peaks above the Tatshenshini River, when they made a remarkable discovery. They had already taken two big rams and were working their way along the edge of a glacier searching for a third when they saw something extraordinary: a piece of wood. Roche was a science teacher, Ward taught English, and Hanlon taught shop at the high school in Nelson, and all three had enough experience in the sterile environment of the glacial highlands to understand that wood of any sort was out of place. A bit farther on they found another piece, and when they put the two pieces together, they formed what looked like a walking stick. Then they spotted a third piece—and this one had a hook carved in one end like an atlatl, a short throwing board used to increase the power of a hurled spear.

"That's when we began to realize we'd come across something really special," Roche later said. Ward used his binoculars to scan the area and quickly spotted a mitten and what looked like a pile of debris out on the glacier. Carefully working their way there, they found something that took their breath away: Wedged in a crevice were the frozen remains of an ancient hunter. Nearby lay a primitive knife with a bone handle in a leather sheath. Next to that was a cloak made of ground squirrel fur and what appeared to be a backpack of some sort.

To their everlasting credit, they understood immediately the magnitude of their discovery and had the presence of mind to spend half an hour carefully marking the location on a map before making the decision to call off their hunt and head back to their base camp. The next morning they started walking out so they could report their find to archaeologists at the Beringia Museum, a hundred miles away in Whitehorse, in the Yukon Territory. They decided to take the knife and sheath along to prove their claim, although Ward later admitted he'd been reluctant to remove anything, saying that he had taught *The Curse of King Tut's Tomb* to his English students for twenty years, and "since all the people involved with that [discovery] died of unnatural causes," it had made him uncomfortable to do so.

As far as I know, no misfortune has befallen the three hunters since their discovery, but the excitement it caused was understandable: It was the first discovery of a human body frozen into a glacier in North America. Eight years earlier a body found in a glacier straddling the border between Austria and Italy had turned out to be 5,300 years old, and some wondered if this was North America's equivalent.

Three days later a helicopter bearing a team of archaeologists and representatives of the Champagne and Aishihik tribes, whose traditional territory included the area where the body had been found, flew into the site to confirm what was there. The next three days were spent carefully surveying and documenting the condition and location of artifacts associated with the body. Then the body was removed by a team of specialists, after being prayed over by Champagne and Aishihik elders, who had given the name Kwäday Dän Ts'ìnchi, or Long Ago Person Found, to their recovered ancestor. What followed was a blending of traditional knowledge and modern forensic technology that allowed the story of Kwäday Dän Ts'ìnchi to unfold in a remarkable way.

Within weeks it had been determined that the warrior had been between nineteen and twenty-one years old when he'd died. The initial radiocarbon dating indicated that he had died approximately five hundred years ago. The examination of bone and tissue samples through stable-isotope analysis and mass spectrometry showed that he had spent most of his life subsisting on a diet of seafood, which indicated that he had been born into one of the coastal bands that harvested salmon, halibut, and shellfish. Next, a chemical analysis of his hair showed that for several months prior to his death he had *not* eaten seafood, but had instead been in the interior, where the Native diet is based on moose and caribou. Pollen and spores from interior plants removed from his clothing confirmed this. Yet most amazing was what the contents of his digestive system revealed: There was partially digested beach asparagus, or glasswort, in his stomach and meat from a crustacean, possibly shrimp. Beach asparagus is a common coastal plant known for its salty, crisp flavor, which I had been hoping to find during the trek to augment my diet of freeze-dried food. It grows only next to salt water.

I dropped my pack to the ground and stared at Grand Plateau Glacier. I was not as tired as I had been after crossing Cape Fairweather, but I was feeling the wear and tear of the past few days in my knees and shoulders. Kwäday Dän Ts'ìnchi had been found 4,500 feet above sea level (which meant that, give or take a few hundred feet for however far the glacier had traveled since he had died, he could have been as high as 5,000 feet or more). Yet glasswort, which has a high water content, is quickly digested, and the location where he was found was *nearly seventy miles from the nearest salt water*. In other words, he had been traveling remarkably fast and light. (Two pieces of dried chum salmon, a species that spawns only in the lower, coastal reaches of the region's rivers, were also found among his things.) The glasswort in his stomach indicated that he had left the coast less than three days before he had died, yet he had already hiked, climbed, and pushed himself to an altitude that even a well-equipped climbing party might take weeks to reach. There, it was thought, he had probably been caught in a storm and died of hypothermia.

I looked at the sweep of the glacier rising into regions of permanent snow and naked stone and wondered what could have sent a young man on such a mad scramble across such inhospitable mountains. The evidence shows that after a life on the coast, he had gone inland for a few months, returned to the coast for a brief period, then turned around and set off again almost immediately on what must have amounted to a headlong run across terrain that usually forces people to move slowly and carefully, or prevents them from traveling at all. The beach asparagus, the salmon, and the pollen found on his clothes indicate that he was almost surely traveling during the first or middle part of August, at the end of the summer, when the chum salmon were spawning, but radiocarbon dating of his equipment indicates that his final journey took place sometime during the tail end of the Little Ice Age, when conditions would have been more extreme than they were by the time I stood on the edge of the lake wondering about his motivation.

I was also puzzled by how he could have been caught by a storm. I do not think it is an exaggeration to say that after decades of living and working at sea and in the wilds of Alaska, I have a "weather eye" that is somewhat more acute than the average city dweller's. Armed with the knowledge and experience of his ancestors, the young warrior must have been able to look at the sky and sniff the wind for approaching weather changes with skills a quantum leap beyond my own. It was hard for me to believe that he didn't know what he was looking at when he saw the sky begin to darken, or when the clouds wrapping themselves around the peaks took on the lenticular shape that means strong winds are blowing aloft. But for some reason he kept going.

Then I remembered how when I'd been in my twenties, I had fallen in love with a dark-eyed girl with a quick smile who lived in

Anchorage, 135 miles from where I was living, in the small town of Seward, at the far end of a narrow, winding highway that was often closed by blizzards and avalanches. I was making my living as a fisherman, longlining halibut during the summer and picking up odd jobs as a carpenter and a sawmill hand in the winter. I owned a 1963 Dodge pickup with 90,000 miles on the odometer that I had bought for three hundred dollars from the U.S. Forest Service at a surplus-equipment auction. Gas was sixty cents a gallon, and love, to paraphrase a country and western song popular at the time, was only three dollars away.

The affair burned like magnesium through July and August, on into autumn, and deep into the heart of winter. By the time that dark-eyed girl called on a stormy December evening to say how much she missed me, frequent trips up and down the highway had worn the tires on the Dodge paper-thin. The only gas station in town closed at six o'clock, and the gas gauge was on empty, but there was a tone in her voice that said she truly wanted to see me that night.

The highway department had already announced that a road closure was imminent due to the avalanche danger, but a sympathetic friend helped me siphon five gallons of fuel from a generator at the sawmill where he was a night watchman. I stuffed three one-dollar bills into an envelope, pushed it under the door of the mill's office, and was on my way, sliding almost out of control in wet snow that was already a foot deep and growing deeper every minute. The barrage of fat, wet flakes was coming down so thick and fast that the windshield wipers could barely keep up with it.

Six hours later I was still crawling along at twenty miles an hour, working the stick shift and trying to stay off the brakes as I slipped past the flashing yellow warning lights 130 miles away, at the northern end of the worst of it. It was one o'clock in the morning before I got to her cabin on the outskirts of Anchorage, but the lamp in the window was still burning.

There is no fever in the world like it, and standing there in the cold north wind, watching ruffled whitecaps roll across Grand Plateau Lake toward me, I remembered how that flaming love had eventually burned down and gone out, then wondered how long, or if, the diminishing fires of my marriage could be kept burning. I had no doubt that Kwäday Dän Ts'ìnchi, after coming of age on the coast, had gone inland, perhaps with a trading party, and met a girl with dark eyes and long black hair who moved in a way that reminded him of tall grass in the wind and touched something inside him he had never known before.

Any serious scientist would rightly scoff at such a notion for lack of evidence, but I had no trouble envisioning Kwäday Dän Ts'ìnchi stumbling back to his home on the coast with his heart still behind him somewhere in the interior. What else could account for a young man in the prime of his life throwing a knife, a few chunks of fish, and some odds and ends into a bag and taking off at what must have amounted to almost a dead run across such hostile territory? What else would push a man up into that world of ice and bald stone by himself, other than the realization that summer was passing, winter was looming, and once the passes closed, it would be another year before he could see her? Maybe he *had* looked at the sky and seen boiling weather approaching, but, just as I had done when I'd gotten a late-evening phone call during a growing storm, he'd said to himself, "I can make it."

But he was wrong.

CHAPTER 24

CROSSING THE LAKE was almost easy. By the time I worked my way to a point well east of the outlet and inflated the kayak, the wind had begun to drop. Dotted among the clusters of softening skim ice out in the middle of the lake were a few icebergs, car-sized bits that had crumbled away from the face of the glacier the previous summer. The wind had slowed to a strong breeze before I had the pack loaded into the kayak and the prayer flag on its raven mast wedged into the bow, but it was still strong enough to push me crabwise across the lake toward the outflow whenever I stopped paddling, so I angled toward the mountains and dipped hard, kneeling in the bottom of the kayak, wishing I had brought a life jacket. A steepled iceberg a quarter of a mile away gave me something to aim for; once I reached it, I knew I was far enough across the lake to tack back toward the northern shore without being blown or sucked into the outflow, which I could hear roaring off to my left like a waterfall. I was sweating under my clothes by the time I pulled up to the beach, unwound my cramping legs, and stepped out into ankle-deep water. I ate an energy bar while I let the kayak deflate, then I rolled it and tied it to the top of the pack, wedging the prayer flag into the lashings, where it could fly upright behind my head.

Getting back to the coast again was almost a mirror image of the morning, with an easy walk on a generally well-defined trail. Here and there it wandered off into red herring byways where bears had decided to divert into thick patches of brush, but these inevitably petered out into riots of thorny, head-high devil's club that quickly turned me around.

It was probably no more than a mile to the beach, and I covered it quickly, in under an hour, but stepping from the sun-dappled forest into the sound of the surf on the north side of the glacier was like walking into a different world. The scope of the sea and the wall of trees were the same, but something simply *felt* different. It was not just that spring seemed more advanced there, although there were fewer snow-banks and more spears of false dogwood and twisted stalk poking up from the moss. It took spotting an axe-cut limb and an arrangement of stones darkened by fire to make the difference apparent; after days of walking through untracked territory, I was once again in the presence of people. A quarter of a mile on, the beach was marked with a set of wind-blurred tire tracks. According to the map, I was only seven miles from the first cabin at the Doame River and another three or so from a branch of the Alsek River. A fisherman had probably been out for a joyride on one of the four-wheelers kept at the camps for moving nets between fishing sites.

I was surprised at the twinge of resentment I felt. The eighty miles of coast between Cape Spencer and Grand Plateau Glacier is some of the wildest in North America, but the sixty miles of broad lowlands from there to Yakutat has always been "people country," ever since the first aboriginals came over the ice from the interior. It was rich land, a cornucopia overflowing with such a wealth of fish, greens, berries, and game that generations of Tlingit had no experience with famine. Centuries of use had scattered the names of a dozen villages across the map.

I stopped to adjust the prayer flag, which had come loose while I was walking, then looked back down the beach at the forest, trying to imagine canoes coming and going, or the smoke of campfires drifting in slow curls above the trees. Traditional Tlingit villages were not, in the Western sense, permanent, in that the residents did not occupy them year-round; they were winter settlements, where a band's members would congregate after spending the spring and summer in scattered hunting and fishing camps, gathering food for winter before coming together to spend the snowbound months dancing and telling stories in the great houses of their respective clans.

According to Lieutenant George Emmons of the U.S. Navy, who along with the anthropologist Frederica de Laguna produced the most thorough ethnographs of life among Alaska's coastal Indians, building a house was the most important event in a Tlingit's life. Enormous amounts of labor were required to cut, transport, form, and fit the huge timbers used to construct the artfully crafted structures, which might be fifty feet wide and sixty feet deep and provide a living space for up to fifty people. The planks, split with mallets and wooden wedges from huge old-growth trees, could be thirty feet long, two or three feet wide, five inches thick, and free of knots for their entire length. To be able to marshal the manpower and resources necessary to build such a structure was a sign of great wealth, as were the intricate carvings and paintings that decorated every surface. Old drawings and photographs of great houses in villages like Klukwan, Yakutat, Angoon, and Sitka show structures so carefully engineered and decorated that it requires no great stretch of the imagination to find comparisons with the early Roman temples or European cathedrals. The comparisons become even more apt when one considers that every step of the building process was accompanied by ceremonies and rituals. From choosing the house site, which required formal consultation with representatives from every clan involved, to the cutting of the trees and their transport by fleets of canoes to the cutting, hewing, and carving of the logs into planks and beams, each act had a requisite ceremony, which Emmons described as being "in every sense a religious observation," meant to honor the spirits of the Tlingit's ancestors. Upon the house's completion, an enormous potlatch was held that often involved the builder's giving away the remainder of his wealth; a name was also given to the house that reflected the history and status of the builder's clan. "It was the ambition of every man to build or rebuild a house," wrote Emmons, "and to that end he saved throughout his life, and if he died before being able to accomplish this, it was a solemn ambition to be carried out by his successor."

From Yakutat to Grand Plateau Glacier there was the Boulder House of the L'uknáx̱adi, or Coho Salmon clan, and the village of Gus'eix̱, with six great houses, including the Frog House, named for a frozen frog found beneath the ground when the hole for the first corner post was dug, which thawed out, came back to life, and hopped away. Gooch Shakkee Aan, the "hilltop town," and Gunaaxoo, lay north and south of Dry Bay, respectively. Clam Hand Fort and Eddy Fort were built up the Alsek River, and I am sure there were others of which I found no record.

Two days of strong north wind had knocked the surf down, and I angled down the beach to walk on the wave-packed sand, thinking about how I, too, had saved all my life to build a home, and about the enormous effort it had required to fall and saw trees, pour concrete, and move truckload after truckload of wood, drywall, glass, metal, tar paper, and insulation up the ridge to the building site, all of which was preceded by an equally demanding effort to build the half mile of gravel road necessary to get trucks to the hill.

This last had been a community effort not unlike the Tlingit building process, with numerous meetings, detailed negotiations, a division of labor, and no small number of barbecues and parties. The neighborhood get-togethers may have fallen short of being true potlatches, because no riches were distributed, but they were often their equal in the amount of fresh crab, salmon, halibut, and berry dishes shared. The ridge I was building on separates two small coves, Amalga and Huffman harbors, along whose shores stand fifteen households constructed on toeholds of postglacial bedrock with their faces to the sea and their backs to the forest. Several of the homesites have been in the same family for generations, and for decades the homes and cabins on the Huffman Harbor side of the ridge were accessible only by

boat or a long hike down a trail so rough it wound up creeks that often
washed out in heavy rains, through berry thickets occupied by browsing bears, and down a rocky gorge so steep and slick with ice in winter
that ascending or descending it required the use of a rope. By the time
I relocated to the area, there were four people in Huffman Harbor over
eighty years old. The trail was getting hard for them, and it was agreed
that what was needed was a road.

Everyone in the neighborhood pitched in. Rob surveyed the route
and drew up the plat; his wife, Kay, kept the books for the project. Bob
was elected "president" of the neighborhood for his skills and patience
in negotiating easements and rights-of-way between all the land-
owners. On a frosty autumn day a librarian, an artist, a dealer in septic tanks, and his brother, who sells glass, shouldered chain saws, axes,
and brush cutters and walked into the forest, followed by a teacher,
a fisheries commissioner, a computer programmer, and a public
employee. A six-year-old girl with a fuzzy yellow dog and her older
brother came behind. Together this unlikely group of neighbors, who
range the political spectrum from ultra-liberal to sternly conservative,
chopped, sawed, dug, burned, stacked, and dragged dozens of trees
and a mountain of brush to clear a sixty-foot-wide swath through the
forest. We labored weekends and evenings, as fall turned to winter
and rain turned to snow, and all through that winter, until the following spring, when trucks came bearing loads of dynamite-blasted rock.
And—miraculously—there was never a cross word among us, in spite
of sprains, sore muscles, and blisters. Instead there was always a thermos of coffee shared around at lunch and a bucket of cold beer at quit-
ting time.

It is a rare thing in modern times to be able to say one lives in a
true community, with the implications of mutual help and concern the
phrase implies, but one of the richest experiences of my life was to par-
ticipate in the building of that road. When I made a stumbling effort to

put my feelings into words, I was saved from my sentimental groping by the grown son of the family four cabins over, who glared at me and growled good-naturedly, "That's why it's called a *neighbor*hood, you jackass." Then he took a slug from a hip flask of whiskey and tossed it over to me. We have picnics and birthday parties together. When my wife and I stood on the unfinished deck of the house and said our vows, they were there, and when one of us dies, we all grieve.

There is little or nothing left of most of the villages along the coast now. The Tlingit survived repeated episodes of dramatic climate change (although the village of Klem-sha-shick-ian, or Sand Mountain Town, in what is now Glacier Bay, was entirely destroyed when a rapidly advancing glacier plowed over it), but they were unable to deal with the diseases that came in the wake of the Russian invaders. Smallpox struck in 1775, measles in 1800, and typhoid fever in 1819. A second wave of epidemics that began in 1836 wiped out entire villages. After typhoid raged along the coast again in 1848 and 1855, there was almost no one left to keep the fires in the great houses burning. Many of the seventy-four clans recorded by Frederica de Laguna have ceased to exist.

The wind died away entirely. To the south a high, thin haze was beginning to creep across the sky. I had walked a mile or more while thinking about the long-gone villages, taking only casual notice of the occasional wolf and bear tracks I crossed. That the Tlingit culture survived at all is a testament to the strength of community. (And survive it has: A totem-pole-raising ceremony I attended in the village of Klawock shortly after my wedding began with a "grand entrance" by over five hundred drumming, singing dancers that literally shook the rafters of the gymnasium where the ceremony took place with their power.) But there are far fewer people north of Grand Plateau Lake now than there were when La Pérouse sailed over the horizon—only a small handful live there year-round—and I had to wonder what vanished songs a descendant of one of the great houses would hear in the wind along the coast today, what forgotten dances he or she would hear in the drumming surf.

I stopped to rest on a log and pulled out the map. According to it, I was sitting in the middle of an estuary big enough to float a small ship, but there was no sign of it; the land had risen so much since the shore had been charted that trees had sprung up in what had once been the estuary's mouth.

I dug out the stove, made a cup of tea, and drank it. I was tempted to throw the nearly useless map into the waves but scribbled a poorly remembered quote from the poet John Keats in the margin instead, something to the effect that "nothing in the world is permanent; uproar's your only music," and put it away.

The day was growing warmer, and the surf, which had been lapping gently at the shore, was beginning to thump with an increasingly insistent rhythm. I put away the stove and started walking again, and thinking about the tragedies the coast has seen made the pack feel even heavier. In addition to the disease-racked villages there were the drownings in the entrance to Lituya Bay and the 1958 tsunami, the victims of murder and hanging at Justice Creek, and the crewmen lost from the *Patterson*. The coast seemed littered with bones.

The prayer flag flicked the back of my head, hung limp for a moment, then flicked again, as if trying to draw my attention to a light breeze filling in from the south. I stopped to fold it away in the pack, and the feel of it in my hands brought to mind again the morning's dream of Luisa, and from there my thoughts skipped to the startling number of deaths that had peppered every circle of my society over the past year. There had been the elderly neighbor I'd found dead in her bedroom and my neighbor with Lou Gehrig's disease, who had succumbed to its slow paralysis; the friend who had died from thirty years of Vietnam-induced post-traumatic stress disorder and alcohol; the stranger who had jumped from the bridge; a cousin dead of a gunshot wound in a park outside Dallas, Texas; and a friend felled by a burst aorta while traveling in Europe.

I kept walking, my boots keeping time with the timpani of cold green waves. Every boom of the surf seemed to add to the mortal litany, and as I walked, my thoughts kept guttering along the lines of wondering why I should bother returning to Juneau to labor on a home that might or might not house an ailing marriage, and contemplating the larger folly of opening one's heart and life to others who must so often die or go away.

I was several miles into this black fugue when a single western sandpiper fluttered past. The sound of its wings brought me out of my funk long enough to notice that the haze moving in from the south had consumed half the sky, a sure sign that the weather was changing. I was glad to see the sandpiper; with the exception of a few ravens I had not seen a living thing for two days—not a single bird, no otters or bears, no ships on the sea or planes. There was only me, alone in a thousand square miles of wilderness, with the wide, open swath of the North Pacific on one side and the hulking, ice-clad mountains on the other. I felt completely isolated and relentlessly gnawed at by the question of life's purpose.

The sandpiper *pip-pip*'d and sped away. Its sudden appearance and disappearance made me feel as if I had been abandoned somehow. Then another bird appeared—a plover this time, in the wild black and gold plumage of a male getting ready to breed—then another and another. Within minutes a small chaos of birds was trickling and stopping, starting and fluttering past me. For the next hour or so plovers, dunlins, sandpipers, and surfbirds twittered and spurted by in groups of two or three, forming a staccato trickle of birds that was broken by long periods when there were none.

Then suddenly it was as if a dam had burst, and the trickle

became a wave. In the space of a few minutes, tens, then hundreds, then literally thousands and thousands of shorebirds appeared out of nowhere, storming north in a veritable tsunami of beating wings.

I thought I knew what was happening. In the North Pacific, low-pressure systems rotate counterclockwise, bringing southerly winds and rain. High-pressure systems spin clockwise, which often means north winds and clear skies along the coast. The stiff north wind that had been blowing for two days had been hitting the migrating flocks dead on the beak and keeping them grounded; now the low-pressure system presaged by the haze moving across the sky was coming, and the birds had gone airborne en masse to gain an energy-saving boost by surfing north on the oncoming pressure wave.

I understood all this intellectually, but there was also something else going on. High overhead I could see a long, wavering line of sand-hill cranes. At sea level flock after flock of phalaropes sped by just outside the breaking waves. Hundreds of dowitchers and turnstones sped up the beach. Most impressive of all were the flocks of sand-pipers, which roared past by the thousands, parting to fly around me like water flowing around a boulder in a stream.

During my forty years in Alaska I had never seen anything like it. Over the sand and the heaving sea, flock after flock rose and fell like ribbons in the wind, twisting and turning, then bending back into themselves like an endlessly writhing animal. Thousands of birds maneuvered as if possessed of a single mind, banking first left, then right, then left again before breaking into separate groups that rose, spiraled, and flowed back together in a tightly braided stream. They seemed to have no fear of me. Clouds of birds passed so close that I imagined I could feel a light turbulence on my face. I put a hand on my hat as if it might be blown away.

Then for a moment—a flash, really, less time than it takes to read this sentence—I saw the sinuous speeding flock as a congregation of souls released from the dead and dying of all humanity, and I understood that the first bird I had seen, the lone fluttering sandpiper that had intensified my morose feelings, was simply that, a single bird, alone in a harsh and vast landscape. In its solitude, it was inconsequential. But a thousand birds, or ten times ten to a hundred thousand, had become a single consciousness, traveling in perfect unison.

I watched as a flock flew up the beach. It moved like a boneless creature or a gossamer curtain blowing loose on the wind, and for that moment it seemed the jubilant, rushing mass was inseparable from all the human souls I imagined to be departing the earth that day, in an uprush from every sickroom, hospital, battlefield, and accident scene on the planet, all flowing in graceful unity toward some distant but promising horizon. In their aggregate, the birds—or souls, if you will have it—were no longer individuals but a single thing.

I knew that many of the birds would not survive the journey. Theirs is a hard life, lived in constant motion, battling weather, scrambling for food, and being chased by the seasons from one part of the globe to the next in the interest of survival and procreation. Every year a large percentage fall prey to starvation and predators. For the individual there is no reasonable hope of a long life, but in the cyclical flocking, migrating, nesting, hatching, and migrating again, over and over through the centuries, there is continuity. And that, I understood, is what truly matters, for we, too, contribute to our own kind's continuation, whether through children and grandchildren or by building a solid home to provide a shelter for coming generations. Though we will inevitably die and be forgotten, as have the majority of kings and generals throughout history, it is a consolation that in the absence of any permanence there is such continuity. In sum, it does not matter if we are forgotten; what matters is the effect we have on those around us and those who come after us. What matters is how our own lives affect the larger, perpetual community of the living.

Slowly the flocks thinned out, and it began to rain. I made camp that evening within a few hours' walk of Dry Bay. Rain drummed on the tent all night, but I was warm and dry inside. And some time in the night I decided to head back to Juneau. As with the birds, I realized, it is a connection with one's own kind that matters. The solitude of the outer coast was a grand, almost overwhelming experience, but now it was time to go home, to be with my neighbors and friends, sharpen my tools, and court my wife again. It was time to catch up with my own flock.

When the sun came up the next morning, I was already walking home.

CHAPTER 25

I FLEW. LIGHT feet, light pack, light heart. I was buoyed up by the numinous experience with the birds, and my boots found sure footing. No rock rolled underfoot, and loose sand felt solid. I did feel a twinge of regret at turning back only a few hours short of completing the circumnavigation of Mount Fairweather. But the hesitation faded quickly, and walking my backtrail gave me a comfortable, familiar feeling, not unlike the faintly remembered childhood sensation of nodding half asleep in the backseat of the family car as the sound of pavement turned to the sound of gravel on a country road, signaling that the long drive to my grandparents' ranch was almost over and would soon be replaced by a grandmother's hugs, a bed of warm quilts, and the feeling of being home at last.

It was warm, and I traveled so fast that I stopped only twice, the first time to strip down to a light shirt under my raincoat and the second time to let a grizzly lingering near the start of the trail to the lake's north shore wander away, which it did, up the trail, in the direction I wanted to go, which compelled me to sit on a log and wait for it to put some distance between us. After half an hour I followed it into the brush, singing Harry Belafonte's "Banana Boat Song" at the top of my lungs in case it was still nearby, giving particular attention to the yodeling chorus of "Daylight *come* and me wan' *go* home" and the "Day-o!" line that follows.

Clearly, it worked (as any such caterwauling probably would), because I saw no sign of the bear other than a darkly fresh calling card of half-digested grass on the trail, and soon enough I stepped out of the woods into a light drizzle at the edge of the lake. A thick layer of low clouds obscured the view of the glacier and mountains, and the gray lake combined with the pale clouds and dark forest along the far shore to form a chiaroscuro of illusion and distance—it could have been a mile across the misty lake or a dozen.

It seems now that it took less time to inflate the kayak, paddle across the lake, and make my way back to the beach on the other side than it does to tell about it, although by the time I covered the additional miles to the small outlet where I had found the driftwood raven stick, my legs were tired and my stomach was growling. Only two days had passed, but the small creek was much higher, and the knee-deep wade it took to get across convinced me that it was time to build a fire, dry out, and sleep for the night.

The mist turned to steady rain around midnight. Late the next morning I woke to the sound of bright chirping and lay puzzled for a moment as I tried to reconcile the drum of rain on the tent with the sound of birds—an unusual thing, since birds do not usually sing in heavy rain—then came fully awake with the recognition that the chirping was the call of a river otter. Family groups use sharp whistles to keep track of each other when they are traveling.

I groped for my watch and compared it with the dull light coming through the tent. I had slept eleven hours. It was the longest rest I had had in years, the thought of which filled me with energy and certainty. But had I possessed some sixth sense attuned to portents and omens, I might have heard the chirping not as the familial call of an otter but as the cry of a *kushtaka*. Maybe some deep, animal gland inside of me *did* recognize it as such, because I was tempted to pull the sleeping bag over my head and stay in the tent. Instead I crawled out, slipped into my rain gear as quickly as I could, and went about making a double helping of instant oatmeal and washing it down with hot chocolate. When I started walking, my feet did not feel as light as they had the previous day, and I had to concentrate on the clicking cadence of the hiking poles to keep up a steady pace.

The wind puffed, and a shower of rain rattled on my hood. The temperature was dropping, but the high, clear note of being homeward bound was still playing in my head, and as I walked, I let myself drift into daydreams of how I might win my wife again. Maybe stop working so much, take a bicycle trip in Europe . . .

I wish now that I had paid more attention to the otter's warning.

The description of what took place over the next few hours that follows here is as accurate as I can make it, though in truth the intense fear of those hours left my memory a jumble of sharp-edged images that continue to disturb my sleep even now, two years later, as I try to sort and assemble them. This shift in the narrative is abrupt, I know, but no more so than the plunge from whistling optimism to a desperate scramble for survival that took place not long after I left the previous evening's camp.

I was walking head down, with my chin to my chest, trying to avoid the pellets of rain being flung at my face by the southwest wind, when I looked up and saw a bear standing at the edge of the forest seventy-five yards away.

I knew there was something wrong as soon as I saw it. It was facing the sea and standing so still that for a long moment I wondered if I was mistaken, if the dark shape might be a root wad or a boulder. The wind stirred the branches behind it, and waves broke on the beach in front of it, but the bear was completely motionless.

I tilted my hat back to watch and leaned on the hiking poles. The bear did not react to my presence. It did not glance in my direction or assume any of the postures that are signs of stress or aggression. But in spite of its stillness it did not seem to be resting. A resting grizzly may sprawl on its back, curl up on its side, or flop down on its belly and nestle its head on its paws, but even a sleeping bear remains to some degree in motion; ears swivel and noses twitch as some part of the

animal's brain continues to sieve the atmosphere around it for information. This one was as still as the rain-darkened rocks. All it did was
stare at the swells rolling in from the horizon.

A worm of unease crawled into my belly. During the forty years I
have lived and worked in Alaska, every one of the hundreds, perhaps
thousands, of black and grizzly bears I have seen was either feeding,
searching for food, walking, running, fighting, or mating. Occasion-
ally there is a burst of roughhouse play. But I had never seen one do
absolutely nothing. And something about the stillness of this bear
seemed to radiate tension the way a deranged, glaring stranger gives off
a dark energy you cross the street to avoid.

I shuffled, unsure of what to do. In the wild, for humans as well
as for animals, anything odd or unknown may mean danger. This ex-
plains why a majority of the grizzlies I had seen since reaching Lituya
Bay had run at the sight of me—most had probably never seen a human before—and I wondered why this one should be different. In any
case, I wanted to get past it and continue on my way home.

I started trying to convince myself that it simply hadn't noticed
me yet because the wind was blowing toward me. If I walked a bit
closer or made some noise, it would sense me and bolt like all the others. But the longer I watched, the louder the alarm inside my head
rang. The bear was too still, and its stillness was too strange. It had not
shifted a millimeter since I had spotted it. Such a lack of activity was
unfathomable.

I had just made up my mind to back away quietly and give it time
to come out of its paralytic state and wander off of its own volition
when something overruled my decision. Whether it was an unconscious motion generated by my indecisive wavering or an eddy of wind
that carried the odor of a man who has not washed in several days to
the bear, I cannot know, but the response was instantaneous.

The grizzly came to life as if a switch had been thrown. Its head
jerked upright, and it turned to look at me. Then it started walking

quickly toward me. It was not charging, but this was not the comfortable, ambling pace of a bear motivated by simple curiosity either, and
the suddenness with which it transitioned from utter stillness to a
rapid, intent gait unnerved me; a normal bear would have reacted by
sniffing the air for a better scent of me, glancing around for other dangers, or, should it have decided that I was a threat, choosing an escape
avenue. A bear may stand upright on its hind legs, but not, as popular
lore would have it, in preparation for rushing forward and grabbing a
victim in a "bear hug"; it's simply trying to get a better view. Bears
usually like to think things over before they act.

Not this one. Everything about it gave me the creeps. I know that
for this to be a proper bear tale, I should say it was a thousand-pound
monster with gnashing teeth and slashing claws, but it wasn't. As grizzlies go, it was rather small, perhaps three hundred pounds, maybe
less, and as it dogtrotted toward me, I could see that it lacked the bulging musculature common to its species. Dreadlocks of matted hair hung
from abnormally lean forelegs, and as it moved, I noted a peculiarity
in its gait, as if its hindquarters were trying to outrun its forelegs by
swinging out to one side.

These were all bad signs. Nothing about this bear was normal.

The alarm in my head escalated to a siren, and I had to will my
feet not to run as I fumbled for the bear spray. Pepper spray has been
proved relatively effective in deterring aggression, but "relatively effective" is a disturbingly weak endorsement when a fist-sized can is
all that stands between you and a strangely behaving grizzly that is
getting closer by the second. The two or three heartbeats it took to
release the canister from its holster and raise it was also long enough
for some part of my shrieking brain to remind me that the effective
range of the spray is no more than thirty feet, pick a spot on the
ground I estimated to be that distance away, and brace myself to fire
when the bear reached it. In the next instant I had to abandon the plan
because the moment I thumbed off the plastic trigger lock, a gust of

wind hit my face. If I fired, the caustic spray would blow back into my eyes.

The bear broke into a loose-footed lope, closing the distance between us so rapidly that I had no time to decide whether to move farther down the beach and try to circle upwind into position to use the spray, or to make a dash for the trees. Before I could do either, it was on me. Without thinking, I snatched off my wide-brimmed hat and held it over my head, yelling, "Stop!" in the loudest voice I could muster. In grizzly society size matters, and stretching myself upright was the only way I had to look bigger.

The bear slowed to a walk but kept coming. It stopped no more than thirty feet away. Then its head dropped, and it sniffed at the ground. When it looked up again, there was something primitive and terrible in the way it stretched out its neck to peer at me. I felt like a rodent being considered by a snake.

Streaks of rain runneled its forehead and muzzle. Its nose was a dark fist pierced by two nostrils. As I write this, I can still see its eyes, like flat black dimes, with no whites or "catchlight," as wildlife photographers call the glint of reflected light that brings an eye to life. More disturbing yet was the way the rubbery black lip swung beneath its lower jaw. There was something obscene in how the fleshy pendulum moved out of synch with the bear's stride as it started moving toward me again.

I yelled louder, fighting to keep my voice from rising to a tremolo. The fight-or-flight response was kicking in, and flight was winning. It was all I could do to hold my ground, but I knew that if I turned to run or backed up, it might trigger an immediate predator-prey response.

The bear stopped a few yards away. I could see the red glint of a deep cut over one eye, and when it gave an odd shake of its head, the wound seemed to wink at me. I forced myself to step forward, bluffing to show I felt no fear.

In this case, the "courteous" approach I normally use with bears would have been as pointless as trying to charm my way past a drunken bar bully who was already advancing on me with an upraised pool cue. Instead I launched into a scold like a pet owner giving a misbehaved dog an angry talking-to, ordering, "Back up! Go away!"

It seemed to work. The bear stood stock-still and stared at me, then shifted its weight from side to side and stared some more. The wind flapped the hood of my raincoat. It is odd how the mind works at such moments, but I remember noticing that the tide was turning; the surf was starting to run farther up the shore. Gulls rose and fell outside the breaking waves. The bear lowered its nose to the ground and sniffed, blowing like a horse. I could see its lips puff out with every snort.

Now there is a tableau in my mind of the bear standing with its nose to the ground and myself poised with my hat extended like a flimsy shield. The spray makes a dull sword at my side. I have no idea how long the pause lasted; there is a record-skip quality to the memory, and the bear and I were both still and silent. I did not know what else to do. The only thing I had resembling a weapon was the plastic flare gun stuffed into a pocket of my pack, and I did not dare take off the pack to reach for it.

Then suddenly it seemed the whole thing was over. The bear looked over its shoulder as if it had forgotten something, then started walking away. I did not move. I could hear the gulls and feel a sprinkle of cold rain against my face. Then without thinking, I put my hat on my head and, keeping my eyes on the bear, bent to pick up the hiking poles.

This was a mistake.

The bear stopped and turned back toward me, stared a moment, and looked away. For a long minute it looked left, then right, then left again, as if still trying to decide something. Then it started coming back for me.

Fear took over, and I started backing up, moving at an oblique angle to the bear's approach, trying to edge upwind. I stumbled on a loose rock and felt the weight of the pack shift. Juggling the pepper spray and hiking poles into one hand, I stooped to pick up the rock and reared back, yelling, "I'll knock your fucking brains out!"

It was trash talk. The squeals of a weakling. My antics had no effect on the bear except to turn it to the side, where it circled, moving to cut off my retreat. I changed direction, and the bear circled the other way. I moved again and it countered me. My back was to the surf. The next move would be checkmate.

The notion of sprinting into the water, where the bear might not come after me, slipped through my mind, but I immediately rejected it as the vision of a wave hurling me back onshore followed; it could snatch me up like a stranded salmon. In any case, the potency of pepper spray can be greatly reduced if used against a soaking-wet bear; spray a grizzly as it climbs out of a river and it may not be effective. Using it in breaking surf would be pointless.

A better plan would be to throw myself facedown on the sand and hope the bear would begin by biting at my pack instead of my limbs. I could cover my head and neck with one arm and fire the spray over my shoulder with the other, while trying to hold my breath and keep my eyes closed to save my mucous membranes; if I survived the mauling, capsicum burns to my eyes and lungs would compound my problems.

I had no illusions about my chances of surviving. Prolonged circling, closing in like a shark, and refusing to be driven off, as this bear was doing, is textbook predatory behavior. This bear meant to eat me. And just as I was under no illusion regarding my hopes for survival, I was under none regarding how it would happen. Most predators kill fairly quickly: Big cats like the leopard go directly for the head, killing with a single bite that penetrates the brain; crocodiles seize their prey and drag it into deep water, spinning over and over to kill by trauma and drowning. Even in the extremely rare case of a giant snake such as an anaconda or a python hunting a human, the victim dies relatively quickly of cardiac arrest as blood flow is interrupted by the crushing pressure of the serpent's coils.*

Not so with bears. When a bear strikes, it simply rushes in like a locomotive with jaws and knocks its prey to the ground. Once the prey is down, the bear pins it with its paws and starts feeding. The worst of it is that a bear may not hurry, but rather, may take its time as it tears random mouthfuls from back, legs, buttocks, and shoulders, or goes in through the stomach for the organs. It does not care if you scream or for how long. It may even feed for a while, then wander away and come back later for another round.

I threw the rock and missed, hitting the sand beside the bear, who seemed not to notice. I bent to grab another rock, and the unwieldy bulk of the pack prevented me from getting much arm in the throw. Nonetheless, the stone glanced off the bear's back, and the animal went airborne, jerking around with such incredible speed that it appeared to turn inside out, landing on its feet, tail tucked and backing away as it looked around for the offending hand that had touched it.

I picked up another rock and winged it. Missing, I bent and groped for another. The bear paused, as if pondering the phenomenon of invisibility, and took another step backward, ignoring me while it looked around in all directions. The fourth throw struck the protruding knob of its hip bone with a satisfying thunk, and the bear bolted, running for the woods so fast that its legs blurred. It smashed into a stand of alder at full speed and disappeared into the crackling underbrush.

I lost no time grabbing my hiking poles and holstering the spray as I hurried away, moving as fast as I could through soft sand studded with boulders. I hugged the surf line, wanting to stay as far from the

---

* There is controversy over whether it is even possible for a large snake to swallow a full-grown human and over whether such an event has ever occurred. Most man-eating-snake stories cannot be documented, and several have been proved false.

edge of the forest as possible, imagining the bear pacing me at a trot among the shadows.

To abbreviate the tale, I should just say that I probably covered less than a mile over the next half hour, but it was enough for me to get my pulse down, swallow the sour taste of adrenaline that frothed from my stomach, and stop looking behind me every few seconds while I cataloged what I had learned; that the bear was apparently injured in some way (the cut over its eye and its odd gait) and that it might be starving (it was so lean its hips were visible). I was also unfathomably grateful to know that a hurled rock was apparently outside its experience or understanding; in the bear's mind, the impact it felt when the rock struck was somehow connected to a threat coming from behind, and although probably not painful, it was still an "unknown" and something to be fled. So it ran and I escaped.

But I was not easy on myself. My fear flipped over into a foot-stomping anger that I had become so cocksure from my previous harmless experiences with bears that I had readily accepted that the odds against an incident were heavily on my side. I kept kicking myself for having decided not to carry a gun. As I skirted a patch of alder and climbed over a drift log, I rehashed my careless bravado when Joel had offered me the .44 Magnum and I had declined, saying it was unnecessary and the extra weight would be too much for the trek.

Four pounds. Maybe five with extra ammo. I threw some profanity in with the mental kicking and slackened my pace. My legs were trembling from the fading adrenaline. My knees and shoulders ached from the jarring of the heavy pack. I was safe, I thought, and I decided I had run far enough to take a break. I needed water and maybe a couple of aspirins.

A drift log with the roots attached made a handy bench to sit down on, and I unbuckled the pack. I let the log take the weight, then eased out of the shoulder straps and lowered it to the ground, unstrapping the top and digging for the small waterproof bag that held my toothbrush, a small bottle of aspirins, and a partial roll of toilet paper. I was into the pack up to my elbow when I glanced back along the beach.

The bear was perhaps two hundred yards away, nose to the ground, snuffling toward me like a bloodhound. I jerked upright and stared as it circled a rib of rock, nosed up the beach, and came on, working precisely along my trail with the unwavering intensity of a bird dog.

In a panic, the mind blurs and seizes. The very words I needed to organize my thoughts disappeared. All I could think of was to run. But where? The bear would keep coming. I could not possibly run far enough or fast enough. I could climb a tree, but then what? I could not climb with my pack, and there was no time to hoist it out of the way before the bear would be on me. If I climbed a tree and left it on the ground, the bear would destroy it. Then I would be stuck in the wild with no tent, sleeping bag, food, or equipment. No way to survive. I also abandoned the impulse to dig out the handheld radio and call for help as fast as it surfaced; even if through some freak of atmospherics I did manage to raise a fishing boat or the Coast Guard, what could they do? It could take hours or even days to arrange a rescue.

I cursed myself again for not carrying a weapon. It took my fear-addled brain a moment to remember the flare gun, the orange plastic pistol designed to fire aerial flares. Coast Guard regulations require every boat owner to carry one, and I had thrown it into my pack at the last minute along with two "meteor" shells, which are designed to streak aloft and burst like bright fireworks, and a third shell designed to create a cloud of orange smoke. I had thought they might come in handy to attract the attention of a passing boat or plane if I got stranded.

I tore into the pack, scattering the contents and ripping open zippers until I found the gun and the flares. My hands were already shaking when I glanced up and saw that the bear had halved the distance. The plastic gun felt like a toy in my hands, and I dithered, trying to choose between a meteor shell and the smoke as the bear got closer.

Again there was an odd moment of clarity in my senses, a surge of calm that made note of a single sandpiper running on toothpick legs along the edge of the surf, its head bobbing as it needled the sand. A raven called *kla-hook* from the trees. It is a hard thing to describe, but somewhere inside of me I heard my own voice say, "Use a meteor. Save the smoke."

It made sense. In mid-May there are eighteen hours of daylight at that latitude and only a brief period of darkness. If I was hurt, a cloud of orange smoke would be more visible to a rescue flight than the burning pinpoint of a meteor shell. In the same wave of clarity I also thought to grab the radio, place it in a small hollow where the trunk of the drift log met the roots, and lay the smoke shell beside it in case I was injured and needed to find them without having to think or search through the mauled remains of my pack. The bear spray went into the front pocket of my rain pants.

When I looked up again, my hands resumed trembling. The bear was a long stone's throw away, coming head-up and sniffing the air. I fumbled a shell into the flare gun and snapped it shut. The bear's ears twitched at the plastic click.

Flare guns are meant to lob a shell skyward in an arc that maximizes "hang time," or how long the pyrotechnics remain visible in the sky, so I aimed high, above the bear's back, imagining the shell's trajectory as a parabola. Thumbing back the hammer, I pulled the trigger. There was a snap, a pause, and the flare ignited.

It missed. The range and power of the flare were much greater than I had thought, and instead of arcing in to hit at the bear's feet, the meteor hissed straight and level, passing a yard above the bear's neck.

The bear did not seem to notice. It did not jerk or flinch. It just kept coming as the flare struck the ground fifty yards beyond it, burst into flames, and started tumbling back and forth in erratic fits.

Smoke curled from the breech of the pistol when I broke it open to pry out the spent round, and the smell of burned propellant filled the air. The second meteor shell fought back as I tried to load it, resisting my efforts to thumb it into the hole, and I had to force myself to take my eyes off the bear, to focus on reloading, to stop trembling and groping, to simply *stop* . . .

I took a deep breath, then willed myself to take another, and the shell went in. Cocking the hammer, I raised the pistol. Sighting down the barrel, I wavered between shooting to hit the bear and firing low, using the speed of the shell to "skip" the flare in so it would burst immediately in front of the animal.

The gun quaked in my hand. Somewhere on the other side of the planet a seismic needle recorded my heartbeat. Using a target shooter's trick, I filled my lungs and let the air out slowly, finger tightening on the trigger, and fired at the bottom of the breath, in that fraction of time when one is breathing neither in nor out and the pulse does not stir the hand. A ball of flame drifted from the muzzle of the gun and floated slowly toward the bear hissing *pleeeaazzzz* . . .

The flare skipped off a patch of gravel a few feet in front of the bear and burst into bright phosphorescence. The bear turned and loped away, looking over its shoulder as it ran, and disappeared into the trees. But a lope is not a run, and I knew it would be back; its departure seemed more strategic withdrawal than retreat. It was clearly not as frightened by the flare as it had been by the rocks I'd thrown earlier.

"Reality" had never seemed so clear. There was the forest with its complex understory of shadows and greens on one hand and the sea unfurling itself against the shore on the other. Overhead were the clouds and the sky. I noticed the weather was changing. The wind was clocking to the northwest and easing. Never had the world felt so huge and so empty, so full of space without safety or refuge; never so wild . . .

And I was nothing. Not a human with centuries of technology and culture and history behind me. Just part of the food chain. Second place.

I started stuffing the scattered contents of my pack back together,

wasting no time on sorting things into their proper place or taking inventory. I had the pack on my back and was leaving when I remembered
the radio and smoke shell, grabbed both off the log, and shoved them
into a pocket of my raincoat, where they beat against my thigh as I ran.

I had gone no more than two hundred yards when I looked back
and saw the bear coming again with the same bloodhound intensity,
its snout in my tracks, snorting at every step. As I watched in growing
horror, it came to me that among all the bears I had watched, photo-
graphed, tracked, and filmed over the past twenty years, I had never
seen one work a scent trail so closely. It is common to see bears hurrying along with their noses lifted to the wind as they seek out the distant source of an interesting odor, or sniffing for rodent nests deep
underground. Researchers have estimated a bear's olfactory senses to
be seven times as sensitive as a bloodhound's and a bloodhound's to
be three hundred times as sensitive as a human's, giving bears an almost supernatural ability to detect the slightest odor. One group of
biologists working in the Arctic documented a male polar bear that
apparently detected a female in estrus from ninety miles away; they
followed by helicopter as it beelined the entire distance without wavering. Some researchers believe that bears may be able to scent a meaty
pile of carrion such as a dead whale from over a hundred miles away,
but I had never seen one hoovering through grass and driftwood, over
logs and through the sand, with such ferocious, single-minded intensity. It never looked up. It just kept coming.

I may have whimpered. I felt like crying. I did not know whether
to run screaming into the trees or hurl myself into the sea and swim
for it—neither of which were truly options. Desperate, I hurried to un-
buckle the pack and drop it to the ground, thinking to sacrifice every
foil-wrapped package of freeze-dried food, candy bar, and dried apple
I had left, scattering them along the ground and across my trail as a
delaying tactic. Maybe the small offering would distract the bear long
enough for me to escape.

Under normal circumstances, giving a bear food is not the last thing you want to do; it is something you *never* want to do. Bears are fast learners, and a single incident of obtaining food from a human may condition a bear to associate all humans with food, which inevitably leads to trouble, as the bear becomes more comfortable raiding campsites and confronting hikers and campers who come after you. But I did not care. The immediacy of the situation easily overruled a lifetime of belief and habit, making me selfish, and it required no effort to convince myself that so few people traversed the area I was in that it was not a concern; nothing I did could make this bear more aggressive. I was more concerned that the idea would not work, that the bear would simply ignore the foil and plastic packages and keep coming, or gobble them up and *still* keep coming. I was reluctant to waste the precious seconds it would take to dig out the food and scatter it. I was still vacillating as I unstrapped the top of the pack and started to empty it. The first item out gave me another idea.

My hands were awkward as I fumbled to unfold the square of waterproof fabric I use as a ground tarp. My fingers felt as if they had been removed and put on backward. For years the black tarp had served as insulation between my tent bottom and soggy ground; now I was hoping it would save my life.

I grabbed a hiking pole and extended it to its maximum length, twisting the knurled locking knob into place. My hand shook so badly that I had difficulty slipping one of the tarp's corner grommets over the spiked tip. It took two or three tries to lash it to the end of the pole with a piece of line.

I stepped behind a thicket of berry stalks, gripping the loose tarp in one hand and the shaft of the hiking pole in the other. Then I waited for the bear. A few years earlier I had run into a medium-sized brown bear on a trail so overgrown and hemmed in by head-high blueberry bushes and devil's club that hiking on it had been like walking down a green hallway. Surprised, the bear lowered its head and came swaggering toward me, popping its jaws and staring, which in bear language is a clear warning that an animal feels crowded. I knew that if I turned around or backed up in that narrow space, it might lunge for me, so while speaking as calmly as I could, I unzipped my raincoat and opened it wide, holding it out to the sides to increase the size of my silhouette. The ruse worked. The bear stopped, and if a bear can be said to look confused, it did so as it backed up a step or two, then crashed off into the brush, apparently flustered by how the small-fry it had thought to bully had suddenly doubled in size.

From my hiding place now I could hear the bear coming. There was the rustle of old grass, and a stick cracked; a muffled snort came, and I eased around the brush. The bear was forty feet away.

Unfurling the tarp, I stepped out, spreading it as wide as I could, clutching a corner with one hand and extending the hiking pole with the other, creating the largest silhouette possible. My legs felt like they weighed a hundred pounds. If I had hesitated, I wouldn't have been able to raise my arms.

I took a step forward, then another until the bear spotted me. It reeled back on its haunches and stared, black eyes impassive, dark nostrils flaring at the end of its muzzle.

I moved forward and shook the tarp.

The bear started to ease away. Taking an agonizingly slow step sideways, it drew its head into its shoulders and tilted its body away from me in a way that made it appear both coiled and indecisive. I had seen the same posture in bears that were being threatened by larger bears, so I did what a bigger bear would do: I charged. Yelling with what I hoped was a roar but probably sounded like a turkey call, I lunged forward, shaking the cloth.

The bear exploded. Its claws threw clots of dark earth and dead vegetation into the air as it spun and ran. I yelled and sprinted a few steps after it. As it ran, it kept its hindquarters tucked toward its stomach as if a larger bear were nipping at its haunches.

I moved just as fast in the opposite direction, stuffing my gear and the tarp willy-nilly into the pack, hoisting the pack on my back, and running. The rising tide had narrowed the beach to a thin slope of sand between the fringe of the forest and the breaking surf. Blankets of foam surged up the beach with every wave. I had covered no more than a hundred yards when I suddenly understood that the bear had been following me with its nose so intently to the ground not because its sense of smell was ungovernably powerful, but because it was not; whatever accident the bear had suffered, whether a fall off a cliff or a beating by another bear, the event had not only affected its ability to feed itself but also curtailed the animal's sense of smell. Otherwise it would have been able to trace me down the beach as any normal bear would have done: head-up, at a dead run if it wanted to. It could only be because it could not do so that it had kept its snout in my tracks, sticking as close to my scent as possible.

Still running—jogging, really, in a stumbling, bent-kneed shuffle, with the heavy pack bouncing from side to side, out of balance from its hurried repacking—I edged down the beach into the froth of the breaking waves. The ground there was soft and sucked at my feet. The larger surges threw a slurry of sand and water over my boots, but I kept plunging, praying that the wash of seawater over my tracks would pale my scent to a point where the grizzly could no longer follow me. A knee-high wave almost knocked my feet out from under me, but I kept running.

CHAPTER 26

Two hours later I ground to a halt, exhausted. It was high tide, late evening, and I felt like I had been beaten with a club. I had no idea how many miles I had covered, but it was not many; for most of that time I had been moving at a pathetic pace, staggering to a near halt every few minutes as the adrenaline faded, then forcing myself back into motion. Every part of my body was in pain or trembling.

A stand of large spruce trees offered a likely stopping spot. It seemed a reasonable bivouac, free of brush, with a clear view in both directions. I had no idea what to expect, whether the bear would keep coming or if I had outwitted it, but I could go no farther, and a rib of rotting snow under the trees would provide a source of water.

Once free of the pack I had to push myself to keep moving, to break out the stove, to think about food, to do everything I needed to do before nightfall. My stomach did flips at the thought of the coming darkness.

The stove hissed beneath a pan of melting snow while I got ready. There was no way I was going to spend the night in the tent, blind to the world outside and wrapped in a sleeping bag like a burrito, so I threw up a rough shelter by tying the corners of the tarp to a spread of limbs and propping one edge up with the kayak paddle. After sorting out a ration of freeze-dried food, the headlamp, the bear spray, a knife, the wire saw, and the flare gun, I used the hundred-foot coil of line to hoist my pack and the remaining food and gear as high as I could into a tree a few yards down the beach. Then I used the knife and the saw to carve an escape route up a tree beside the shelter, clearing branches out of the way until I had a series of hand- and footholds I could find in the dark. I should be able to get twenty or thirty feet up the tree in seconds.

Climbing was no guarantee of safety. There is a common belief that grizzlies cannot climb trees, but this is inaccurate; brown bears climb well when they want to, particularly the smaller ones. Only two years earlier, in June 2005, a thirty-six-year-old woman had been pulled from a tree and killed by a grizzly in Alberta, Canada. By all accounts Isabelle Dube had been exceptionally fit and athletic, a champion mountain biker, but she had not been able to climb high enough or fast enough to get away from the two-hundred-pound bear that had gone after her.

I tried not to think about it as I arranged my getaway. Dube had been young, fit, and fast; I was on the downslope of middle age and felt like I had been in a car wreck. I also tried, and failed, to block out the thought that she had been jogging with friends near a popular golf course, while I was a long way from the nearest human. And I could not help thinking about the victim of the last fatal attack in Glacier Bay, a man named Alan Precup who had disappeared in 1976 while on a camping trip. Precup had been killed thirty years earlier, sixty-five miles away, and across two deep fjords and a whole slew of ice fields and mountain ranges, but I knew that all that had remained of him when they'd found him had been one hand, his booted feet, and his camera, which had contained photographs of a small, undernourished grizzly like the one that had been stalking me. So distracted and exhausted was I that I did not realize until I'd finished eating that I had completely forgotten one of the most basic tenets of traveling and camping in bear country: Only a fool cooks in the location where he will be sleeping.

It is difficult to describe the state I was in, other than to compare it with the numb exhaustion of an ambush or artillery-barrage survivor. I was depleted. My mind was out of gear, yet my body felt electrified. I couldn't stop twitching; I barely noticed the fluttering calls of a flock of whimbrels flying along the beach, but the tap of a spruce cone falling on the tarp made me jump. Determined not to sleep, I looped the headlamp around my neck, arranged the flare gun close at hand, and nestled into the moss at the base of the tree. Pulling my sleeping bag over my waist, I leaned against the trunk with the pepper spray in my hand and the knife, absurdly, tucked in my boot. Then I prepared myself to wait.

Dawn.

A thrush trilling. Waves hushing themselves against the shore. The first thing I felt was my feet. They were freezing. My boots were still wet, and when I threw off the sleeping bag and tried to stand, I was sore all over. I was lying on the flare gun and had to look around for the pepper spray; it had slipped from my hand while I slept and was under the sleeping bag. An ember of pain smoldering between my shoulder blades burst into flame when I forced myself upright; my right arm was numb and tingling. The jolting of the pack as I'd run had irritated the pinched nerve in my neck.

Moving carefully, I filled a pan with snow and melted it, drank a large cup, then another, and melted some more to make tea. Then I took four aspirins and dug through my pack for dry socks. The rain had eased a bit, but I hardly noticed. Every step shot a dull pain through my heel.

Wolfing down a handful of nuts and dried fruit with a second cup of tea, I melted more snow to refill the water bottle, then shouldered my pack and started walking.

My journal stops at the confrontation with the bear. I made no more notes, scribbled no thoughts, penciled nothing in the margin of the map. Every bit of the elevation I had found in the rushing migration of the birds was gone. There was only the walking, at the edge of the surf, as far as I could get from the forest, looking over my shoulder, jumpy as a whipped dog. The weather had closed in again, blanketing the coast with rain and fog, and there was an odd, disoriented interval when I did not know if I had walked two miles or twenty, until I found myself standing on the bank of a swollen river. The swath of gray water poured across the beach so fast that looking at it gave me vertigo.

Coming up against the flooding river felt like finding myself at a dead end in a dark alley in the worst part of town. With the bear still somewhere behind me, I wanted badly to get across, but the creek, which had been hip-deep only a few days earlier, was now rushing wildly from bank to bank. If I had been with a group or a partner, it might have been possible to fasten one end of the hundred-foot line to the kayak, have one person paddle like mad for the far shore while someone else tended the line, and then rig a second line to "ferry" the kayak back and forth, but being alone made that impossible. I was not strong enough to take on this river, and I knew it. If I tried to paddle across, I would be swept into the surf. If I tried to ford it, I would drown.

The blowing rain was working its way down my collar. I stood there so long watching clumps of grass and roots wash by while I tried to figure out what to do that a chill set in. The sensible thing to do would have been to set up the tent, build a fire, and get warm, but all I could think about was how to cross the river, keep walking, and get home.

I started up the riverbank, listening to the sound of cobblestones being rolled downstream along the bottom of the river by the force of the current. Rain rattled on my raincoat like thrown gravel. A gust of wind twisted through the trees. Paddling across a river would usually mean scouting the opposite side for a back eddy of calm water behind a point or obstruction, then launching the kayak far enough upriver to aim for a safe landing in the eddy while being swept downstream, but there were no eddies in sight. The river ran full and straight between its banks.

I squatted on the riverbank and huddled in my raincoat as I tried to come up with a plan. Gravel trickled from the lip of the bank in front of me. The trickle grew and the bank collapsed. The river was still rising, undercutting its banks. The longer I waited, the more difficult it would be to cross.

My only choice was to go upriver until I found an eddy on the other side where I could land without flipping the kayak. But going upstream would mean going into the forest.

I did not want to go into the forest.

Let me repeat that: I did *not* want to go into the forest. Going into the forest would mean pushing through heavy brush, making my way through dense alder, and searching for a way through thick stands of trees, any one of which might hold a bear. The thought of leaving the beach, where I could see in all directions, and stepping into the dark understory made me queasy.

I was shivering. Another piece of the riverbank caved in.

I had no choice. I pushed myself to my feet and went in.

I do not know how long or how far I went, only that everything inside of me was stretched drum tight and more than once I thought to turn around, although the going was not as difficult as I had feared. In places the river ran in braids across a plain of sand and water-scoured stones where I could walk out in the open on gravel bars. In others I had to scout a way through tangled brush, swinging inland around the worst parts, then back to the river every hundred yards or so to look for an eddy. I found no place to cross.

It was early afternoon by the time I came to a fork in the river, where it split into a tumbling rush of concrete-colored water to the left, closest to me, and a shallower stream of clear water to the right. The silty water appeared to be coming from a glacier and made up the bulk of the flow, but the watercourse it flowed through was narrow.

Upstream of the fork it ran even faster because of the constriction. As I moved inland, patches of snow became more frequent, and the undergrowth grew thicker.

Slogging through the thickets was exhausting. The pinched nerve in my neck was aching, and I was on the verge of giving up and heading back to the beach, when I spotted a downed tree on the opposite side of the river. The trunk lay in the water pointing upstream; downstream, in the lee of the roots, was a small eddy.

A skim of old leaves and debris swirled slowly in a weak countercurrent below the roots; the slick surface of the eddy was not much larger than the kayak. Upstream, on my side of the river, I could see no place to launch, no obstruction that would provide a place to slide the kayak into the water without it being snatched away.

The noise of the rushing current ate at my confidence; if I tried to cross and missed the eddy, I would spin off downstream on a wild, plunging ride that in all likelihood would end with the kayak's being overturned.

I spent the next half hour searching up and down a quarter-mile stretch of the river, trying to think of a way to get the kayak in the water without being swept away and trying in vain to convince myself that I could make it across and spear the blunt, unwieldy inflatable into the tiny opening before I blew past it. But after I tossed a stick into the water to measure the speed of the current, I knew it was not possible; I simply did not have the skill required. It was not far—the river had narrowed to no more than fifty or sixty feet—but I knew I was not proficient enough to hit such a small target in such swiftly moving water.

My only chance was to get the rope across and pull myself over. But how? It was too far to lasso a tree or boulder like a cowboy; all I could do was try to throw the line across and hope it snagged on something. If I could throw it over a branch on the far side, it might snarl and hold somehow.

I tried several times to lash a rock to the end of the line as a weight, to make it easier to throw, but the knot kept slipping. When that failed, I broke out the wire saw and cut a length of alder, fastened the line to it, swung it, and tossed it.

The line dropped into the stream halfway across, and a stab of pain shot through my shoulder. I reeled the line in, coiling it carefully for a second try, then a third and a fourth, but each fell short; I tried underhand, overhand, and a lunging, full-bodied throw, but none carried the line far enough. Every try made my shoulder worse.

I blew out my lips in frustration. Any second-string Little League player could have tossed a ball into the underbrush on the other side underhanded, but with my neck flaring up, my right arm was nearly useless, and when I attempted to use my left, the result was so uncoordinated that I gave up after a single try.

I felt defeated, stuck, incompetent. For a moment I considered tying one end of the line to my pack and the other around my waist, then flinging myself into the river in an attempt to swim across, thinking that if I made it to the far shore, I could pull the pack across behind me and then figure out a way to deal with the wet gear and clothes. I dropped the idea after visualizing becoming tangled in the line or exhausting myself in the current and being washed away. I told myself that if I had brought a life jacket, I might have tried it, but a deeper part of me knew that I would have still been afraid. The thought of going into the rushing water was just too much.

I was stymied until a small, niggling idea began to take form, first as a piecemeal memory, then as a solid shape. More than a decade earlier I had worked with a BBC film crew on a documentary about eagles, part of which had required placing a small platform high in a tree near a nest, where a cameraman could squat inside a blind, waiting to capture footage of the eagles feeding their chicks. The production company's rigger, a squat, immensely strong fellow with ice blue eyes and a jaw darkened by three days of beard, had used a pistol-sized crossbow to shoot a "messenger" line of thin cord across a stout limb eighty or ninety feet up the tree. The messenger line had then been used to pull a proper climbing rope aloft, giving us a means to go up and down the tree as we'd hoisted the preassembled platform into position.

At first I tried to think of a way to make a small crossbow or to use the flare pistol to fire a messenger line across—perhaps by carving a stick to fit into the barrel, then emptying the smoke-producing compound out of the remaining shell and using the detonator and propellant to fire the stick and an attached line across. Except I did not have a small-diameter line long enough, and besides, unlike with the tree limb, where gravity had dropped the end of the messenger line back down to us, I would have no way to retrieve a messenger line and thus no way to use one to get the heavy line across and secured.

But a larger crossbow might work. I started searching for a stick or branch to make into a bow, but the brush was all too small or twisted. A waterlogged branch I dragged out of the river snapped when I flexed it.

I had to search for a while before I found what I needed—a young spruce tree growing in the middle of a patch of alder. Then it took some time, having wormed my way into the alder, to use the saw to cut the sapling down and whack off enough of the limbs to drag it out of the thicket. But another hour of work and I had the slender trunk trimmed down into a tall pole as thick as my wrist. When doubled and twisted, one of the small-diameter cords I had used to rig the ground tarp as a shelter was strong enough to serve as a bowstring.

Green spruce is amazingly flexible, and Sitka spruce is the strongest wood for its weight in the world. It took a couple of tries before I figured out how to butt one end into the ground against a tree root and use the tree trunk as a fulcrum to bend the sapling. I had to brace one knee against the tree and pull with both hands to fit the string. Stringing the bow around the tree left the trunk of the tree between the shaft and the bowstring, which made it easy to use another cord from the ground tarp to lash the bow horizontally to the trunk. The bow was so stiff I had to hold the bowstring with both hands to draw it, but when I let go, it snapped forward with a satisfying thunk.

Next came the arrow, or bolt, as a crossbow projectile is called. I needed something heavy enough to carry the line across the river and substantial enough to penetrate the growth on the other side. A four-foot chunk of the spruce sapling did the job. I trimmed and smoothed it with the knife, hacked a deep V in the end to fit the bowstring, then cut a groove around one end for the line. After thinking a moment, I reconsidered and carved a second groove near the middle, then retied the line; the bolt was more likely to tangle and hold if it could "toggle," or twist sideways, in the brush on the other side.

I tied the remaining end around a tree and laid the body of the line out in careful coils, making sure there were no snags that might interfere. I wanted the line to pay out with as little drag on the bolt as possible.

I notched the bolt into the drawstring, muttering a small prayer that amounted to nothing more than "please, please, please," and flexed the bow to make sure the line was clear. I did not really expect the crude contraption to work, but if it failed, I would just have to keep trying until it succeeded.

I gripped the bowstring on either side of the bolt and reared back, pulling hard and angling the bow a few degrees skyward. I heard wood fibers start to crack and let go. The string snapped, the bow jumped, and the bolt shot across the river in a shallow arc that carried it straight into a copse of trees, leaving me staring openmouthed as the line fell into the water and the current snatched the slack down-river.

I dashed for the line and grabbed it, hauling it in hand over hand until I felt resistance on the other end, then stopping, hesitant to tug too hard and pull it loose. I need not have worried. I pulled, then pulled harder, and nothing gave, even after I reared back and put my full weight against it. The toggle had worked. The bolt turned sideways and lodged between two trees. I walked downstream and jerked, but the line held.

I was almost jubilant until I realized I had another problem. With the line knotted around a tree on my side of the river, if I pulled myself across in the kayak, I would have no way to retrieve it. I would have to abandon it, but there were more rivers to cross, and I might need it.

I tugged on the line and paced back and forth, trying to imagine a slipknot of some sort or a way to cut the line after I was across, maybe by wedging a sharp stone or my knife between the tree trunk and the knot, then working the line back and forth from the other side until it parted . . . but it might not work . . . or if the line got cut before I was across, the kayak would swing downstream and . . .

That was the answer. With the line fixed on the far shore, all I had to do was secure the kayak to the line, turn it loose, and let the current swing me across like a pendulum. It was pure luck that I had chosen a tree upstream of the root wad to use as a base for the cross-bow; this made it an easy matter to estimate the distance from where the line was toggled into the brush downstream to the eddy and to measure the same distance back along the line, which gave me the point at which I could fasten the kayak in order to have the current ferry me across. If I was right, the arc would carry me into the calm water below the root wad.

While I pumped up the kayak, I went through the procedure in my head, trying to imagine everything that could go wrong, thinking about how the force of the current would act on the kayak and the line, and wondering if I should try to steer with the paddle or just hang on. My stomach rolled at the thought of getting into the kayak without a life jacket, and what it would be like if the kayak flipped and I made it to shore but lost my gear. I might be able to make it to Lituya Bay and the emergency supplies I had stashed in the river bag on the beach there, but it would be a long, cold walk with no dry clothes and no sleeping bag.

After inflating the kayak, I dug out the small waterproof bag that held my toothbrush, toilet paper, and aspirin, and added a film canister of waxed matches, the remaining half of a chocolate bar, a pair of dry socks, the knife, and the handheld radio. Then I took off my belt, placed it crossways on the foam sleeping pad, and folded the pad over and over around the leather belt until it formed a thick roll, which I secured with the silver tape I had wrapped around the hiking poles while I was preparing for the trek. With the belt buckled around my chest below my armpits, the pad made a plausible if uncomfortable life vest. After trying it on, I decided to wrap the ground cloth around the pad as well; I could use it as a shelter if I needed it. With the bag clipped to the belt and the knife, the bear spray, and a foil bag of freeze-dried potatoes and eggs in my pockets, I was as ready as I could be to go.

I noticed a light tremor in my hands as I pulled the line tight, knotted a loop into it, and ran a second, shorter piece of line from the bow of the kayak through the loop. The kayak bucked and jumped when I slid it into the water, as if it was trying to get away. I secured it to a root protruding from the bank with a slipknot and dangled the free end of the line where I could reach it after I was seated in the kayak.

I tossed the pack into the heaving boat and strapped it in, then put the paddle on the bank where I could reach it. Getting into the kayak required a fumbling squirm to lower my butt into the lurching craft without losing my balance. Once I was in, with my knees tucked under me and the slipknot in my hand, the kayak suddenly seemed much too small, the river too swift, the whole thing absurd.

I jerked the knot loose. The kayak slipped backward, the bow falling off downstream as I grabbed the paddle and started thrashing at the water, trying to gain control; the boat spun halfway around, wobbled over a boiling surge of water, and started plunging downstream sideways. A wave sloshed aboard, and a gout of cold water hit my face. Just as I thought the whole thing was going out of control, the line began to tighten and the bow swung upstream.

The kayak bumped and slewed in the current, but slowed and began moving across the stream, swinging in an arc that carried it swiftly toward the root wad. There was a heart-seizing moment when I thought the line would be too long or too short and I would miss the eddy, or it would tangle in a snag hanging out from the bank, but instead the kayak slipped into the still water behind the root wad as calmly as a horse stepping into a stall.

I was across. I was on my way home.

EPILOGUE

THE REST OF the trek back to Lituya Bay was uneventful except for finding the cache of food I had left at Cape Fairweather gone. Something small had gotten into it, perhaps squirrels or a marten, and there was nothing left but a litter of shiny, finely gnawed scraps of foil strewn across the ground. I was on short rations for the next few days, but there were no more floods, no aggressive bears, and the weather turned fine. The *Wilderness Swift* was where I had left it, riding peacefully at anchor when I paddled up, although a shattered coffee cup and a jumble of books on the cabin sole told me it had ridden through at least one gale-tossed night. The voyage from Lituya Bay back to Juneau was easy, with ten knots of wind and following seas across the gulf, followed by a stop in the tiny village of Elfin Cove for fuel and a phone call to my wife.

She did not answer. It is autumn now as I write this, and she has been gone for two years. It turned out that getting a divorce in Alaska is not hard. She moved out the day after I got home. There were papers to sign and a waiting period. We held hands as the magistrate dropped the hammer and went for coffee afterward. A week later she left for Italy with her lover. Our own love, she said, had simply faded; people change and grow apart; she did not blame me. There was more, but it was difficult to respond to such well-practiced lines.

Now, at the end of a long, hot summer that saw temperatures in Southeast Alaska soaring into the eighties, the salmon are massing at the mouth of the creek near the house, blackening the water with the sheer number of their bodies, waiting for a rising tide to push them up a small waterfall that stairsteps down a face of jagged rocks. Once above the falls, the salmon will swim inland, spawn, and die. Their decomposing bodies will then release nutrients into the stream that will fertilize the tiny plants and feed the insects that in turn will provide food for the salmon's offspring until they are strong enough to swim downstream into the ocean. Only a few of the fry will survive life among the predators of the open sea long enough to reach adulthood, and 90 percent of these will be caught by fishermen or eaten by seals, sea lions, or killer whales before they can return to their natal stream. Of those that make it back into the river, still more will be consumed by bears.

It is tempting to dismiss the salmon's perseverance in hurling themselves upstream to spawn and die as simple instinct, but as with all migrating animals—birds, whales, caribou, even the wildebeests in Africa—everything they do, whether by instinct or consciously, is for the benefit of the coming generations.

I lost traction for a while after the divorce, downshifting from working seven days a week to days of sitting on the unfinished porch or in a chair by an upstairs window. When his own wife left him for a London playboy, the British satirist Evelyn Waugh wrote in a letter to his friend Harold Acton that he "did not know it was possible to be so miserable and live," adding, perhaps as an afterthought, "I am told it is a common experience." Were it not for my own friends, who pushed back my drift toward reclusion with insistent invitations to dinners, hikes, and evenings out, it would have been difficult, or perhaps impossible, to rise out of the sump of doubt and confusion one falls into when forced to acknowledge the remarkable capacity of the human heart to see what it wants to see and believe what it wants to believe in the face of all reason and evidence. And it was the kindness of neighbors who shoveled a path through hip-deep snow to the house to keep an eye on things when I left town for the winter that showed me how when the bottom drops out, it is the gentle, unspoken web of community that breaks the fall and catches you.

Eventually, of course, I returned to working on the house, but there was no longer a rush, and now my days rarely end in exhaustion. Yesterday I started making a closet door out of two planks that at one time might well have gone into the firewood pile. The first is riven with wind shake scars, dark, jagged cracks formed when the tree was still living, and the second is plagued with knots. It will require hours of sawing, planing, and sanding to turn the wounded wood into panels, but the slow work of deciphering an attractive pattern in the deformities will be worthwhile if it allows me to turn something so deeply flawed into something beautiful. The house is well built; it could stand for a hundred years. With proper attention to detail, it may provide a comfortable, *wabi-sabi* home for the generations that come after me.

It took a while to sink in, but in the end the extremity of the trek, from the heart-lifting experience among the migrating birds to the screeching terror of being stalked by the bear, also made the transition easier; after all, being peeled down to the point where you are nothing more than just another mammal trying desperately to stay alive puts things in perspective. Looking into the dull eyes of that grizzly undressed me in a way that I had never been undressed before, reminding me that the "real" world is still out there, and that it is a medieval place where nature is not always pretty and humans are not always in charge.

Balance this with the experience with the birds. There are six billion people on the planet, and life is short; we flicker and disappear like sparks rising from the campfires of the gods, who sit in the heavens watching ice ages come and go, mountains rise and fall, and civilizations disappear. But as with the enormous flock of migrating shorebirds, it is the *totality* of the organism that matters, an ongoing unison of such scale that the sheer abundance of its moving parts makes it seem infallible. There is continuity. We stand smack in the middle of life, evolution, and history, and we are vital parts of the system. No one can be certain, of course, what Kwäday Dän Ts'inchi was doing up on that glacier when he died, but studies have established to a remarkable degree who he was, if not by his given name, then by his lineage; DNA samples gathered from 250 members of the Champagne and Aishihik bands in the interior and the Tlingit communities in the coastal areas have positively identified seventeen living relatives. Tlingit culture is matrilineal, based on two descendant groups designated as Eagle and Raven; all of Kwäday Dän Ts'ìnchi's relatives are of the Eagle moiety. Even in death, some part of the young warrior lives on through his mother's line.

There is almost no chance the bear is still out there. When I described the animal's initial motionless state to a biologist, he noted that the behavior was consistent with a loss of vision. The odd gait indicated neurological damage. An animal so badly wounded almost certainly died of starvation, leaving its body to be consumed by scavengers or melt away into nutrients that fertilized the grass. We are all inevitably a source of life for something else. "Loss," wrote Marcus Aurelius, "is nothing but change, and change is nature's delight."

The novelist Leif Enger wrote that "drift is the bane of the epilogue," but there is one more thing I want to share with you, so please bear with me.

The last day of the long run home from Lituya Bay back to Juneau was also the day of Luisa's memorial service. From Elfin Cove, on Cross Sound, through the Inian Islands into Icy Strait, and all the way north around the farthest tip of Admiralty Island, the sea was as flat as a plate of mercury. Rags of mist hung along the shore. The horizon came and went between brushstrokes of rain. The ceremony in remembrance of Luisa's life was scheduled to begin at four P.M., a few minutes before the day's lowest tide.

I could have been there. In such calm weather it would have been a simple matter to lay a course from the north end of Admiralty Island down around the bottom of Shelter Island, then shoot east across Favorite Channel to the beach where she and Joel had built their home. But after the immense solitude of the outer coast and the intensity of my experiences there, I was not ready to mingle with the hundreds of people I knew would be present. And while friends were flying in from all over the globe to say goodbye to Luisa, dropping anchor in front of such a crowd and rowing ashore would have felt like grandstanding. Instead, I went south, running along the shore of Admiralty Island until I came to a small cove at the foot of a mountain I knew was visible from Joel and Luisa's front window. At 3,600 feet Mount Robert Barron is the highest peak on Admiralty Island, and Luisa had immersed herself in its view as she'd lain in the front room with the hummingbirds hovering outside the window during the last days of her life. By three o'clock the *Wilderness Swift* was anchored in the cove, and I was rowing ashore with the prayer flag, a coil of line, some tarred seine twine, the hip flask of scotch, and a thermos of hot tea in my pack. A smear of rain drifting down the channel caught up with me as I stepped ashore and became a pelting shower.

The tide was an hour from low and still falling, so I balanced the skiff's small mushroom anchor on the bow, looped a line through the eye, and waded out as far as I could go without water going over the top of my rubber boots, pushing the skiff in front of me. Then I gave the skiff a shove, watched it drift to the end of the tether, and gave the line a yank, pulling the mushroom off the bow into the water to anchor it. Barnacles crunched under my boots as I walked ashore.

I stopped at the edge of a grassy isthmus beside a spreading spruce tree, took off the pack, and pulled out the prayer flag. It took a couple of tries to toss the coiled line over a wrist-thick limb ten feet above my head and my full weight to bend the branch down far enough to reach the tip. Standing on the line to hold the branch in place was awkward, but I cut two pieces of twine and used them to lash the prayer flag to the end of the branch, working slowly, using the knife to trim away smaller branches so the flag could flutter without becoming snarled. After securing two corners of the flag with round turns and finishing the lashings with square knots, I stepped back, took my weight off the line, and let the branch rise. There was no wind. The flag hung as limp as sodden laundry, a scrap of cloth out of place in a tree.

The rain began to fall harder, coming down with enough velocity to rattle off the brim of my hat and spackle the surface of the cove with overlapping circles. I sank to a seat on a stone with the pack between my knees and pulled my raincoat around me. Then I dug out the thermos, unscrewed the cap, and poured. A trickle of rain inched its way under my collar, but the cup of tea in my hands was warm. I took a sip and closed my eyes, trying to think of Luisa.

I am not sure what I was expecting. I suppose some part of me thought a swarm of hummingbirds might appear, or a deer, or an eagle would drift low overhead to inspect the prayer flag. A few years earlier Luisa, Joel, and I had gone with a group of friends to a creek on the eastern shore of Admiralty Island to hold a memorial ceremony for an older, wilderness-loving friend who had died a year earlier of thyroid cancer. Stan Price had homesteaded at Pack Creek for nearly thirty years, living cheek by jowl with a couple dozen grizzlies who had become so familiar with his comings and goings, as had he with theirs, that it was not unusual to find a bear sleeping under the porch of his cabin or see one wander into his shop while he was working. When a young bear walked out of the brush during our informal ceremony and lay down a few yards away, put its head on its paws, and listened until we were finished, then got up and ambled away, we all agreed that in some fashion the bear was Stan's spirit, dropping by to hear what we had to say. Now a part of me was hoping for something similar, some sign I could interpret as an assurance that those we love never truly leave us.

The rain became a downpour. It gushed and pounded, falling so thick and fast that rivulets began to trickle from the brim of my hat into the cup of tea. I sat for half an hour, still hoping. Nothing moved. Just the rain.

At four o'clock I gave up and tossed the diluted remains of the tea on the ground, then pulled out the scotch, tipped a shot into the cup, and raised it to the prayer flag in lieu of a prayer. The smoky liquid burned as it went down. I was not sure if the tears trickling down my cheeks were from the scotch, for Luisa, or just the rain.

I was on my feet, coiling the line in preparation for leaving, when it started.

First the rain stopped. It ended so abruptly that it was like having a roaring engine or a blaring radio switched off, leaving only the sounds of water dripping from the trees and runoff trickling through the rocks. Then a raven called and another answered. An eagle I had not seen perched in the top of a tree overhead shrieked and shrieked again, its falsetto cry tapering off into a tremolo. Next came the back-and-forth buzz of several thrushes from deep within the trees, and within a few seconds a mob of crows, jays, robins, ravens, eagles, and a dozen species I cannot name were cawing, calling, whistling, singing, and chirping from the sky, the forest, and the grass covering the isthmus. A flock of herring gulls appeared overhead, arguing and screeching. The musical cacophony swelled until I stopped in my tracks, looking in all directions for the cause of it.

It lasted at most half a minute. Then one by one the calls stopped. Before I knew what to make of the frenetic chorus, it was over, leaving me standing on the beach with the half-coiled line in my hand, listening to a single distant gull yammer at a passing crow . . .

Everything went still again. It grew so quiet I could hear the faint pop of bubbles rising through the seaweed at the water's edge, exposed barnacles and mussels closing with tiny clicks.

After waiting a minute or two, I finished coiling the line, threw the pack over one shoulder, and walked down the beach to pull the skiff in. The tide was changing, the sea starting to rise. I stepped into the skiff and fitted the oars into the oarlocks. For three weeks I had been traveling in the wake of people with remarkable endurance—Chirikov,

La Pérouse, and Jim Huscroft; the crews of the *Badger* and the *Edrie*, who rode out the world's largest tsunami; Hans and Hannah Nelson, whose marriage endured a winter of murder and privation; the cast-aways of the *Patterson* and their rescuers; and last, the Tlingit people, who continue to salvage their culture from the devastation of the past.

The oarlocks squeaked in time with my strokes. I was in no hurry to get back to the boat. We are all the end product of a million years of survivors; your mother and father both had to be sufficiently strong and healthy as babies, children, and young adults to live long enough to meet, mate, and produce you, often against the incalculable odds of disease, war, famine, and troubles beyond name and number. Consider their parents—your grandparents—and this run of luck has happened five times. Go back to the time of Edgar Allan Poe or Lincoln, and we are the direct descendants of approximately 240 very strong, lucky people. By La Pérouse's day, the number reaches one thousand. At twenty generations, it breaks a million, all of who possessed the fortitude and fortune to live long enough to throw their genetic material into the relentless collusion that would culminate in you. Scramble back down the evolutionary ladder far enough, and the odds against being here to read or write these words reach into the trillions.

I pulled alongside the *Swift* and climbed aboard, locked the skiff into the davits, and started the engine. There would almost certainly be rough seas ahead—friends would die, relationships stumble, sooner or later my body would decide not to do all I asked—but for now just being alive was miracle enough. There won't be anything I cannot handle.

As for the last few miles of the unfinished circumnavigation of Mount Fairweather, I will save it for my dotage. A level hike on a broad beach might be just the thing when I am seventy or eighty. This winter, instead of chipping ice off the table saw and fighting blizzards, I may go for a walk across the island of Hawaii—a warm, 120-mile hike from a protected beach at sea level, up, over, and around a pair of 14,000-foot volcanoes, then down through an ancient koa forest and grasslands, until I drop into a deep valley that broadens into blue surf and gentle trade winds at its mouth. It will be easy; there are no rivers to cross and no bears.

Or maybe I will just rent a car and drive around the island. Why not? I am fifty-five years old; they are *all* victory laps now.

ACKNOWLEDGMENTS

I relied on the help of far too many people in the writing and preparation of this book to adequately acknowledge each and every one, so I should start with a blanket expression of gratitude to the numerous biologists, geologists, guides, rangers, researchers, fishermen, and mariners who shared their often hard-earned knowledge with me so generously.

Next comes a very large debt to Gayle Goedde, Jim Simard, Gladi Kulp, and the rest of the staff at the Alaska State Historical Library, without whose help much of this book would have been thin on facts. My appreciation for you all is incalculable.

A very special thank-you is owed to Ed Huizer, without whose help, support, and steady stream of doughnuts this book might have never been written and the house I now call home would certainly never have been built. Ed, thanks for sharing both your memories of Alaska during its territorial days and so many volumes from your personal collection of Alaskana. They all have been invaluable.

I must also say thanks to the numerous writers and historians whose work over the past two hundred years played such a large part in igniting my interest in Lituya Bay. No one planning to visit the outer coast of Glacier Bay National Park should do so without carrying along a copy of Francis E. Caldwell's *Land of the Ocean Mists*, which was so expertly edited by Alaska's finest living historian, Robert N. DeArmond. If space in one's backpack or boat locker allows, Philip L. Fradkin's *Wildest Alaska* is a truly fun read as well.

And last, to the Tlingit Indian elders and storytellers who have dedicated themselves to preserving the traditions and history of their people, I send my very small and inadequate *Gunalch'eesh*!

Lynn Schooler
Juneau, Alaska
2005

Lynn Schooler is the critically acclaimed author of *The Blue Bear* and *The Last Shot*. He has lived in Alaska for almost forty years, working as a commercial fisherman, a shipwright, a wilderness guide, and an award-winning wildlife photographer.